PERSPECTIVES

4

Amanda **JEFFRIES**

Lewis **LANSFORD**

Daniel **BARBER**

NATIONAL
GEOGRAPHIC
LEARNING

Australia · Brazil · Mexico · Singapore · United Kingdom · United States

NATIONAL GEOGRAPHIC
L E A R N I N G

Perspectives 4
**Amanda Jeffries, Lewis Lansford,
Daniel Barber**

Publisher: Sherrise Roehr

Executive Editor: Sarah Kenney

Publishing Consultant: Karen Spiller

Senior Development Editor: Brenden Layte

Senior Development Editor: Lewis Thompson

Editorial Assistant: Gabe Feldstein

Director of Global Marketing: Ian Martin

Product Marketing Manager: Anders Bylund

Director of Content and Media Production:
Michael Burggren

Production Manager: Daisy Sosa

Media Researcher: Leila Hishmeh

Manufacturing Customer Account Manager:
Mary Beth Hennebury

Art Director: Brenda Carmichael

Production Management and Composition:
3CD

Cover Image: © Alexander Remnev / Aurora
Photos

For product information and technology assistance, contact us at
Cengage Learning Customer & Sales Support, cengage.com/contact
For permission to use material from this text or product,
submit all requests online at **cengage.com/permissions**
Further permissions questions can be emailed to
permissionrequest@cengage.com

Student Edition: Level 4
ISBN: 978-1-337-27715-0

National Geographic Learning
20 Channel Center Street
Boston, MA 02210
USA

National Geographic Learning, a Cengage Learning Company, has a mission to bring the world to the classroom and the classroom to life. With our English language programs, students learn about their world by experiencing it. Through our partnerships with National Geographic and TED Talks, they develop the language and skills they need to be successful global citizens and leaders.

Locate your local office at **international.cengage.com/region**

Visit National Geographic Learning online at **NGL.Cengage.com/ELT**
Visit our corporate website at **www.cengage.com**

Photography Credits **4** (tl1) © Will Stauffer-Norris, (tl2) © Shao Feng, (cl) CB2/ZOB/Breef/Newscom, (bl1) © Devlin Gandy, (bl2) Blaine Harrington III/Corbis Documentary/Getty Images, **5** (tl1) © Ryan Lash/TED, (tl2) © James Duncan Davidson/TED, (cl) © Ryan Lash/TED, (bl1) © James Duncan Davidson/TED, (bl2) © Bret Hartman/TED, **6** (tl1) © Nigel Dickinson, (tl2) Ton Koene/Alamy Stock Photo, (cl) © Tyrone Bradley, (bl1) © Karolis Janulis/Offset, (bl2) © Marla Aufmuth/TED, **7** (tl1) © Marla Aufmuth/TED, (tl2) © TED, (cl) © James Duncan Davidson/TED, (bl1)) © Ryan Lash/TED, (bl2) © TED, **8-9** (spread) © Will Stauffer-Norris, **10-11** (spread) Anadolu Agency/Getty Images, **13** Chayanee Jongthai/EyeEm/Getty Images, **14** Carsten Peter/National Geographic Creative, **15** David Grossman/Alamy Stock Photo, **16-17** (spread) © Ryan Lash/TED, **18-19** (spread) Joe Morahan/NewSport/Zumapress.com/Newscom, **20-21** (spread) © Shao Feng, **22-23** (spread) Natthawat/Moment Open/Getty Images, **25** (bgd) Matthieu Paley/National Geographic Creative, (tc) © 1983 by Harcourt, Inc. Book design by Lizzie Scott, (tr) © Northwestern Universoty Press, 2002, **26** Stefano Politi Markovina/Alamy Stock Photo, **27** PA Images/Alamy Stock Photo, **28-29** (spread) © James Duncan Davidson/TED, **30-31** (spread) Panoramic Images/National Geographic Creative, **32-33** (spread) CB2/ZOB/Breef/Newscom, **34-35** (spread) © Enric Sala, **37** (t) (ct) (cr) (bl) (bc) Steve Boyes/National Geographic Creative, **38** Ralph Lee Hopkins/National Geographic Creative, **39** Michael Nolan/robertharding/Getty Images, **40-41** (spread) © Ryan Lash/TED, **42-43** Rich Carey/Shutterstock.com, **44-45** © Devlin Gandy, **46-47** NASA/JPL-Caltech/MSSS, **49** Robert Clark/National Geographic Creative, **50** Erik Simonsen/Getty Images, **51** Merydolla/iStock/Getty Images, **52-53** © James Duncan Davidson/TED, **54-55** John Mccarhty/EyeEm/Getty Images, **56-57** (spread) Blaine Harrington III/Corbis Documentary/Getty Images, **58-59** (spread) © Joao Pina/Redux, **61** Blend Images/AlamyStock Photo, **62** Zuma Press, Inc./Alamy Stock Photo, **63** © Purnima Sriram Iyer, **64-65** (spread) © Bret Hartman/TED, **66-67** (spread) Patti McConville/Getty Images, **68-69** (spread) © Nigel Dickinson, **70-71** (spread) Jan Riephoff/laif/Redux, **73** Christian Kober/robertharding/Getty Images, **74** Jonas Gratzer/LightRocket/Getty Images, **75** Abir Abdullah/European Pressphoto Agency/Dhaka/Bangladesh/Newscom, **76-77** © Marla Aufmuth/TED, **78-79** (spread) China Daily/Reuters, **80-81** (spread) Ton Koene/Alamy Stock Photo, **82-83** (spread) Nigel Hicks/National Geographic Creative, **85** Robert Clark/National Geographic Creative, **86** Ricardo Ribas/Alamy Stock Photo, **87** © Pim Hendriksen, **88-89** (spread) © TED, **90-91** (spread) Xinhua News Agency/eyevine/Redux, **92-93** (spread) © Tyrone Bradley, **94** (bl) Jodi Cobb/National Geographic Creative, (br) Lucas Vallecillos/Redux, **95** (bl) Dan Kitwood/Getty Images News/Getty Images, (br) Bloomberg/Getty Images, **97** Alberto E. Rodriguez/Getty Images Entertainment/Getty Images, **98** Glow Asia/Alamy Stock Photo, **99** redsnapper/Alamy Stock Photo, **100-101** (spread) © James Duncan Davidson/TED, **102-103** (spread) © Juan Pablo Velasco, **104-105** (spread) © Karolis Janulis/Offset, **106-107** (spread) NurPhoto/Getty Images, **109** Gianluca Colla/National Geographic Creative, **110** ivstiv/E+/Getty Images, **111** SolStock/E+/Getty Images, **112-113** © Ryan Lash/TED, **114-115** (spread) © Marla Aufmuth/TED, **116-117** (spread) Adrian Sherratt/Alamy Stock Photo, **118-119** (spread) Top Photo Corporation/Alamy Stock Photo, **118** (cl) National Geographic Learning, **121** NASA, **122** General Photographic Agency/Hulton Archive/Getty Images, **123** JOSÉ LUIS SALMERÓN/NOTIMEX/Newscom, **124-125** © TED, **126-127** (spread) Kevin Winter/WireImage/Getty Images.

Text Credit **25** (tl) From "An African in Greenland" by Togolese writer Tete-Michel Kpomassie, 1981 published by the New York review of Books,Inc (24 April 2003) ISBN-10: 0940322889 ISBN-13:978-0940322882, (tr) From "House of Day, House of Night" by Olga Tokarczuk, 2003.

Printed in Mexico
Print Number: 04   Print Year: 2022

ACKNOWLEDGMENTS

Paulo Rogerio Rodrigues
Escola Móbile, São Paulo, Brazil

Claudia Colla de Amorim
Escola Móbile, São Paulo, Brazil

Antonio Oliveira
Escola Móbile, São Paulo, Brazil

Rory Ruddock
Atlantic International Language Center, Hanoi, Vietnam

Carmen Virginia Pérez Cervantes
La Salle, Mexico City, Mexico

Rossana Patricia Zuleta
CIPRODE, Guatemala City, Guatemala

Gloria Stella Quintero Riveros
Universidad Católica de Colombia, Bogotá, Colombia

Mónica Rodriguez Salvo
MAR English Services, Buenos Aires, Argentina

Itana de Almeida Lins
Grupo Educacional Anchieta, Salvador, Brazil

Alma Loya
Colegio de Chihuahua, Chihuahua, Mexico

María Trapero Dávila
Colegio Teresiano, Ciudad Obregon, Mexico

Silvia Kosaruk
Modern School, Lanús, Argentina

Florencia Adami
Dámaso Centeno, Caba, Argentina

Natan Galed Gomez Cartagena
Global English Teaching, Rionegro, Colombia

James Ubriaco
Colégio Santo Agostinho, Belo Horizonte, Brazil

Ryan Manley
The Chinese University of Hong Kong, Shenzhen, China

Silvia Teles
Colégio Cândido Portinari, Salvador, Brazil

María Camila Azuero Gutiérrez
Fundación Centro Electrónico de Idiomas, Bogotá, Colombia

Martha Ramirez
Colegio San Mateo Apostol, Bogotá, Colombia

Beata Polit
XXIII LO Warszawa, Poland

Beata Tomaszewska
V LO Toruń, Poland

Michał Szkudlarek
I LO Brzeg, Poland

Anna Buchowska
I LO Białystok, Poland

Natalia Maćkowiak
one2one, Kosakowo, Poland

Agnieszka Dończyk
one2one, Kosakowo, Poland

The author and publishers would like to thank
the following for their help: Dr. Emily Grossman; Ms. Li.

Perspectives teaches learners to think critically and to develop the language skills they need to find their own voice in English. The carefully-guided language lessons, real-world stories, and TED Talks motivate learners to think creatively and communicate effectively.

In *Perspectives*, learners develop:

● AN OPEN MIND

Every unit explores one idea from different perspectives, giving learners opportunities for practicing language as they look at the world in new ways.

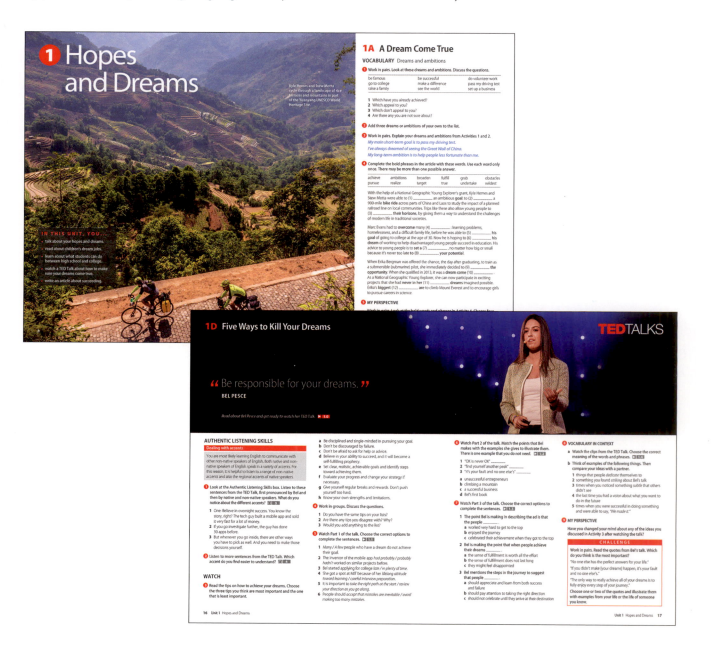

● A CRITICAL EYE

Students learn the critical thinking skills and strategies they need to evaluate new information and develop their own opinions and ideas to share.

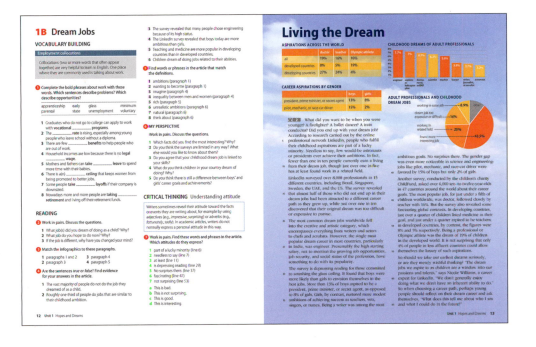

● A CLEAR VOICE

Students respond to the unit theme and express their own ideas confidently in English.

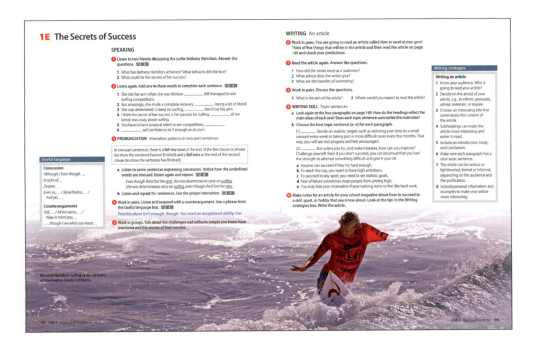

CONTENTS

GRAMMAR	TED TALKS		SPEAKING	WRITING
Continuous and perfect aspects	**Five ways to kill your dreams**	**BEL PESCE** Bel Pesce's idea worth spreading is that we're more likely to achieve our dreams if we follow a few basic principles. **Authentic listening skills** Dealing with accents	Concession and counter-arguments **Pronunciation** Intonation patterns in two-part sentences	An article **Writing skill** Topic sentences
Narrative tenses and future in the past **Pronunciation** Using stress to change meaning	**My year reading a book from every country in the world**	**ANN MORGAN** Ann Morgan's idea worth spreading is that books and stories can help us see the world through different eyes and connect us across political, geographical, cultural, social, and religious divides. **Authentic listening skills** Following a narrative	Telling and responding to a story	A story **Writing skill** Using colorful language
Third and mixed conditionals; *I wish / If only* **Pronunciation** Contractions	**An underwater museum, teeming with life**	**JASON DECAIRES TAYLOR** Jason deCaires Taylor's idea worth spreading is that we need to open our eyes to the amazing beauty, imagination, and fragility of nature. In this way, we will be inspired to cherish and protect our environment. **Authentic listening skills** Chunking	Making and explaining promises	Informal emails **Writing skill** Informal language
Passives; Passive reporting structures **Critical thinking** Information order	**The boiling river of the Amazon**	**ANDRÉS RUZO** Andrés Ruzo's idea worth spreading is that we should allow our curiosity to lead us to discover the unknown wonders of the world. **Authentic listening skills** Engaging the listener's attention	Describing benefits and clarifying	A discussion essay **Writing skill** Hedging
Cleft sentences **Pronunciation** Contrastive stress	**What does it mean to be a citizen of the world?**	**HUGH EVANS** Hugh Evans's idea worth spreading is that we are first and foremost not members of a state, nation, or tribe, but members of the human race. We need to seek global solutions to global challenges. **Authentic listening skills** Rhetorical questions	Making suggestions and requests; Resisting and persuading	A formal letter **Writing skill** Making a point

CONTENTS

GRAMMAR	TEDTALKS	SPEAKING	WRITING

GRAMMAR	TEDTALKS		SPEAKING	WRITING
Passive *-ing* forms and infinitives	**LINDA CLIATT-WAYMAN** Linda Cliatt-Wayman's idea worth spreading is that a successful school needs a strong leader with a positive attitude to challenges and unconditional love for the students. **Authentic listening skills** Deducing the meaning of unknown words	How to fix a broken school? Lead fearlessly, love hard	Agreeing and disagreeing **Pronunciation** Rise-fall-rise intonation	An opinion essay **Writing skill** Avoiding repetition
Nominalization **Pronunciation** Words with two stress patterns	**WANIS KABBAJ** Wanis Kabbaj's idea worth spreading is that we can find inspiration in human biology to design efficient and elegant transportation systems for the future. **Authentic listening skills** Predicting what comes next	What a driverless world could look like	Asking for and giving information	A report **Writing skill** Expressions of approval and disapproval
Expressing habitual actions and states	**SARAH-JAYNE BLAKEMORE** Sarah-Jayne Blakemore's idea worth spreading is that the human brain undergoes profound changes during the teenage years, making it an amazing time for learning and creativity. **Authentic listening skills** Preparing to listen	The mysterious workings of the adolescent brain	Showing understanding, offering encouragement and help **Pronunciation** Intonation to show understanding	An essay comparing advantages and disadvantages **Writing skill** Interpreting essay questions
Articles	**KENNETH SHINOZUKA** Kenneth Shinozuka's idea worth spreading is that smart uses of sensory technology can improve our lives as we age, particularly for Alzheimer's patients and those who care for them. **Authentic listening skills** Understanding fast speech	My simple invention, designed to keep my grandfather safe	Discussing, summarizing, and responding to proposals **Pronunciation** Intonation in responses	A proposal **Writing skill** Impersonal style
Subordinate and participle clauses	**CHRIS ANDERSON** Chris Anderson's idea worth spreading is that a great idea is the core ingredient to a truly great talk because our ideas have the potential to change someone else's perspective for the better or inspire someone to do something differently. **Authentic listening skills** Collaborative listening	TED's secret to great public speaking	Giving a presentation **Pronunciation** Intonation of signpost expressions	A review **Writing skill** Reference

1 Hopes and Dreams

IN THIS UNIT, YOU...

- talk about your hopes and dreams.

- read about children's dream jobs.

- learn about what students can do between high school and college.

- watch a TED Talk about how to make sure your dreams come true.

- write an article about succeeding.

1A   A Dream Come True

VOCABULARY   Dreams and ambitions

1 Work in pairs. Look at these dreams and ambitions. Discuss the questions.

be famous	be successful	do volunteer work
go to college	make a difference	pass my driving test
raise a family	see the world	set up a business

1 Which have you already achieved?
2 Which appeal to you?
3 Which don't appeal to you?
4 Are there any you are not sure about?

2 Add three dreams or ambitions of your own to the list.

3 Work in pairs. Explain your dreams and ambitions from Activities 1 and 2.

My main short-term goal is to pass my driving test.

I've always dreamed of seeing the Great Wall of China.

My long-term ambition is to help people less fortunate than me.

4 Complete the bold phrases in the article with these words. Use each word only once. There may be more than one possible answer.

achieve	ambitions	broaden	fulfill	grab	obstacles
pursue	realize	target	true	undertake	wildest

With the help of a National Geographic Young Explorer's grant, Kyle Hemes and Stew Motta were able to (1) _____ an ambitious **goal**: to (2) _____ a 900-mile **bike ride** across parts of China and Laos to study the impact of a planned railroad line on local communities. Trips like these also allow young people to (3) _____ **their horizons**, by giving them a way to understand the challenges of modern life in traditional societies.

Marc Evans had to **overcome** many (4) _____ : learning problems, homelessness, and a difficult family life, before he was able to (5) _____ his **goal** of going to college at the age of 30. Now he is hoping to (6) _____ his **dream** of working to help disadvantaged young people succeed in education. His advice to young people is to **set a** (7) _____ , no matter how big or small because it's never too late **to** (8) _____ **your potential.**

When Erika Bergman was offered the chance, the day after graduating, to train as a submersible (submarine) pilot, she immediately decided to (9) _____ **the opportunity**. When she qualified in 2013, it was a **dream come** (10) _____ . As a National Geographic Young Explorer, she can now participate in exciting projects that she had **never in her** (11) _____ **dreams** imagined possible. Erika's **biggest** (12) _____ **are** to climb Mount Everest and to encourage girls to pursue careers in science.

5 MY PERSPECTIVE

Work in pairs. Look at the bold words and phrases in Activity 4. Choose four phrases and ask and answer questions using them.

What obstacles at school have you had to overcome?

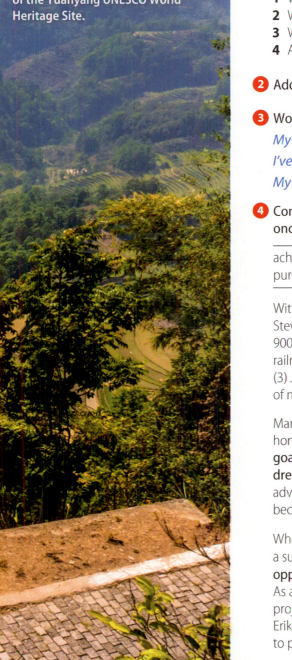

Kyle Hemes and Stew Motta cycle through a landscape of rice terraces and mountains in part of the Yuanyang UNESCO World Heritage Site.

LISTENING

6 Listen to four people talking about a dream or ambition. What dream or ambition is each one talking about? 🎧 **1**

7 Work in pairs. Which of the speakers (1–4) mentions the following? There may be more than one correct answer. Listen again and check your ideas. Write any words or phrases that support your answers. 🎧 **1**

a developing a talent recognized by others
b setting targets to achieve their goal
c a problem with work-life balance
d disappointment at not realizing a dream
e working with other people
f having to wait patiently to reach their goal
g realizing there will be hard work ahead
h being tested
i determination to realize a dream

GRAMMAR Review of tenses

Future forms

a *He and his partner **are opening** a new restaurant next month.*

b *Even a half marathon is hard for me, so it's **going to be** tough…*

c *… but hopefully I'**ll be able to** do it.*

d *… I'**m definitely going to try** again next time.*

e *The class **starts** next September…*

f *… so I'**ll be practicing** hard all next summer.*

g *… as soon as I start the class I'**ll have** the chance to pick up another instrument.*

h *It'**ll probably** be the piano…*

8 Look at the Grammar box. Match the sentences with their uses.

1 a prediction based on something you know in the present
2 a firm intention
3 an action that will be in progress at a point in the future
4 a fixed plan, often involving other people
5 a future event with a timetable
6 a prediction of something certain
7 a prediction of something possible
8 a hope or belief for the future

Check your answers on page 128. Do Activity 1.

9 Work in pairs. Read the article and choose the options that are <u>not</u> possible. Cross out one in each case.

I've always had a fascination with books. Since elementary school, my ambition has been to be a writer, and now it looks like my dream (1) *will come / comes / is going to come* true. After winning first prize in a short-story competition for a national magazine, I was approached by an editor who encouraged me to develop the story into a novel, which I did. The editor loved it, so my first novel (2) *is going to be / is / will be* published! It (3) *is / will be / is being* the publishing company's tenth anniversary next month, and the book is being released online on the first of the month. An annual bookfair (4) *is going to take / is takes / takes* place in October, and the company (5) *will probably print / is probably printing / probably prints* the book for that. (6) *I meet / I'll meet / I'm meeting* my editor next week to talk about translations. The company (7) *will be translating / is translating / will be translate* the book into Spanish, and there are several other possibilities. Once the promotion of this book is over, (8) *I'll start / I'm starting / I'm going to start* thinking about my next one. I can't wait!

10 Look at the Grammar box. Answer the questions.

Present and past tenses

a ... my dad **had been working** at a really stressful job...

b ... every day he **was leaving** home at six in the morning...

c ... the business **is going** strong.

d And they're absolutely **loving** it!

e Running **is becoming** really popular where I live...

f I'd never **been** very athletic before...

g I've always **been** interested in stargazing...

h I've **been taking** cello lessons since I was a kid.

i And then the chance **came up**... so I **grabbed** the opportunity.

j ... as soon as I've **started** the class...

1 Which sentence describes a series of actions in the past?
2 Which sentence describes repeated actions in the past?
3 Sentences c, d, and e are all in the present continuous. What does it express in each case? Which one might be considered unusual? Why?
4 Which four sentences describe an action starting in one time and continuing up to another?
5 Which one is followed by a future tense if the sentence is complete?

Check your answers on page 128. Do Activities 2 and 3.

11 Complete the article with the correct tense of the verbs in parentheses.

Im Dong-Hyun is a perfect example of following your goals. The South Korean archer (1) _____ (target) gold at the London Olympics of 2012, and for a while it (2) _____ (look) as though this was a real possibility when Im (3) _____ (break) the world record in the qualification round and was ranked first going into the knock-out rounds. In fact, he (4) _____ (already / help) his national archery team to gold in the 2004 and 2008 Olympics but (5) _____ (miss) out on an individual medal both times. So Im (6) _____ (anticipate) this moment for years, but unfortunately, his dream was not to be: despite being ranked first, Im (7) _____ (be) knocked out before he (8) _____ (even / reach) the quarter-final stage. So why is this story so unusual? Im Dong-Hyun is legally blind and (9) _____ (struggle) even to read a newspaper, yet his disability (10) _____ (never / prevent) him from trying to achieve his goal.

12 MY PERSPECTIVE

Work in pairs. What do you think of Im Dong Hyun's achievement? Is it very special? Do you know of anyone who has achieved a goal, or almost achieved a goal, when the circumstances were difficult?

13 Make a timeline of something you have achieved in your life. It could be something to do with sports, school, or something you have done for your community. Then include something you might do in the future (connected with what you achieved). Discuss your timelines in groups.

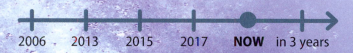

2006   2013   2015   2017   **NOW**   in 3 years

A photographer watches the Perseid meteor shower in eastern Turkey.

1B Dream Jobs

VOCABULARY BUILDING

Employment collocations

Collocations (two or more words that often appear together) are very helpful to learn in English. One place where they are commonly used is talking about work.

1 Complete the bold phrases about work with these words. Which sentences describe problems? Which describe opportunities?

| apprenticeship | early | glass | minimum |
| parental | state | unemployment | voluntary |

1 Graduates who do not go to college can apply to work with **vocational _____ programs**.
2 The **_____ rate** is rising, especially among young people who leave school without a diploma.
3 There are few **_____ benefits** to help people who are out of work.
4 Household incomes are low because there is no **legal _____ wage**.
5 Mothers and fathers can **take _____ leave** to spend more time with their babies.
6 There is a(n) **_____ ceiling** that keeps women from being promoted to better jobs.
7 Some people **take _____ layoffs** if their company is downsized.
8 Nowadays more and more people are **taking _____ retirement** and living off their retirement funds.

READING

2 Work in pairs. Discuss the questions.

1 What job(s) did you dream of doing as a child? Why?
2 What job do you hope to do now? Why?
3 If the job is different, why have you changed your mind?

3 Match the infographics to these paragraphs.

1 paragraphs 1 and 2   3 paragraph 4
2 paragraph 3   4 paragraph 5

4 Are the sentences *true* or *false*? Find evidence for your answers in the article.

1 The vast majority of people do not do the job they dreamed of as a child.
2 Roughly one third of people do jobs that are similar to their childhood ambition.

3 The survey revealed that many people chose engineering because of its high status.
4 The LinkedIn survey revealed that boys today are more ambitious than girls.
5 Teaching and medicine are more popular in developing countries than in developed countries.
6 Children dream of doing jobs related to their abilities.

5 Find words or phrases in the article that match the definitions.

1 ambitions (paragraph 1)
2 wanting to become (paragraph 1)
3 imagine (paragraph 4)
4 inequality between men and women (paragraph 4)
5 rich (paragraph 5)
6 unrealistic ambitions (paragraph 6)
7 natural (paragraph 6)
8 think about (paragraph 6)

6 MY PERSPECTIVE

Work in pairs. Discuss the questions.

1 Which facts did you find the most interesting? Why?
2 Do you think the surveys are limited in any way? What else would you like to know about them?
3 Do you agree that your childhood dream job is linked to your skills?
4 What do you think children in your country dream of doing? Why?
5 Do you think there is still a difference between boys' and girls' career goals and achievements?

CRITICAL THINKING Understanding attitude

Writers sometimes reveal their attitude toward the facts or events they are writing about, for example by using adjectives (e.g., *impressive*, *surprising*) or adverbs (e.g., *fortunately*, *sadly*). In academic articles, writers do not normally express a personal attitude in this way.

7 Work in pairs. Find these words and phrases in the article. Which attitudes do they express?

1 part of a lucky minority (line 6)
2 needless to say (line 7)
3 at least (line 11)
4 is depressing reading (line 29)
5 No surprises there. (line 37)
6 fascinating (line 47)
7 not surprising (line 53)

a This is bad.
b This is not surprising.
c This is good.
d This is interesting.

Living the Dream

ASPIRATIONS ACROSS THE WORLD

	doctor	teacher	Olympic athlete
all	19%	16%	10%
developed countries	8%	5%	19%
developing countries	27%	24%	4%

CAREER ASPIRATIONS BY GENDER

	boys	girls
president, prime minister, or secret agent	13%	8%
pilot, mechanic, or race-car driver	15%	2%

CHILDHOOD DREAMS OF ADULT PROFESSIONALS

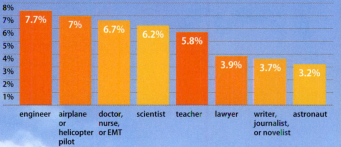

engineer 7.7% | airplane or helicopter pilot 7% | doctor, nurse, or EMT 6.7% | scientist 6.2% | teacher 5.8% | lawyer 3.9% | writer, journalist, or novelist 3.7% | astronaut 3.2%

ADULT PROFESSIONALS AND CHILDHOOD DREAM JOBS

working in same job — 8.9%
other
dream job too expensive or difficult — 16%
working in related field — 21%
found more interesting job — 43.5%

🎧 **2** What did you want to be when you were younger? A firefighter? A ballet dancer? A train conductor? Did you end up with your dream job? According to research carried out by the online
5 professional network LinkedIn, people who fulfill their childhood aspirations are part of a lucky minority. Needless to say, few would-be astronauts or presidents ever achieve their ambitions. In fact, fewer than one in ten people currently earn a living
10 from their dream job, though just over one in five has at least found work in a related field.

LinkedIn surveyed over 8,000 professionals in 15 different countries, including Brazil, Singapore, Sweden, the UAE, and the US. The survey revealed
15 that almost half of those who did not end up in their dream jobs had been attracted to a different career path as they grew up, while just over one in ten discovered that their original dream was too difficult or expensive to pursue.

20 The most common dream jobs worldwide fell into the creative and artistic category, which encompasses everything from writers and actors to chefs and acrobats. However, the single most popular dream career in most countries, particularly
25 in India, was engineer. Presumably the high starting salary, not to mention the growing job opportunities, job security, and social status of the profession, have something to do with its popularity.

The survey is depressing reading for those committed
30 to smashing the glass ceiling. It found that boys were more likely than girls to envision themselves in the best jobs. More than 13% of boys aspired to be a president, prime minister, or secret agent, as opposed to 8% of girls. Girls, by contrast, nurtured more modest
35 ambitions of achieving success as teachers, vets, singers, or nurses. Being a writer was among the most

ambitious goals. No surprises there. The gender gap was even more noticeable in science and engineering: jobs like pilot, mechanic, and race-car driver were
40 favored by 15% of boys but only 2% of girls.

Another survey, conducted by the children's charity ChildFund, asked over 6,000 ten- to twelve-year-olds in 47 countries around the world about their career goals. The most popular job, for just under a fifth of
45 children worldwide, was doctor, followed closely by teacher with 16%. But the survey also revealed some fascinating global contrasts. In developing countries, just over a quarter of children listed medicine as their goal, and just under a quarter aspired to be teachers;
50 in developed countries, by contrast, the figures were 8% and 5% respectively. Being a professional or Olympic athlete was the dream of 19% of children in the developed world. It is not surprising that only 4% of people in less affluent countries could allow
55 themselves the luxury of such aspirations.

So should we take our earliest dreams seriously, or are they merely wishful thinking? "The dream jobs we aspire to as children are a window into our passions and talents," says Nicole Williams, a career
60 expert for LinkedIn. "We don't generally enjoy doing what we don't have an inherent ability to do." So when choosing a career path, perhaps young people should reflect on their dream career and ask themselves, "What does this tell me about who I am
65 and what I could do in the future?"

People explore canyons in New South Wales, Australia.

1C Bridging the Gap

GRAMMAR Continuous and perfect aspects

1 Work in pairs. Read the text and answer the questions.

1 What is a gap year? What can people do during one?
2 Are gap years something that graduates in your country often take? Why?
3 Do you know anyone who has taken a break from studying?
4 Do you think that young people can benefit from a break between high school and college, or is it more likely to be a disadvantage?

Gap-year dreams

Have you ever dreamed of taking time off to see the world or do something completely different? These days, more and more young people are taking a gap year between high school and college. The idea of the gap year started in the UK in the 1960s, and its popularity is still growing—and not only in the UK. The number of students in the US taking time off has been increasing since 2006, and gap years are now known in countries as diverse as Venezuela and Ghana. It is commonly believed that a gap year helps young people broaden their perspectives and gain maturity. What do you think?

COMMENTS:

Susie   I'm currently working in Costa Rica for three months as part of my gap year. I'm helping young students with their English. I think I've grown up a lot, and I'm sure my future studies will benefit from it.

Enrique   I'm at the end of a few months in Shanghai, China. I've been volunteering at a law firm. I'd been studying law for a year before I came here, but this has made law real for me. I've also made some good friends and connections, and we'll definitely keep in touch.

2 Look at the Grammar box. Match the sentences with the questions. You can use the sentences more than once.

The continuous and perfect aspects

a … more and more young people **are taking** a gap year…

b … the number of students in the US… **has been increasing** since 2006…

c I'm currently **working** in Costa Rica…

d I think I**'ve grown up** a lot, and I'm sure my future studies will benefit…

e I**'ve been volunteering** at a law firm.

f I**'d been studying** law for a year before I came here…

g I've also **made some** good friends…, and we'll definitely keep in touch.

Which sentence(s)…

1 describe temporary actions or situations?
2 describe ongoing actions or situations?
3 describe a completed action or situation?
4 describe a past action that links with the present / future?
5 describe a past action which relates to a more recent past action?

3 Choose the correct options to complete the descriptions of the continuous and perfect aspects.

The continuous aspect describes actions or situations that are (1) *ongoing / short or complete* and usually ones that are (2) *permanent / temporary*.

The perfect aspect usually describes an action that comes (3) *before / after* another action and creates a link between two (4) *places / times*.

Check your answers on page 128. Do Activities 4 and 5.

4 Work in pairs. Read these statements from a gap-year student. Decide which options are possible and discuss the difference in meaning, if any.

1 This is the first time I *work / 've worked / 'd worked* abroad.
2 I *'ve wanted / 've been wanting / 'd wanted* to experience a different culture for a long time.
3 The last group of volunteers *were leaving / had left / left* when we arrived.
4 I *'m working / 've worked / 've been working* here for almost four months now.
5 Every day I *experience / 'm experiencing / 've experienced* something new.
6 I *'ve made / 've been making / 'm making* two very good friends while I've been here.

5 Complete the sentences with these pairs of verbs. Use a correct present or past form.

apply + increase	be + grow	be matched + grant
rise + start	take + rise	

1 Each year in the United States around 8,000 students _____ a gap year. The figure _____ steadily for the last few years.
2 Until 2012, the most popular destination for gap-year students from the US _____ Southeast Asia. The popularity of South America as a destination _____ until it finally surpassed Southeast Asia that year.
3 This year more students in the UK _____ to study medical subjects at college than anything else. Applications _____ by four percent since last year.
4 In some countries, the number of students taking gap years _____ for some time. In Denmark, for example, in 2009, the government _____ to reward students who go straight into higher education after school.
5 The increase in the number of Chinese students applying for visas to study in Australia _____ by the number of visas the Australian authorities _____ , an increase of over 22 percent since 2016.

6 Make notes about these things. Then discuss them in groups.

1 something I've done that I'm proud of
2 something I've been doing for the past few years
3 something I do regularly that I'd rather not do
4 something that's changing in my life
5 something I think I'll be doing in two years

7 MY PERSPECTIVE

Where would you like to go on a gap year? Why would you like to take one? How do you think a gap year could benefit you?

8 CHOOSE Choose one of the following activities.

- Choose a country you'd like to visit. Search for "gap year in (country)" online and find as much information as you can. Present it to your classmates.

- Work in pairs. Make a list of things that you think would be good to do in a gap year (in your town / country or abroad). Decide on the best two or three. Then discuss your choices with another pair and decide on the two best activities.

- Think of something interesting you have done outside of school, for example a job over school vacation, or something you have done with family members or friends. Write a short blog explaining what it was and why you did it.

A high school teenager works with younger children in an educational after-school program in New York City, US.

" Be responsible for your dreams. "

BEL PESCE

Read about Bel Pesce and get ready to watch her TED Talk. ▶ **1.0**

AUTHENTIC LISTENING SKILLS

Dealing with accents

You are most likely learning English to communicate with other non-native speakers of English. Both native and non-native speakers of English speak in a variety of accents. For this reason, it is helpful to listen to a range of non-native accents and also the regional accents of native speakers.

1 Look at the Authentic Listening Skills box. Listen to these sentences from the TED Talk, first pronounced by Bel and then by native and non-native speakers. What do you notice about the different accents? 🎧 **3**

1 One: Believe in overnight success. You know the story, right? The tech guy built a mobile app and sold it very fast for a lot of money.

2 If you go investigate further, the guy has done 30 apps before.

3 But whenever you go inside, there are other ways you have to pick as well. And you need to make those decisions yourself.

2 Listen to more sentences from the TED Talk. Which accent do you find easier to understand? 🎧 **4**

WATCH

3 Read the tips on how to achieve your dreams. Choose the three tips you think are most important and the one that is least important.

a Be disciplined and single-minded in pursuing your goal.
b Don't be discouraged by failure.
c Don't be afraid to ask for help or advice.
d Believe in your ability to succeed, and it will become a self-fulfilling prophecy.
e Set clear, realistic, achievable goals and identify steps toward achieving them.
f Evaluate your progress and change your strategy if necessary.
g Give yourself regular breaks and rewards. Don't push yourself too hard.
h Know your own strengths and limitations.

4 Work in groups. Discuss the questions.

1 Do you have the same tips on your lists?
2 Are there any tips you disagree with? Why?
3 Would you add anything to the list?

5 Watch Part 1 of the talk. Choose the correct options to complete the sentences. ▶ **1.1**

1 *Many / A few* people who have a dream do not achieve their goal.
2 The inventor of the mobile app *had probably / probably hadn't* worked on similar projects before.
3 Bel started applying for college *late / in plenty of time*.
4 She got a spot at MIT because of her *lifelong attitude toward learning / careful interview preparation*.
5 It is important to *take the right path at the start / review your direction as you go along*.
6 People should *accept that mistakes are inevitable / avoid making too many mistakes*.

6 Watch Part 2 of the talk. Match the points that Bel makes with the examples she gives to illustrate them. There is one example that you do not need. ▶ **1.2**

1 "OK is never OK" _____
2 "find yourself another peak" _____
3 "it's your fault and no one else's" _____

a unsuccessful entrepreneurs
b climbing a mountain
c a successful business
d Bel's first book

7 Watch Part 3 of the talk. Choose the correct options to complete the sentences. ▶ **1.3**

1 The point Bel is making in describing the ad is that the people _____ .
    a worked very hard to get to the top
    b enjoyed the journey
    c celebrated their achievement when they got to the top

2 Bel is making the point that when people achieve their dreams _____ .
    a the sense of fulfillment is worth all the effort
    b the sense of fulfillment does not last long
    c they might feel disappointed

3 Bel mentions the steps in the journey to suggest that people _____ .
    a should appreciate and learn from both success and failure
    b should pay attention to taking the right direction
    c should not celebrate until they arrive at their destination

8 VOCABULARY IN CONTEXT

a Watch the clips from the TED Talk. Choose the correct meaning of the words and phrases. ▶ **1.4**

b Think of examples of the following things. Then compare your ideas with a partner.

1 things that people *dedicate* themselves to
2 something you found *striking* about Bel's talk
3 times when you noticed something *subtle* that others didn't see
4 the last time you had a *vision* about what you want to do in the future
5 times when you were successful in doing something and were able to say, *"We made it."*

9 MY PERSPECTIVE

Have you changed your mind about any of the ideas you discussed in Activity 3 after watching the talk?

CHALLENGE

Work in pairs. Read the quotes from Bel's talk. Which do you think is the most important?

"No one else has the perfect answers for your life."

"If you didn't make [your dreams] happen, it's your fault and no one else's."

"The only way to really achieve all of your dreams is to fully enjoy every step of your journey."

Choose one or two of the quotes and illustrate them with examples from your life or the life of someone you know.

1E The Secrets of Success

SPEAKING

1 Listen to two friends discussing the surfer Bethany Hamilton. Answer the questions. 🎧 **5**

1 What has Bethany Hamilton achieved? What setbacks did she face?
2 What could be the secrets of her success?

2 Listen again. Add one to three words to complete each sentence. 🎧 **5**

1 She lost her arm when she was thirteen _____ still managed to win surfing competitions.
2 But amazingly, she made a complete recovery, _____ losing a lot of blood.
3 She was determined to keep on surfing, _____ she'd lost her arm.
4 I think the secret of her success is her passion for surfing. _____ all her family was crazy about surfing.
5 You have to have a natural talent to win competitions, _____ .
6 _____ , self-confidence isn't enough on its own.

3 PRONUNCIATION Intonation patterns in two-part sentences

> In two-part sentences, there is a **fall-rise tone** at the end of the first clause or phrase (to show the sentence has not finished) and a **fall tone** at the end of the second clause (to show the sentence has finished).

a Listen to some sentences expressing concession. Notice how the underlined words are stressed. Listen again and repeat. 🎧 **6**

> *Even though she'd lost her <u>arm</u>, she was determined to keep on <u>surfing</u>.*
> *She was determined to keep on <u>surfing</u>, even though she'd lost her <u>arm</u>.*

b Listen and repeat the sentences. Use the proper intonation. 🎧 **7**

4 Work in pairs. Listen and respond with a counterargument. Use a phrase from the Useful language box. 🎧 **8**

Practice alone isn't enough, though. You need an exceptional ability, too.

5 Work in groups. Talk about the challenges and setbacks people you know have overcome and the secrets of their success.

Useful language

Concession

Although / Even though…,
In spite of…
Despite…
Even so,… / Nevertheless,… /
* And yet,…*

Counterarguments

Still,… / All the same,… /
* Keep in mind you,…*
…, though I see what you mean…

Bethany Hamilton surfing at the US Open at Huntington Beach, California.

WRITING An article

6 Work in pairs. You are going to read an article called *How to excel at your sport*. Think of five things that will be in the article and then read the article on page 149 and check your predictions.

7 Read the article again. Answer the questions.

1 How did the writer excel as a swimmer?
2 What advice does the writer give?
3 What are the benefits of swimming?

8 Work in pairs. Discuss the questions.

1 What is the aim of the article?   **2** Where would you expect to read the article?

9 **WRITING SKILL** Topic sentences

a Look again at the four paragraphs on page 149. How do the headings reflect the main ideas of each one? Does each topic sentence summarize the main idea?

b Choose the best topic sentence (a–e) for each paragraph.

(1) _____ Decide on realistic targets such as reducing your time by a small amount every week or taking part in more difficult races every few months. That way, you will see real progress and feel encouraged.

(2) _____ But unless you try, and make mistakes, how can you improve? Challenge yourself. Even if you don't succeed, you can be proud that you had the strength to attempt something difficult and give it your all.

a Anyone can succeed if they try hard enough.
b To reach the top, you need to have high ambitions.
c To succeed in any sport, you need to set realistic goals.
d Fear of failure sometimes stops people from aiming high.
e You may lose your motivation if your training starts to feel like hard work.

10 Make notes for an article for your school magazine about how to succeed in a skill, sport, or hobby that you know about. Look at the tips in the Writing strategies box. Write the article.

Writing strategies

Writing an article

1 Know your audience. Who is going to read your article?

2 Decide on the aim(s) of your article, e.g., to inform, persuade, advise, entertain, or inspire.

3 Choose an interesting title that summarizes the content of the article.

4 Subheadings can make the article more interesting and easier to read.

5 Include an introduction, body, and conclusion.

6 Make sure each paragraph has a clear topic sentence.

7 The article can be serious or lighthearted, formal or informal, depending on the audience and the publication.

8 Include personal information and examples to make your article more interesting.

2 Reading the World

- talk about books and movies.

- read about thought-provoking attitudes about travel.

- learn about a creative reading project.

- watch a TED Talk about the challenge of reading a book from every country in the world.

- write a story using colorful language.

A modern bookstore
in Yangzhou, China

2A Telling a Story

VOCABULARY Describing books or movies

1 Work in pairs. Look at the photo and read the caption. Discuss the questions.

1 What is a book to you? Is it entertainment? Homework? Education? History? Boring? A way of traveling? A story?
2 What book are you reading now or have you read recently?
3 What was your favorite book as a child?
4 What book or movie has made a huge impact on you?
5 What type of books do you like?
6 Do you read in print or electronically? Why?
7 What kinds of movies do you like and dislike?

2 Look at the adjectives. Answer the questions.

accessible	boring	entertaining	gripping
intriguing	moving	overrated	sentimental
slow-moving	thought-provoking	touching	witty

1 Which adjectives have a positive meaning? Which have a negative meaning?
2 Do you think any could have both?

3 Match the words in Activity 2 with the comments about books and movies. More than one answer may be possible.

1 I was in tears at the end when the boy was reunited with his father.
2 It got five-star reviews, but to be honest, I found it pretty disappointing.
3 I was yawning the entire time. I prefer action movies—something with a little more excitement.
4 It was so boring that I lost interest halfway through and walked out.
5 I really enjoyed it. Great acting, fabulous photography, and the plot was very interesting. All in all, a fun evening.
6 The author is very smart and funny. I kept laughing out loud. It was absolutely hilarious!
7 It was a very difficult topic, but the narrator explained the facts really clearly and made it easy to understand.
8 It grabbed my attention from the opening scene and from then on, I was on the edge of my seat.
9 I loved the part where the boy gave his friend his own paper plane. It was so sweet.
10 It opened my eyes to why people might turn to crime. It really made me think.
11 The title caught my eye. I wanted to find out more, so I watched the trailer.
12 A typical blockbuster. No depth to the characters and a happy ending that, to be honest, left me cold.

4 Look at the comments in Activity 3 again. Which ones refer to a book? Which refer to a movie? Which could refer to either?

5 Work in pairs. Find two or three books you have both read or movies you have both seen. Which adjectives would you use to describe them? Why?

LISTENING

6 Listen to two descriptions of books. Complete the table. 🎧 9

	Lucas	Beatriz
Title of book		
Author	Galsan Tschinag	Isabel Allende
Type of book		
Would the speaker recommend it?		

7 Listen again. Complete the summary. 🎧 9

Lucas talks about *The Blue Sky*, which is (1) _____ Mongolia. The main character is a small boy who lives with his family in a yurt*. The book describes his experiences working as a (2) _____ after he comes of age. It describes his everyday (3) _____ , both the good and the bad. Lucas thought it was a little (4) _____ , but overall he recommends it.

Beatriz has just read *The House of the Spirits* which is a (5) _____ saga. It has a very complex (6) _____ . It describes the lives of (7) _____ of two families in twentieth-century Chile. Allende uses magical realism, which is a mixture of real and fantasy events, which Beatriz loved. Clara is one of the (8) _____ and can see into the future.

yurt *a large, circular tent*

8 Work in pairs. Discuss the questions.

1 Do the books in Activity 6 appeal to you? Why?
2 Ask and answer questions about the things you talked about in Activity 1. Use different adjectives to describe them.

Does it have a good plot? What are the characters like? Is it realistic? Where is it set?

GRAMMAR Modifying adjectives

9 Read the movie review and underline the adjectives.

Gravity is a movie by highly acclaimed Mexican director Alfonso Cuarón. This incredibly exciting movie, starring George Clooney and Sandra Bullock, focuses on two astronauts. As an absolutely terrifying situation develops in space, a very moving human drama unfolds inside the space capsule. The very long opening shot, a full seventeen minutes, is visually amazing. It's an outstanding movie. You shouldn't miss it.

Gradable and ungradable adjectives

Gradable adjectives (e.g., *cold*, *difficult*, and *tired*) express degrees of a quality. They can be modified or compared (e.g., *too cold*, *very tired*, and *more difficult than*).

Ungradable adjectives (e.g., *freezing*, *impossible*, and *exhausted*) express the limit of a quality. They can only be modified with certain adverbs, such as *absolutely* or *totally* (e.g., *absolutely freezing* and *totally impossible*). They can't be compared: *more freezing than*.

10 Read the Grammar box. Then answer the questions about the review in Activity 9.

1 Why does the writer use *absolutely terrifying* but *very moving*?
2 Which adjectives are gradable? Which are ungradable?

Check your answers on page 130. Do Activity 1.

11 Match the gradable adjectives in A with the ungradable adjectives in B with similar meanings.

A	angry	clever	funny	interesting
	pleased	sad	scared	surprising

B	amazing	brilliant	delighted	fascinating
	furious	heartbroken	hilarious	terrified

12 Complete the sentences with the correct adjectives from Activity 11.

1 We were very _____ to get tickets for the first night of the Harry Potter play!

2 I find historical novels absolutely _____ . History is one of my main interests.

3 His new comedy is very _____ but not as good as his last one.

4 Sara was completely _____ when her favorite actor said he was retiring.

5 I was totally _____ by the end of James Patterson's new thriller. It's really frightening.

Adverbs of degree

A

It's really moving.

It's fairly slow-moving at times. The plot is very complex.

It's pretty accessible.

B

Her descriptions are incredibly vivid.

An absolutely terrifying situation develops…

…which makes it totally gripping.

13 Look at the sentences in the Grammar box. Underline the adverbs. Then answer the questions.

1 Which adverbs are usually used with gradable adjectives? Which are used with ungradable adjectives?

2 Which of these adverbs would you put under A? Which would you put under B?

a bit / a little	completely	extremely
fairly	not very / not all that	really
slightly	somewhat	very

3 Which adverbs intensify the adjective? Which ones weaken the adjective?

Check your answers on page 130. Do Activity 2.

14 Work in pairs. Cross out the incorrect option.

1 I think documentaries are *very / somewhat / absolutely* boring.

2 I'm a huge fan of thrillers and horror movies; I find them *totally / completely / slightly* gripping.

3 Movie adaptations of books can often be *kind of / very / simply* disappointing.

4 I think comedies are *barely / extremely / really* hilarious.

5 Hollywood blockbusters tend to leave me cold. They are *so / not all that / really* predictable.

6 I enjoy watching independent movies; they are often *pretty / really / a bit* intriguing.

7 I'm not *too / pretty / very* into movies; I'd rather watch TV shows.

15 Choose three opinions from Activity 14 that you agree with and three you don't. Discuss them in groups.

> *I agree that documentaries can be somewhat boring. What do you think?*

> *Well, I think some of them can be very interesting. I saw one about lions that was absolutely fascinating.*

16 MY PERSPECTIVE

Work in pairs. You discussed what a book was to you in Activity 1. Have you changed your mind?

Goats and sheep are kept by many families and can be seen wandering among the yurts in Mongolia.

2B Travel Broadens the Mind

VOCABULARY BUILDING

Phrasal verbs with two particles

Some phrasal verbs have three parts: a verb and two particles. The object comes after the particles.

*The author always **comes up with** great ideas.*

1 Complete the sentences with these words. Match the meanings of the words in parentheses.

around to	away with	forward to
out of	up to	up with

1 In my opinion, e-readers will eventually *do* _____ the need for books. (remove)

2 I have so much homework that I don't often *get* _____ reading for pleasure. (find time for)

3 I love making up stories. Sometimes I *come* _____ an idea for a book or a movie. (think of)

4 That director is amazing. I'm really *looking* _____ her new movie. (be excited about)

5 I often find that sequels *don't live* _____ the original movie. (are not as good as)

6 I used to like reading comics when I was a child, but I've *grown* _____ them now. (am too old for)

2 What is the normal position of the object with these verbs?

3 Work in pairs. Discuss whether the sentences in Activity 1 are true for you. Why?

READING

4 Work in pairs. Read the three excerpts, two from a memoir and one from a novel. Which excerpt mentions:

1 an attempt to understand another person's thoughts?

2 the birth of an ambition?

3 a new experience?

5 Find words in the extracts that mean:

1 approached (excerpt A)

2 impressed (excerpt A)

3 caused (excerpt A)

4 deep desire (excerpt A)

5 produce an emotional response (excerpt A)

6 a storm with snow and wind (excerpt B)

7 broke into small pieces (excerpt B)

8 walked confidently with long steps (excerpt B)

9 complete uselessness (excerpt C)

10 survive (excerpt C)

6 Underline evidence for these statements.

Excerpt A

1 The author was a child when the event took place.

2 He found the book visually appealing.

3 The book had a powerful effect on him.

Excerpt B

4 It took time for the sea to freeze over.

5 Watching the sea freeze over reminded the author of an earlier experience.

6 He had mixed feelings about walking on the ice.

Excerpt C

7 Marta felt that there is no point in leaving home.

8 Marta believed that travel distracts people from seeing the world.

9 Marta thought that you can learn more about the world by staying at home.

7 Work in pairs. Discuss the questions.

1 How would you describe the narrator and Marta? Thoughtful? Curious? Fearful? Something else? Why?

2 How do you think the excerpts might continue? Which would you most like to continue reading? Why?

CRITICAL THINKING Figurative language

> Writers sometimes make comparisons using *similes* and *metaphors*. Similes compare one thing to another (i.e., using *like*); metaphors say one thing actually is another thing.

8 Look at these sentences from excerpt B. Underline the similes and circle the metaphors. What effect do they have? What happens if you remove them?

I kept a keen watch on this furious battle of cold and waves and ice.[…] Eventually the surface of the bay was nothing but a vast white stretch of pavement strewn with numerous black or blue patches that made it look rather like marble.

9 Read these excerpts from the books. Use a dictionary if you need to. Underline metaphors and similes. How does each one make the writer's meaning more vivid?

1 The orchard stretched down to the forest, stopping at a dark wall of spruces, standing there like soldiers.

2 The windmill stood down below, its restless arms a landmark for the village.

3 Slabs of broken ice bobbed on the waves like great white water lilies.

4 The great feather dusters of the coconut trees… were swaying above our heads like gigantic parasols.

An African in Greenland

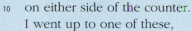
One morning, when my
brothers had left early for the
coconut plantation and there
was no-one left at home to take
5   me for a walk along the
seashore, I went out alone and
visited the Evangelical
Bookshop. Inside, there were
two shelves against the walls
10 on either side of the counter.
I went up to one of these,
attracted by a book laid flat on a half-empty shelf,
with a cover showing a picture of a hunter dressed in
clothes made of animal skins and leaning on a spear*.
15 I was struck at once by the title: *The Eskimos* from
Greenland to Alaska* by Dr. Robert Gessain. The book
was illustrated with photographs and engravings*. I
liked the look of it, bought it, then went on my way
to the beach. By noon, I had finished my new book,
20 the first I had read about the life of the little men of
the north. Was it the author's praise of their hospitality
that triggered my longing for adventure, or was it fear
of returning to the sacred forest? I hardly remember.
But when I had finished reading, one word began to
25 resonate inside me until it filled my whole being. That
sound, that word was Greenland. In that land of ice, at
least, there would be no snakes!
[…]

B

During the previous two weeks, ice had started to build
up each day, but each time a blizzard shattered it.
30 … That was my first sight of the sea freezing over, and
I kept a keen watch on this furious battle of cold and
waves and ice. It was the same fascination I had felt in
my childhood when, hidden behind a tree, I'd watch
a battle to the death between two snakes. Eventually
35 the surface of the bay was nothing but a vast white
stretch of pavement strewn with* numerous black
or blue patches that made it look rather like marble.
When I first walked out on the frozen sea, it gave
me an unforgettable sensation, at once pleasant and
40 frightening. While others strode out firmly, I planted
my feet with care. I was scared but refused to show it.
What if the ice, which was not supported by anything
underneath, should suddenly break?

House of Day, House of Night

C

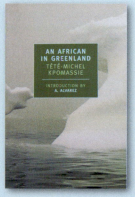

"You don't have to leave home
45 to know the world," said Marta
suddenly as we were shelling
peas* in the steps in front of
her house.

I asked how. Maybe she meant
50 by reading books, watching the
news, listening to the radio,
surfing the internet, or going
to the shop for gossip. But what
she had in mind was the futility
55 of travel.

When you're traveling, you have to take care of
yourself in order to get by, you have to keep an eye
on yourself and your place in the world. It means
concentrating on yourself, thinking about yourself,
60 and looking after yourself. So when you're traveling,
all you really encounter is yourself, as if that were
the whole point of it. When you're at home you
simply are; you don't have to struggle with anything
or achieve anything. You don't have to worry about
65 railway connections and timetables; you don't need to
experience any thrills or disappointments. You can put
yourself to one side—and that's when you see the most.

She said something like that and fell silent. It surprised
me, because Marta has never been further than
70 Wambierzyce, Nowa Ruda, and Wałbrzych.

Some of the peas were maggoty*, so we threw them
into the grass. Sometimes I suspect that whatever Marta
has said is completely different from what I have heard.

spear *a long pointed stick used as a weapon*
Eskimos *natives of Greenland, today known as Inuits*
engravings *types of printed pictures*
strewn with *covered with*

shelling peas *taking peas out of their natural covering*
maggoty *full of insects*

Frozen sea in East Greenland

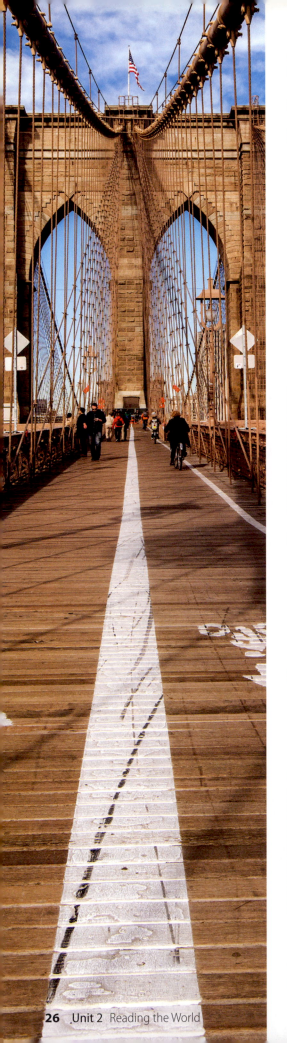

2C Moments of Inspiration

GRAMMAR Narrative tenses and future in the past

1 Read about the Reading Project.

Shaheryar Malik came up with the idea for the Reading Project one day in 2015, as he was walking across the Brooklyn Bridge in New York. He was going to take a selfie and had been taking out his phone to share the moment with his friends when a thought suddenly struck him. Instead of doing something that people had done a million times before, he would share something different with the world. So he went back home, picked 40 books from his bookshelves, ranging from fiction to gardening guides and history books, and carried them back to the bridge. Then he left the books with a note encouraging people passing by to take one for free, read it, and email him to let him know which book they had taken and where they had ended up. The Reading Project would become famous all over New York. Months later, after leaving a total of 250 books in eight different locations in New York, he had received more than 60 emails from people in more than 30 different countries, from Belgium to Singapore.

Narrative tenses
The narrative tenses (i.e., the simple past and past continuous, and the past perfect and past perfect continuous), are used to tell stories. We can also use time conjunctions followed by a verb tense and time prepositions followed by the *-ing* form of the verb. … *when a thought suddenly struck him. Instead of doing*…

2 Look at the Grammar box. In the text in Activity 1, underline examples of:

1 the simple past.
2 the past continuous.
3 the past perfect.
4 the past perfect continuous.
5 time conjunctions followed by a verb tense.
6 time prepositions followed by the *-ing* form of the verb.

3 Which of the tenses in Activity 2 (1–4) are used to describe:

a completed past actions at the time of the narrative?
b completed past actions before the time of the narrative?
c an action in progress at a time in the past?
d an action in progress before a time in the past?

Check your answers on page 130. Do Activity 3.

Future in the past
There are different ways to talk about a future action or event as seen from the past. a *He was just about to get out (on the verge of getting out) his phone… when a thought suddenly struck him.* b *He was going to take (was hoping to take) a selfie…* c *The Reading Project would (was to) become famous all over New York.*

The pedestrian walkway on the Brooklyn Bridge, New York, where Shaheryar put his books

4 Look at the Grammar box. Answer the questions.

1 Which of the sentences (a–c) could describe:
- a future event that *took place*, as seen from the past?
- an imminent future event, that *perhaps did not take place*, as seen from the past?
- a more distant future event that *did not take place*, as seen from the past?

2 Which of the sentences are more formal?

Check your answers on page 130. Do Activities 4 and 5.

5 PRONUNCIATION Using stress to change meaning

a Listen to these clauses and underline the stressed word(s). In which clauses (1 or 2) are we sure that the action did not take place? 🎧 **11**

1 I'd been thinking of visiting New York…
2 I had been thinking of visiting New York…

1 I was going to stay with relatives…
2 I was going to stay with relatives…

b Listen again and repeat the sentences. Then finish them in an appropriate way. 🎧 **11**

6 Read about how author J. K. Rowling started writing about Harry Potter. Choose the correct option.

J. K. Rowling (1) *came / had come* up with the idea of Harry Potter while (2) *traveled / traveling* on a train from Manchester to London. At that time, she (3) *was living / had lived* in London, but she (4) *had spent / was spending* the weekend in Manchester where she (5) *looked / had been looking* for an apartment. As she (6) *was looking / had been looking* out the window at some cows, she (7) *suddenly thought / would suddenly think*: "Boy doesn't know he's a wizard—goes off to wizard school." She (8) *had been writing / was writing* since she was six, but she (9) *was never / had never been* as excited about a potential book before. She (10) *forgot / had forgotten* to bring a pen, and since she was too shy to ask anyone for one, she (11) *spent / had spent* the entire four-hour journey thinking up all the ideas for the book. When she (12) *arriving / arrived* at her London apartment, she immediately (13) *began / was beginning* to write *The Sorcerer's Stone*, although it (14) *would take / had taken* several years to finish.

7 Complete the sentences with the correct form of the verbs. More than one answer may be possible.

1 After _____ (complete) *Harry Potter and the Sorcerer's Stone*, J. K. Rowling _____ (look for) a publisher.

2 She decided she _____ (not / give up) until she _____ (find) a publisher.

3 After _____ (approach) twelve publishers, she _____ (eventually / find) one that _____ (want) to publish it.

4 She _____ (think) of writing for adults but _____ (decide) to write for children instead.

5 She _____ (never / imagine) that the book _____ (become) the best-selling children's book of all time.

8 Work in pairs. Complete the sentences in an interesting way.

1 I was going to… , but I realized I had no money.
2 I was about to… when all of a sudden the lights went out.
3 I was just about to… when my friend called.
4 When I caught the bus, I never imagined I would…

9 MY PERSPECTIVE

What do you do when you finish reading a book? Do you put it on a shelf or give it to a friend? What other ways are there of reusing books? Discuss in pairs.

10 CHOOSE Choose one of the following activities.

- Work in small groups. Remember how Shaheryar Malik and J. K. Rowling had a moment of inspiration that led to a change of plans? Talk about a time when you changed a plan (e.g., a plan to go out, visit someone, or buy something). Say why you changed your plan.

- Work with a partner. Write a summary about a book or movie that inspired you to change your way of doing or thinking about things.

- Research the life of a writer, artist, or other famous person. Give a short presentation about a turning point in their life and the impact it would have on their future.

J. K. Rowling reading from one of the Harry Potter books

more alive than ever before to the richness, diversity, and complexity of our remarkable planet. **"**

ANN MORGAN

Read about Ann Morgan and get ready to watch her TED Talk. ▶ **2.0**

AUTHENTIC LISTENING SKILLS

Following a narrative

Speakers often use longer sentences when they are narrating events, especially in more formal or scripted speech. When you hear words and phrases like *as soon as*, *while*, or *after*, be ready for what comes in the next part of the sentence.

1 Look at the Authentic Listening Skills box. Then look at the extracts from the TED Talk. Choose the more likely ending. Listen and check. 🎧 **12**

1 Discovering this massive, cultural blind spot in my reading came as quite a shock. And when I thought about it, *it seemed like a real shame / I managed to find a book.*

2 When I looked back at much of the English-language literature I'd grown up with, for example, *using an e-reader is more convenient / I began to see quite how narrow a lot of it was.*

3 These days, when I look at my bookshelves or consider the works on my e-reader, *I accepted enthusiastically / they tell a rather different story.*

2 Listen to three more extracts from the talk. With a partner, guess how they might continue. Then listen and check your ideas. 🎧 **13**

1 What do my bookshelves say about me? Well, when I asked myself this question a few years ago,…

2 Having spent my life reading almost exclusively British and North American books,…

3 Four days after I put that appeal online,…

WATCH

3 Work in pairs. Discuss the questions.

1 Make a list of writers you have heard of from countries other than your own.

2 Make a list of books you have read by foreign writers (either in the original language or in translation).
   • How many different countries are on your list?
   • If there are very few, why do you think that is?
   • Do you have a favorite book by a foreign writer?

3 What can you learn from reading books by foreign writers?

4 What is on your bookshelf? What isn't? What does your bookshelf say about you?

4 Watch Part 1 of the talk. Answer the questions. ▶ **2.1**

1 What did Ann discover about herself when she looked at her bookshelves?

2 What kind of books did she mainly have?

3 What kind of books were largely missing?

4 Why did 2012 feel like a good year to start her project?

5 What exactly did she decide to read during the year?

5 Watch Part 2 of the talk. Complete the summary with a number or percentage. ▶ **2.2**

Ann calculated that she would have to read approximately (1) _____ books a week in addition to working about (2) _____ days a week. She was afraid that she might not find enough books because roughly (3) _____ of the books published in the UK are translated from another language.

6 Watch Part 3 of the talk. Label the events in the order (1–8) they happened. ▶ 2.3

_____ **a** She asked for translators.
_____ **b** A team of people translated an entire book for her.
_____ **c** She asked for help on a blog.
_____ **d** Friends and colleagues offered to help her.
_____ **e** Many people all over the world became involved in picking books.
_____ **f** She could not find a book in translation.
_____ **g** A stranger offered to select books for her.
_____ **h** She received two books from a distant country.

7 Watch Part 4 of the talk. Read the opinions about reading books from all over the world. Which point does Ann not make? ▶ 2.4

1 It helps you see the world from other people's point of view.
2 It can sometimes be difficult to accept viewpoints that are different from your own.
3 It can make you question your own ideas and realize what you don't know.
4 It gives you a clear understanding of the way of life in another country.
5 It can help to create greater harmony and understanding between cultures.
6 The more people start asking for books in translation, the more books will become available.

8 **VOCABULARY IN CONTEXT**

a Watch the clips from the TED Talk. Choose the correct meaning of the words and phrases. ▶ 2.5

b Think of a time when the following things happened to you. Then compare your examples in pairs.
1 Somebody *went out of their way* to help you or make you feel welcome.
2 You had to start learning or doing something *from scratch*.
3 You had difficulty *getting hold* of something you needed.
4 You *stuck to your word*, even though it was difficult.

9 **MY PERSPECTIVE**

Work in pairs. Which book from your country would you recommend if someone wanted: to know more about your culture? an interesting read?

CHALLENGE

Choose a book written in your language and find a paragraph or short extract to translate into English. Use dictionaries and other reference books (e.g., a thesaurus, dictionary of collocations) to help you. Then work in groups.

1 Read your translations. Compare the similarities and differences between group members' translations.
2 What were the most interesting and most difficult parts of doing the translation?
3 What has the experience taught you about translation and what can get "lost in translation"?

2E To make a long story short…

1 Listen to someone telling a friend a story. Then answer the questions. 🎧 14

  1 What kind of experience was it?
  2 Where and when did the story take place?
  3 What had happened before the story?
  4 What exactly happened?

2 Work in pairs. Can you remember:

  1 what words the speaker uses to start the story?
  2 what words the listener uses to respond to the story or ask questions?
  3 what words the speaker uses to end the story?

3 Listen again and check your answers. 🎧 14

4 **PRONUNCIATION** Using intonation to express attitude

Listen to four ways of saying *Really*. Match each to the attitude expressed. Then listen and repeat. 🎧 15

  _____ interest   _____ sympathy
  _____ surprise   _____ impatience

5 Listen to some short excerpts from stories. Respond using a phrase from the Useful language box. 🎧 16

6 Prepare to tell a story about something that happened to you, a friend, or a family member on a vacation, a day trip, or a journey. It can be a true story or one you make up. Make notes about the following.

  • what kind of experience it was
  • where and when the story took place
  • what you were doing and / or what was happening when the story started
  • what exactly happened and how you felt at the time

7 Work in pairs. Tell each other your stories and respond appropriately.

8 Now work with another partner and repeat your story. Was it better the second time? If so, how exactly?

Useful language

Starting a story

Have I told you about the time when…?

Have I told you about my (trip / vacation to…)?

I had the most (embarrassing / amazing) experience when…

Responding

How annoying!

What a nightmare!

Oh, no!

How scary!

That's too bad!

What a relief!

Sounds wonderful!

Great!

That was lucky!

Showing interest

Oh, OK.

Uh-huh.

Yeah.

Really? / Is it? / Did he?

Ending

Anyway, to make a long story short,…

Luckily, it all worked out in the end.

It was a really terrifying / hilarious / amazing experience.

Munich Airport, Germany

WRITING A story

9 Read the story on page 149. Put these stages of a story in a logical order (1–6).

a something that went wrong
b a planned action
c how the situation was resolved
d a new plan for the future
e the setting (time, place, protagonist)
f how the protagonist reacted

10 **WRITING SKILL** Using colorful language

Find synonyms for these words in the story. Do the synonyms improve the story? If so, how?

1 singing	**4** walked	**7** looked hard	**10** flew
2 drank	**5** gave	**8** made	**11** took
3 thought about	**6** opened	**9** threw	**12** flew up

11 Underline an expression in the story that means *he was unhappy to find that*. Then complete these sentences in your own words. Write three more sentences of your own using the words in the Useful language box.

1 I opened my suitcase and discovered that to my horror…
2 I looked for my wallet and found that to my utter embarrassment…
3 I opened the letter and saw to my relief that…
4 We arrived home and saw that to our disbelief…

12 Match these emotions with the expressions describing emotion in the Useful language box.

a embarrassment
b anger
c surprise
d amusement
e unhappiness
f disappointment
g relief
h fear

13 Choose three or four expressions of emotion. Write a sentence that could come before or after each one.

14 Plan a story about travel / broadening perspectives, the kindness of strangers, or an idea of your own. Use the different elements in Activity 9. Make notes using key words.

15 Write your story. Give it a title. Check that it includes:

- the correct use of tenses.
- a range of time expressions.
- colorful language and expressions.

Useful language

Describing reactions

I saw to my absolute (horror / embarrassment / relief / disbelief / delight / dismay / disappointment) that…

Expressions describing emotion

My heart sank.
I could hardly believe my eyes.
I was blind with rage.
I couldn't stop laughing.
I felt like bursting into tears.
My face turned red.
I sighed with relief.
I was shaking like a leaf.

Pristine Places

IN THIS UNIT, YOU...

- talk about how to protect the ocean and the environment.
- read about an expedition into the Okavango Delta.
- learn about World Heritage Sites.
- watch a TED Talk about creating underwater sculpture parks.
- write informal emails.

An underwater sculpture in the Coral Reef Sculpture Garden in the Bahamas

3A Deep Blue Sea

VOCABULARY Ocean environment

1 Work in pairs. Look at the photo and read the caption. Why do you think the sculptor chose the ocean as a place to put his art? Do you think it will encourage people to see the oceans as places worthy of protection?

2 Guess the correct options. Do any of the facts about oceans surprise you?

- The oceans cover just over (1) *30% / 70%* of the planet. They are the Earth's largest life-support system.
- About (2) *50% / 70%* of the oxygen we breathe is produced by the oceans.
- An estimated (3) *30%–50% / 50%–80%* of all life on Earth is found in the oceans.
- The world's fisheries employ about (4) *180 million / 18 million* people and feed billions.
- Sea levels have risen (5) *10–25 cm (3.9–9.8 in) / 25–50 cm (9.8–19.7 in)* over the past 100 years.
- The largest living structure in the world is the Great Barrier Reef. It measures around (6) *500 kilometers (310 miles) / 2,600 kilometers (1,615 miles)* in length.
- There are many endangered species, including whales, dolphins, sharks, and turtles. As many as (7) *1 million / 100 million* are killed each year for their meat.
- Just over (8) *2% / 10%* of the ocean is protected by marine reserves and no-fishing zones.

3 Match words in box A with words in box B to make compound nouns. Then complete the article with the compound nouns.

A	climate	coral	endangered	flood	fossil	global
	greenhouse	~~marine~~	oil	polar	sea	renewable

B	change	defenses	energy	fuels	gases	ice caps
	levels	reefs	refineries	~~reserve~~	species	warming

The world's largest (1) _marine reserve_ , covering 830,000 square kilometers (515,738 square miles), has been created around the remote Pitcairn Islands in the South Pacific. These waters contain some of the few pristine (2) _____ left on the planet, which are home to a huge number of sharks and other large fish. Scientists hope that initiatives like this can protect oceans from pollution caused by the dumping of chemicals, plastics, and other trash and by accidental spills from (3) _____ .

(4) _____ is the term used to describe an increase in the average temperature of the Earth's atmosphere and its oceans. This is the cause of longer-term (5) _____ . Many scientists believe that this is largely due to (6) _____ such as carbon dioxide in the atmosphere. This has meant that the (7) _____ in the Antarctic and Arctic are melting, threatening the habitats of (8) _____ such as polar bears. It also results in rising (9) _____ , which threaten the existence of many low-lying islands and other countries and create a need for strong (10) _____ . Many people believe that we should reduce our use of (11) _____ and invest more in (12) _____ sources such as solar, wind, and tidal power.

4 **PRONUNCIATION** Compound noun stress

Listen and check your answers. Then underline the stressed part of each compound noun. Is there a general rule about where the stress is? 🎧 **17**

LISTENING

5 Work in groups. Read the opinions about ecological issues. Choose one or two opinions to discuss.

- The dangers of global warming have been exaggerated.
- We should reduce our reliance on fossil fuels and invest in renewable energy sources.
- People do not do enough to protect the environment or the oceans from pollution.

6 Listen to Enric Sala, a National Geographic explorer and marine ecologist. Answer the questions. 🎧 **18**

1 What is the name of Enric's project and what is its aim?
2 What three threats to the ocean does he mention?
3 What two pieces of advice does he give?

7 Listen again. Complete the statements with no more than three words. 🎧 **18**

1 Enric prefers to spend his time _____ rather than at the office.
2 Enric's work involves using scientific research as well as films, articles, and _____ .
3 Because of overfishing, fish cannot _____ quickly enough.
4 Over the last century, _____ of the large fish in the ocean have disappeared.
5 If the current trend continues, we will lose the majority of the _____ in the world.
6 We've already lost _____ of the world's coral reefs.
7 Enric advises against eating large fish like tuna, sharks, and _____ because they may contain mercury.

8 MY PERSPECTIVE

Work in pairs. Discuss the questions.

1 What is the most interesting thing you have learned about the ocean in this lesson?
2 Do you or your family often eat fish? If so, what kinds? Would you change your eating habits to protect the ocean?

GRAMMAR First and second conditional

First and second conditional
a If *we **don't change** our course before 2050, most of the fisheries of the world **will have collapsed**.*
b If *everyone **made** smart choices, it **would make** a huge difference.*
c *Coral reefs **would not be disappearing** so fast if there **were** more marine reserves.*
d If *we **can inspire** world leaders to create marine reserves, we **will be able** to protect more species.*

9 Look at the Grammar box. Answer the questions.

1 Which sentences refer to:
- a real future possibility?
- a hypothetical or unlikely situation in the present or future?
2 Which modal verbs in bold could you replace with *may*, *might*, or *could*?
3 Which sentences could you rewrite using *unless*?
4 In **d**, replace *if* with *as long as*. Does it make the condition *more* or *less* necessary in order to get the result?

Check your answers on page 132. Do Activities 1 and 2.

Enric Sala uses his photos as a teaching tool. This one shows a coral reef in Palau.

10 Work in pairs. Match the sentence halves. Do you agree with the statements?

1 If you eat more vegetables,
2 If everyone bought fish from sustainable sources,
3 Unless we eat less fish / reduce our fish consumption,
4 Unless sea levels stop rising,
5 If there were no fish farms,
6 As long as governments act now to stop pollution,

a some low-lying islands may have vanished by 2050.
b some large species, like sharks, will become extinct.
c overfishing would definitely increase.
d you will be more healthy.
e we could preserve endangered species like tuna and sharks.
f we will be able to preserve our coral reefs.

11 Look at the Grammar box. Answer the questions.

Conditional variations

We can form conditionals in different ways to express different levels of likelihood and formality.

First conditional

a *If you **see** someone dumping chemicals into the ocean, please **report** it immediately.*

Second conditional

b *If people **stopped** dumping chemicals into the ocean, there **would be** less pollution.*

1 In this sentence, is the condition (the *if* clause) more or less likely than in example sentence a?
If people were to stop dumping chemicals into the ocean, there would be less pollution.

2 In this sentence, is the style more or less formal than in example sentence b?
Were people to stop dumping chemicals into the ocean, there would be less pollution.

12 Complete the questions about these topics in your own words. Then ask and answer in pairs.

endangered species	a flood	global warming
plastic bags	pollution	saving energy
tidal energy	a wind farm	

1 What would happen if…?
2 If everyone would…, ?
3 How would you feel if…?
4 If the government…, ?
5 Should there be…, ?

13 MY PERSPECTIVE

Work in groups. What can you do at home or at school to reduce your impact on the environment? What will the consequences be?

3B Into the Okavango

VOCABULARY BUILDING

Greek prefixes

Parts of speech can be borrowed from one language to another. One case where this is common is in the number of prefixes that are borrowed from Greek to English. These prefixes are common, and they can help you guess the meaning of new words, so they are useful to learn.

1 Work in pairs. Look at the pairs of words (1–8). Match the prefixes in bold with the meanings in the box. Use a dictionary if necessary.

environment	extremely small	land	large
life	more than usual	one	opposed to

1 biology	**bio**graphy
2 ecology	**eco**system
3 microscope	**micro**chip
4 monologue	**mono**tonous
5 geography	**geo**logy
6 hyperactive	**hyper**sensitive
7 antisocial	**anti**biotic
8 macroeconomy	**macro**climate

2 Work in pairs. Guess the meaning of these words. Do you know any other words with these prefixes?

antidepressant	biodiversity	eco-friendly
ecotourism	geophysics	hypercritical
macro lens	microsurgery	monolingual

READING

3 You are going to read about the Okavango Delta. What would you like to learn from the article? Write three questions. Then read the text to check whether your questions were answered.

4 Read the text again. Find evidence for these statements.

1 The Delta is a unique natural environment.
2 There are many species of wildlife and vegetation there.
3 The Delta now has special international protection.
4 The mission of the expedition is to protect the Delta.
5 The team traveled as local people have always done on the river.
6 The Cuito River starts and ends in different countries.
7 The explorers wanted people to follow the expedition online, as it happened.

5 Which posts (A–D) mention themes 1–7? Underline the information that talks about each theme.

1 appreciation of others on the expedition
2 encouragement to learn more about the expedition
3 difficulties that are currently being experienced
4 appreciation of online followers
5 a journey into the unknown
6 encouragement to appreciate nature
7 a reflection on past challenges on the trip

6 Work in pairs. Match these comments* to the photos and their posts. Write a response to two of the posts.

1 Wish I was out there with you around the fire to share memories of the trip.
2 I've really enjoyed seeing the world through your eyes. Can't wait to follow the expedition!
3 Wow! Stunning image and amazing detail.
4 Sounds scary! Good luck with the rest of the trip!

* The comments were created for this activity.

7 Work in pairs. Discuss the questions.

1 Would you have liked to go on the expedition? Why?
2 Have you ever posted photos on a photo-sharing site? What were they? What kind of response did you get?
3 How do you think expeditions like these can help protect wildlife? Talk about publicity, funding, and tourism.
4 What comforts would you miss if you went on an expedition like this? What would you take with you?

CRITICAL THINKING Emotional responses

One way of involving and inspiring people is to create an emotional response in readers.

8 What do you think the writer's purpose was in the posts? Check all that apply. Compare answers in pairs.

☐ to inform people about the expedition
☐ to make people feel involved
☐ to inspire people to protect the natural world

9 Work in pairs. Find examples of the following in the posts. How does each add to the emotional experience?

1 sharing personal feelings
2 highlighting beauty
3 appealing to the senses
4 addressing the reader directly
5 use of colorful language (especially adjectives)
6 use of informal language and exclamation points

10 Complete the sentences. Compare your answers in pairs.

1 My favorite post was the one about…
2 My favorite photo was the one of…
3 It made me feel…
4 It made me want to…

Exploring the Okavango Delta

🎧 **19** *The Okavango Delta in northern Botswana is one of the last wetland wildernesses in Africa. It contains a variety of habitats and is home to a diverse range of flora and fauna. In 2014, the Delta was designated the one thousandth UNESCO World Heritage Site. Dr. Steve Boyes, a conservation biologist and National Geographic Fellow, and his brother, Chris Boyes, are dedicated to the preservation of the Okavango Delta. With a small team of scientists, engineers, local guides, and other experts, they led an expedition over 2,414 kilometers (1,500 miles) down the length of the Okavango River, paddling in traditional dugout canoes down the Cuito River—a source river starting in Angola—to the river's end on the sands of the Kalahari Desert in Botswana. On the way, they broadcast the sights, sounds, and ideas surrounding them through social media and a blog, intotheokavango.org.*

grueling, and exactly what we love most—exploration, research, and pure wilderness living! Here we go for #Cuanavale16.

♡ 💬

B If you keep on looking, there is always more beauty to find! We walked past this so many times while setting up camp, but only later in the day, while walking around to collect biodiversity data, did I focus on this incredibly beautiful flower already overlooked so many times and captured it with the macro lens. There is beauty everywhere, even in your backyard. You just have to take the time to crouch down and take a closer look!

♡ 💬

C The moisture still hasn't fallen from the sky! In the mornings the mist is thick, and everything is covered in dew. With swarms of bees chasing us out of camp so early every morning, we have no time to let our stuff dry,

so tents are always packed sodden*. The bee invasion began a day into our river expedition as an incessant buzz consumed our camp. They are a force to be reckoned with, and every day we expect stings! This place is not easy to live in, but wow—it is amazing to be out here!

♡ 💬

D Our last night around the campfire, the center of our outdoor home in the Angolan wilderness! This is a thank-you to the river team for being so miraculously persistent. A thank-you for getting up every morning and measuring strange fish in the cold, for paddling in the afternoon heat, for braving boiling rapids and angry hippos and burrowing worms. For eating oatmeal 17 weeks in a row, for walking on blistered feet, for staying up late to tweet and post photos online and to upload data. For 122 amazing days. For enduring. It's also a thank-you to all 50,000 of you for following along, for your words of encouragement, your inquisitive nature, and your passion for what we're doing. We know that all of you will act as ambassadors for this crucially important ecosystem. Check out intotheokavango.org for more information on how to get involved!

sodden *very wet*

♡ 💬

A Today we embarked on our journey down the length of the Caunavale River! This is estimated to be 400–500 km (249–311 miles) of narrow, fast-flowing river cutting its way through the Kalahari sands. We have no idea what to expect over the next couple of weeks, but we are sure it will be incredibly beautiful, incredibly

Iguazu National Park, Argentina

3C World Heritage Sites

GRAMMAR Third and mixed conditional sentences

1 Work in pairs. What do you know about UNESCO World Heritage Sites?

2 Read the text and check your ideas. Then answer the questions.

UNESCO is a UN organization that works to preserve important cultural sites (like the Great Wall of China, the Incan ruins of Machu Picchu in Peru, and Krakow's Historical Center in Poland) for the benefit and inspiration of future generations. But did you know UNESCO also works to protect natural places like Iguazu National Park in Argentina and Brazil and the Great Barrier Reef in Australia? Today there are over 1,000 sites in 163 countries around the world. Can you imagine a world without these beautiful sites? If UNESCO had not protected them, some would not have survived, and the world today would be a lot poorer. Now, UNESCO is exploring how it may one day be able to protect wonders of the ocean, which do not belong to any particular country, such as giant underwater volcanoes, coral islands, and floating rainforests.

1 What are World Heritage Sites?
2 Why has UNESCO protected them?
3 What may UNESCO do in the future?

Third and mixed conditional sentences

a *If UNESCO **had not protected** the sites, the world today **would be** a lot poorer.*

b *If the ocean sites **belonged** to particular countries, UNESCO **might have protected** them before now.*

c *If UNESCO **had been able to protect** the ocean before now, it **would have saved** more species from extinction.*

---

3 Look at the Grammar box. Match the sentences (a–c) to the descriptions (1–3).

1 Third conditional: a hypothetical (unreal) situation in the past and its hypothetical result in the past _____
2 Mixed conditional A: a hypothetical situation in the past and its hypothetical result in the present _____
3 Mixed conditional B: a hypothetical situation in the present and its hypothetical result in the past _____

4 Read these variations of the third conditional. Cross out the sentence that has a different meaning from the others.

1 Had UNESCO helped, the sites would not have been preserved.
2 Had UNESCO not helped, the sites would not have been preserved.
3 Had it not been for UNESCO's help, the sites would not have been preserved.
4 If not for UNESCO's help, the sites would not have been preserved.

Check your answers on page 132. Do Activities 3 and 4.

5 Listen to a talk on the Galapagos Islands. Answer the questions. 🎧 20

1 What happened in 1978?
2 How many species are the islands home to?
3 What happened in 2010?

6 Work in pairs. Choose the correct option.

1 If the islands *would not have / did not have* their unique location, they *would not have developed / did not develop* such a rich ecosystem.

2 If the Galapagos Islands *had not become / did not become* a World Heritage Site, they *would not have received / had not received* so much help to protect their wildlife.

3 If UNESCO *had not helped / had helped* with the project, some species *might become / might have become* extinct.

7 PRONUNCIATION   Contractions

a Rewrite these sentences about visiting the Galapagos Islands using contractions where possible. Then say the sentences. How are the contracted verbs pronounced?

1 If the islands were closer, I would have visited them.

2 If I had had more money, I might have gone on a tour.

3 If I had not lost the guide book, I could have been reading about the history.

4 If I had not visited the marine reserve, I could not have taken so many photos.

5 If I had gone on the tour, I would know more.

6 If I had not gone on the tour, I might not be feeling so tired now.

b Listen and check. Underline the words which carry the main stress in each clause. Then listen again and repeat. 🎧 21

8 Read some quotes from a visit to the Galapagos Islands. Complete the second sentence with a conditional sentence relating to the first.

1 We didn't bring enough water, so we got very thirsty.
Had _____

2 The sea was very rough, so we couldn't go on the boat trip.
Had the sea _____

3 Thanks to our GPS, we were able to find our way home.
If not for _____

4 I felt tired, so I missed the tour.
Had _____

5 We didn't get bitten by mosquitoes because we had insect repellent.
Had it _____

I wish / If only

9 Look at the Grammar box. Choose the correct option to complete the sentences.

1 In **a**, the speaker *did / didn't* lose the guide book.

2 In **b**, the speaker *did / didn't* go on the tour.

3 *I wish* and *If only* + past perfect express a desire for the *present / past* to be different.

10 Underline the expressions that show regret.

1 Thank goodness I brought my binoculars.

2 I regret not taking more photos.

3 Luckily, we had an excellent guide.

4 I'm glad we planned the trip carefully.

5 I would have liked to stay there longer.

6 We really should have brought hiking boots.

Check your answers on page 132. Do Activity 5.

11 Look again at the situations in Activity 8. With a partner, write sentences expressing regret or lack of regret.

12 CHOOSE   Choose one of the following activities.

- Think about vacations, day trips, or walks you have been on in the past. Write six sentences expressing regret or lack of regret using third or mixed conditional sentences. Share your sentences with a partner.

- Research and write a paragraph about a UNESCO World Heritage Site. Include third or mixed conditional sentences. Present your research to the class.

- Work in groups. Read the facts below and imagine what might have happened in the past or the present if things had been different. Discuss your ideas using third or mixed conditional sentences.

  a In 1997, 84 countries signed the Kyoto Protocol to reduce greenhouse-gas emissions.

  b For many centuries, people in the Netherlands have built flood defenses along the coast.

  c Dinosaurs became extinct 65 million years ago when an asteroid hit the Earth.

A Galapagos iguana sits on a volcanic rock.

artist ...ul ever with f..r. "

JASON DECAIRES TAYLOR

Read about Jason deCaires Taylor and get ready to watch his TED Talk. ▶ **3.0**

AUTHENTIC LISTENING SKILLS

| Chunking |

When people are speaking to an audience, and especially if they are reading aloud, they often break up their sentences into short meaningful sections, or chunks, to make it easier for the listeners to follow.

1 **Look at the Authentic Listening Skills box. Then listen to an extract from the TED Talk. Mark the pauses.** 🎧 **22**

/ I'm standing here today / on this boat in the middle of the ocean, and this couldn't be a better place to talk about the really, really important effect of my work. Because as we all know, our reefs are dying, and our oceans are in trouble.

2 **Read another extract from the TED Talk. Mark where you think the pauses will be. Then listen and check.** 🎧 **23**

Ten years ago I had my first exhibition here. I had no idea if it would work or was at all possible, but with a few small steps and a very steep learning curve, I made my first sculpture called "The Lost Correspondent." Teaming up with a marine biologist and a local dive center, I submerged the work off the coast of Grenada in an area decimated by Hurricane Ivan.

WATCH

3 **Work in pairs. Discuss the questions.**

1 Why would someone want to put sculptures in the ocean?
2 What do you think the sculptures represent?
3 What could happen to the sculptures after they have been underwater for a while?
4 Jason calls the sculpture parks "an underwater art museum, teeming with life." Why do you think he compares them to a museum? What life does he mean?
5 What effect might the sculptures have on a) visitors and b) the local environment?

4 **Watch Part 1 of the talk. Are the sentences *true*, *false*, or is the information *not given*?** ▶ **3.1**

1 Jason's first underwater exhibition was carefully planned.
2 The underwater museum developed very slowly.
3 In Mexico, he made sculptures of people who lived nearby.
4 Many people have visited Jason's sculptures.
5 "Ocean Atlas" was bigger than his previous sculptures.
6 He paints the sculptures underwater.

5 **Watch Part 2 of the talk. Write down notes answering the questions. Write only key words, not full sentences. Compare with a partner. Watch again to check your notes.** ▶ **3.2**

1 Why is the ocean "an amazing exhibition space"?
2 What does Jason consider to be "the really humbling thing about the work"?

6 Watch Part 3 of the talk. Choose the correct options. ▶ **3.3**

1 "Banker" is Jason's most popular sculpture because _____ .
   a it draws attention to the threats facing the ocean
   b it is widely shared on social media

2 Visitors to the Marine Park in Cancun _____ .
   a have had a positive effect on the environment
   b have had a negative effect on the environment

3 People who visited "Ocean Atlas" _____ .
   a helped to clean up the coast
   b drew attention to an environmental problem

4 The Sculpture Park in Grenada _____ .
   a has increased tourism in the area
   b provided money for a local environment project

5 According to Jason, if we value places or works of art _____ .
   a we protect them better
   b we understand them better

6 Jason says that people _____ .
   a don't appreciate the ocean enough
   b are more aware now of the ocean's fragility

7 Watch Part 4 of the talk. Answer the questions. ▶ **3.4**

1 Why does Jason say "this is just the beginning of the mission"?
2 What is the main message Jason wants to convey? Do you think he succeeds in conveying the message?

8 **VOCABULARY IN CONTEXT**

a Watch the clips from the TED Talk. Choose the correct meaning of the words and phrases. ▶ **3.5**

b Complete the sentences with your own words. Then compare your sentences in pairs.
   1 When I took up _____ , there was *a steep learning curve.*
   2 Something that really *blew my mind* in the talk was _____ .
   3 I think people shouldn't *take* _____ *for granted.*

9 **MY PERSPECTIVE**

Work in pairs. Discuss the questions.

1 What was the most powerful message in the talk? Why?
2 What was your favorite sculpture in the talk?
3 Would you like to visit one of his museums? Why?

CHALLENGE

Jason said, "Let's think big, and let's think deep. Who knows where our imagination and willpower can lead us?" With a partner, think about a sculpture or installation you would like to create to raise awareness of a fragile or endangered environment. Take notes about these questions.

• What would you want to draw attention to?
• Where would you put the sculpture?
• What would it look like?

Describe your sculpture to another pair. How similar were your ideas?

3E World Oceans Day

SPEAKING

1 Read about *Wave for Change*. Answer the questions.

Every year on June 6th, people all over the world celebrate World Oceans Day to raise awareness of the ocean and encourage people to protect it. In *Wave for Change*, people make a specific promise to help the ocean, then record a video clip, stating their promise and doing the wave. Finally they post their videos and encourage others to join them by using the hashtags #WaveForChange and #WorldOceansDay.

1 What is World Oceans Day?
2 What three things do people do in *Wave for Change*?

2 Match the suggestions for helping save the ocean with the explanations.

1 Watch your carbon footprint and cut energy use. _____
2 Eat sustainable seafood. _____
3 Use fewer plastic products. _____
4 Keep beaches and waterways clean. _____
5 Use fewer chemicals in home and garden products. _____
6 Support organizations that work to protect the ocean. _____
7 Influence change in your community. _____
8 Educate yourself about oceans and marine life. _____

a Prevent pollution.
b The more you learn, the more you'll want to help.
c Stop using harmful chemical products that might end up in the ocean.
d Be conscious of your energy use.
e Organize campaigns to educate friends and family about the oceans.
f Get involved in an organization that is fighting to protect ocean habitats.
g Eat less fish. Choose seafood that is sustainable.
h Carry reusable water bottles and recycle.

3 Listen to someone talking about a pledge she made for World Oceans Day. Answer the questions. 🎧 24

1 What does she value about the ocean?
2 What is she worried about?
3 What promise does she make?
4 What does she hope to achieve?

Useful language

Making promises

I never realized…
I promise / pledge to…
My promise is to…
I promise that I'll / I'm going to…

Explaining promises

Let me explain how that's going to work.
Hopefully by doing this, I / we'll be able to…
The more we…, the more / better / less…

Campaigns like *Wave for Change* are bringing attention to issues that affect the ocean. One of the most important issues is pollution. What can you do to help solve this issue?

4 Decide on a pledge you want to make to protect the oceans. Use the information in Activity 2. Make notes on what you want to do, using the questions in Activity 3 and Useful language box to help you.

5 Work in groups. Take turns saying your pledges. Decide whose idea was a) the most practical, b) the easiest, c) the most challenging, and d) the most fun.

WRITING Informal emails

6 Read the emails on page 150. Answer the questions.
1 What event happened on June 8th?
2 Who played, who organized, and who attended?
3 What is the relationship between the people?
4 Underline examples in the emails of:
   a an invitation   **c** acceptance   **e** an offer
   b a request   **d** giving thanks   **f** good and bad news

7 **WRITING SKILL** Informal language

a Read the advice about writing informal emails. Are the statements *true* or *false*? Find examples of each correct (or corrected) statement in the emails.
1 Begin with *Hi* or *Hello* + name.
2 Don't use contractions (*I've / he's / don't*, etc.).
3 Don't use multi-word verbs (*go back*, *get into*, etc.).
4 It is common to use exclamation points (!), dashes (-), and ellipses (…).
5 It is common to use informal language (*guys*, *kids*, etc.).
6 It is not common to leave out words (subjects, *be*, auxiliary verbs).
7 It is common to use abbreviations (AM, ASAP, etc.).

b Find informal expressions in the emails that mean the same as these formal ones.
1 I am writing to express my appreciation of…
2 I hope you are well.
3 I look forward to hearing from you.
4 I apologize for the delay in writing to you.
5 Thank you very much for your email.
6 I am writing to tell you…

8 Make a list of five people you might send an email to. When is it appropriate to use an informal style and when is it not appropriate?

9 Write an informal email to make an invitation or a request or to express thanks. Include personal news and a variety of informal expressions. Send your email to someone in the class. Answer the email you receive.

Useful language

Responding to news
I'm glad / sorry to hear that…
Congratulations on…

Expressing thanks
This is just to say thanks so much for…
I loved / appreciated…

Making and responding to an invitation
Do you feel like / want to?
Sounds great / I'd love to, but…

Making a request
It would be great if you could…
Is there any way you could… ?

Making an offer
I could… if you like.
Should I… ? / I'll…

4 Discovery

National Geographic explorer and TED speaker Andrés Ruzo taking water samples at the Boiling River, Peru.

4A Voyages of Discovery

VOCABULARY Exploration

1 Work in pairs. Look at the photo and read the caption. Discuss the questions.

1 What is the difference between exploration and discovery?
2 What qualities and skills do you think you need to be an explorer?
3 Why do you think people explore?

2 Complete the sentences about exploration and discovery with the correct form of these pairs of words.

endurance + try	launch + boundary	map + seek
mission + hypothesis	motivate + thrill	settlement + network
trek + circumnavigate		

- Part of Sir Edmund Hillary's (1) _____ to climb Mount Everest was for the (2) _____ of being the first. "No one remembers who climbed Mount Everest the second time," he said.
- More than a thousand years ago, it's likely that the islands of Polynesia became overpopulated. This caused Polynesians to explore the oceans by canoe and establish (3) _____ on islands around the Pacific. They set up extensive trading (4) _____ , exchanging many types of plants and animals, including sweet potatoes, chickens, and dogs.
- Isabella Bird was a fearless solo traveler. In the second half of the nineteenth century, she explored the United States, Australia, and Hawaii, where she (5) _____ up an active volcano. At the same time, Annie Londonderry became the first woman to (6) _____ the world on a bicycle. She did it to show just what a woman could achieve on her own.
- The (7) _____ of Apollo 8 in December of 1968, marked a turning point in space exploration because it was the first manned craft to leave Earth's orbit. It showed that the human race was pushing the (8) _____ of our knowledge about the universe.
- The Irish polar explorer Ernest Shackleton tested the limits of his, and his crew's, (9) _____ by sailing in a small open boat for 720 miles across the South Atlantic to try to reach civilization after their ship had been destroyed by ice in the Antarctic. He (10) _____ to do something never attempted before and successfully reached help.
- NASA's robotic explorer, Curiosity, landed on Mars in 2012. Its (11) _____ is to gather scientific data on the climate and geology of the planet and to test the (12) _____ about the existence of water.
- It's never been easier to explore the world thanks to modern technology. We have to thank the explorers who (13) _____ the world like Zheng He, Vasco de Gama, and James Cook. They wanted to better humanity, not just (14) _____ fame and fortune.

3 Read the sentences in Activity 2 again. Answer the questions.

1 What were the different things that motivated the explorers?
2 What do you think was the most important achievement?

4 Work in pairs. Which explorers have you learned about in school? Talk about:

- where they went.
- their achievements.
- their motivation.

LISTENING

5 Work in pairs. How much do you know about these explorers? Complete as much of the chart as you can.

	Nationality	When	Where
Christopher Columbus			
Zheng He			
Leif Erikson			
Neil Armstrong			
Muhammad Ibn Battuta			

6 Listen to a radio show about the explorers. Check your answers and complete the chart. 🎧 **25**

7 Listen again. According to the speaker, are the statements *true*, *false*, or *not stated*? 🎧 **25**

1 Columbus hoped to reach Asia by sea.
2 The Vikings wanted to set up trading networks.
3 The Americans went to the Moon primarily to gather scientific data.
4 Ibn Battuta's journals made people aware of other ways of life.
5 The main motivations of Ibn Battuta and the Spanish were trade and cultural exchange.
6 Modern voyages of discovery are more successful than those of the past.

GRAMMAR Modals of deduction and probability

8 Look at the sentences from the radio show in the Grammar box. Underline the modal verbs.

Modals of deduction and probability

a A major motivation **may have been** curiosity.

b Viking explorers **must have reached** the coast of America in the eleventh century.

c Zheng He **may have gotten** to the Americas before Columbus.

d The world **must be** round.

e There **can't be** life on the Moon.

f Life **could exist** elsewhere in the universe.

9 Complete rules 1–4 with one or more of the modal verbs. Which sentences refer to the past, and which to the present?

1 If you are certain that something is true based on evidence, use _____ .
2 If you are certain that something is not true based on evidence, use _____ .
3 If you are not sure whether something is true, use *might*, _____ , or _____ .
4 To increase the possibility, use *could*, _____ , or *might* followed by *well*.

NASA's Curiosity Mars rover exploring the surface of Mars. The rover's wheels are incredibly only 50 centimeters (19.7 inches) in diameter and about 40 centimeters (15.7 inches) wide.

10 Rewrite these sentences using the words in parentheses.

1 It is possible that Europa, one of the moons of Jupiter, has oceans 30 miles deep. (could)

2 It seems like there is some evidence that the sun is getting hotter. (be)

3 It is likely that Mars formed less than 5 billion years ago. (have)

4 Maybe the solar system formed when a dust cloud exploded. (might)

Check your answers on page 134. Do Activities 1 and 2.

11 **PRONUNCIATION** Deduction stress

> When a speaker is deducing information or expressing probability, you can often tell how certain they are by how they stress the modal. 🎧 **26**

Listen to the sentences. Underline the stressed words. How sure is the speaker in each sentence?

1 There must be life somewhere in the universe.

2 Mars has signs of water, so it might have plant life.

3 We couldn't have walked on the Moon and learned nothing!

12 Read the predictions about space exploration. The level of probability is expressed by modal verbs, adjectives, or adverbs. Underline the modal expression in each one.

1 Robots, like the Mars Rover, and telescopes could completely replace manned space missions in the near future.

2 By the end of this century, we may have discovered life on another planet.

3 Humans will definitely go back to the Moon in the coming decades.

4 People won't lose interest in space exploration.

5 My country might send a rocket into space.

13 Does each prediction express a future possibility, probability, or certainty?

14 Look at the predictions in Activity 12. Which ones do you agree with? Which ones do you disagree with? Why? Work in pairs. Compare your opinions.

15 Work in pairs. Make predictions about space exploration. Use these ideas or ideas of your own.

- colonize the Moon
- vacations in space
- set foot on Mars

4B Discovering the Past

VOCABULARY BUILDING

Suffix -ity

The suffix -ity can be added to some words to mean "the state or condition of."

antique ⟶ antiquity, human ⟶ humanity

Note that there are some irregular formations.
celebrate ⟶ celebrity, simple ⟶ simplicity

1 The suffix -ity is often added to adjectives. What adjective is each noun formed from? Which are regular?

1 curiosity
2 creativity
3 authenticity
4 clarity
5 possibility
6 necessity
7 humidity
8 mentality
9 intensity
10 civility

READING

2 Work in pairs. You are going to read an article about space archeology. Before you read, discuss these questions.

1 What do you think space archeology might be?
2 What technology do you think space archeologists use?
3 How do you think it works?

3 Read the first paragraph and check your ideas.

4 Read the article. Match the sentences with paragraphs 1–5. There is an extra sentence.

a Moreover, with each new batch of images, it is becoming increasingly clear that archeologists have underestimated the size of past human settlements.

b Space archeology not only helps with the discovery of new sites, but it is also helping to protect them.

c Strange as it may seem, archeologists often look to the sky to discover sites buried deep beneath the Earth.

d Parcak embraces the comparisons to Indiana Jones. Her Twitter handle is @indyfromspace, but she also stresses that the analogy isn't perfect.

e Global Xplorer could help democratize archeology and answer some of the field's oldest and biggest questions.

f The project works like this.

5 Cross out the information that is not given in the article.

1 Space archeology…
   a is much cheaper and quicker than traditional methods.
   b shows there are more sites than people thought.
   c will one day replace traditional methods.

2 Satellites can…
   a show where to find ancient settlements that are invisible on the ground.
   b take accurate photographs of ancient sites.
   c help archeologists see significant changes to the surface of the land.

3 Sarah Parcak's project will…
   a help to recover artifacts stolen by smugglers.
   b involve ordinary people in archeological work.
   c help to tackle the problem of looting.

4 People working on the project will…
   a study a small area of the Earth.
   b learn how to recognize ancient sites.
   c know exactly where sites are being looted.

5 Sarah Parcak's aim is…
   a to learn more about ancient history.
   b to encourage more people to be archeologists.
   c to encourage people to value their past.

CRITICAL THINKING Balanced arguments

Writers do not always present both sides of an argument or a complete list of advantages and disadvantages. They often present arguments that support their own point of view. As a reader, you sometimes need to think about what they are *not* saying as well as what they are saying.

6 Work in groups. Discuss the questions.

1 Does the writer present a *positive*, *negative*, or *balanced* evaluation of the technique? How do you know this?

2 Which of the points are mentioned in the article?
   a It enables archeologists to locate sites very quickly and accurately.
   b It could create problems related to privacy.
   c Global Xplorer could inspire many more people to be interested in their past.
   d Training volunteers could be complicated and time-consuming.
   e It is difficult to protect sites from looting.
   f Untrained volunteers may make errors.
   g It enables archeologists to make new discoveries about the past.
   h Technology might replace archeologists one day.

3 Which points from question 2 are possible advantages and which are possible disadvantages?

7 Was your impression of remote sensing influenced by the article? How could you check the advantages and disadvantages by yourself?

Space archeologist needs your help

"Satellite imagery lets us see the invisible. Now we can discover and explore far more of Egypt's ancient treasures faster than ever before. Technology of the future is helping us save our past." — SARAH PARCAK

🎧 **27** 1 _____ Space archeology, or "remote sensing," refers to the use of high-resolution satellite imaging and lasers to map and quantify ancient ruins and protect humanity's past. The process is helping archeologists plan and map their excavations and surveys more precisely and discover an invisible world of lost tombs, temples, and pyramids—even an entire Egyptian city buried for 3,000 years. Satellites cannot literally "see" beneath the ground, but satellite imagery allows scientists to detect subtle short- and long-term changes to the Earth's surface. This is because buried archeological remains affect the overlying vegetation, soil, and even water in different ways, depending on the landscape.

2 _____ Egyptologist Sarah Parcak estimates that less than one percent of ancient Egypt has been discovered and excavated. Millions of sites are believed to remain undiscovered in the Egyptian desert. Of course, any discoveries made by satellite cameras will still need to be confirmed by teams of archeologists digging on the ground, but the time and cost savings of satellite technology are enormous.

3 _____ In recent years, many ancient sites across the Middle East have been damaged, destroyed, or looted, and the stolen artifacts are being sold by networks of antiquity smugglers. Parcak estimates that if nothing changes, all of Egypt's sites will be affected by looting by 2040. So when she won the $1 million TED Prize in 2016, she announced that she will spend the money on developing a cutting-edge computer technology—which she is calling Global Xplorer for now—to combat looting. Her vision is to engage people around the world in a project of archeological discovery and create a new citizen-science technology for mapping and protecting ancient sites.

4 _____ When people join, they are given a card with a small satellite image covering somewhere between 400 and 2,500 square meters (1,312–8,202 square feet) of ground and with only a general idea of the location, which protects the sites. They are then shown examples of what an ancient tomb, village, or looter's pit would look like from space and asked to look for these features on their own card. The resulting data from all the different cards will then be shared with archeologists and government authorities. "The big dream is that ultimately we will map the entire world," says Parcak. "You'd have a global alarm system where areas would glow red when they are being looted."

5 _____ Why did the Pyramid Age end, and why did ancient Egypt collapse? Why did the flow of the Nile River change over time? How did humans shape landscapes, and how did landscapes shape us? "A hundred years ago, archeology was for the rich; fifty years ago it was mainly for men; now it is primarily for academics. Our goal is to allow anyone to participate," says Parcak. By introducing school children to the excitement of exploration and discovery, she also hopes to educate a future generation about the importance of archeological sites and the pressing need to protect the world's cultural heritage. "I think the only solution for stopping looting globally is to get people to buy into the idea that our human history is important," she says.

4C Satellite Technology

GRAMMAR Passives

1 Work in pairs. List three things you can remember about Sarah Parcak.

2 Look at the Grammar box. Underline the passive forms.

Passives
a *Parcak estimates that less than one percent of ancient Egypt has been discovered and excavated…*
b *… millions of sites are believed to remain undiscovered in the Egyptian desert.*
c *… the stolen artifacts are being sold by networks of antiquity smugglers.*
d *… if nothing changes, all of Egypt's sites will be affected by looting by 2040.*
e *When people join, they are given a card with a small satellite image…*
f *They are then shown examples of what an ancient tomb, village, or looter's pit would look like…*

3 Answer the questions.

    1 Which tenses are the verbs?

    2 Why is the passive used in each example?

    3 Which two examples include the agent (doer) of the passive verb? How is the agent introduced?

    4 Look at examples **e** and **f**. What is different about them? (Think about the objects of the verbs.) Can you think of another way of expressing them?

    5 Which example expresses a thought or idea felt by many people? Can you change the sentence to start with *It is…* ?

Check your answers on page 134. Do Activity 3.

4 Work in pairs. What do you know about the history and use of satellites? Complete the article with verbs in the passive or active of the correct tense.

The world's first artificial satellite, Sputnik 1, (1) _____ (launch) by the Soviet Union on October 4, 1957. It (2) _____ (follow) four months later by the first US satellite, Explorer 1. The space race was on, and with it came a new way of looking at the Earth. **The first aerial photographs** were taken a century earlier by a French hot-air balloonist. **Balloons** (3) _____ (briefly use) to gather military intelligence during the US Civil War, and **other attempts to view the ground** (4) _____ (make) by attaching tiny cameras to kites and even to pigeons. Jump forward to the end of the 20th century and thousands of satellites (5) _____ (orbit) the planet, many of them providing steady streams of scientific data, along with views of the Earth that (6) _____ (never dream) of before. **Satellite imagery** (7) _____ (revolutionize) our lives: images (8) _____ (regularly bring) to us from around the globe. It (9) _____ (enable) us to produce accurate maps of the Earth and even to predict the weather. Over 6,500 satellites (10) _____ (estimate) to (11) _____ (put) into orbit, of which only about 1,000 (12) _____ (still use). The rest are basically just space trash now!

This US satellite is used for communications.

Passive reporting structures

5 Look at sentence a in the Grammar box. The structure can be changed and the meaning stays the same. Look at sentences 1–8 about the pyramids. Write a second sentence so that it has the same meaning as the first.

1 It is known, however, that they acted as burial chambers. *They… are known to have acted as burial chambers.*

2 People think that some pyramids are over 4,500 years old. *Some pyramids…*

3 It is estimated that the Great Pyramid of Giza weighs 6.5 million tons. *The Great Pyramid…*

4 It is believed that the pyramid was built as a burial chamber for the Egyptian Pharaoh Khufu. *The pyramid…*

5 It is estimated that over two million stones were used to build each pyramid. *Over two million…*

6 It is believed that the Egyptians transported the stones by river. *The Egyptians…*

7 Some early Arab historians thought it was built as an observatory. *It…*

8 It is reported that the pyramids are visited by over two million people each year. *They…*

6 Work in pairs. Think about news you have seen or heard recently. Start with these reporting structures and use the passive where appropriate. Then present the same news in an alternative way.

It is reported / believed / known / estimated / considered…

> It is reported that seven people have been injured in an earthquake in New Zealand.

> Seven people are reported to have been injured in an earthquake in New Zealand.

Check your answers on page 134. Do Activity 4.

CRITICAL THINKING Information order

Sometimes, words will refer to something that you have previously read. These are called referents. The things they refer to are called antecedents. They refer to the same thing.

*The people watched **the satellite** as it flew overhead.*

7 Look at the words in bold in the article in Activity 4. They all refer to something from the previous sentence. What is it in each case?

8 Choose the most natural follow-up sentence.

1 Satellites send detailed images of archeological remains.
   a This data is then studied by archeologists.
   b Archeologists then study this data.

2 The Earth is orbited by the Moon.
   a Thousands of man-made satellites also orbit the Earth.
   b It is also orbited by thousands of man-made satellites.

3 Many motorists use GPS systems in their cars.
   a These help them to find their way to a destination.
   b Destinations can be found quickly this way.

Check your answers on page 134. Do Activity 5.

9 Read about another type of satellite. Rewrite the underlined sections to make the text flow better. Use passives where necessary.

Many satellites orbit the Earth to monitor changes in the environment.

(1) We know these as Earth Observation Satellites, and they record data on gases in the atmosphere, the condition of the oceans, and vegetation changes. (2) Scientists then examine this information in order to make comparisons over time. (3) Projections about environmental change are made from the comparisons.

Earth Observation Satellites orbit the Earth about 800 kilometers (497 miles) above the Earth. (4) The delicate instruments that they carry need a relatively low altitude, and (5) a constant distance from the sun also helps them.

10 MY PERSPECTIVE

Work in pairs. Have you learned more about satellite technology? Make a list of as many uses of satellite technology as you can think of. Do you know any new ones?

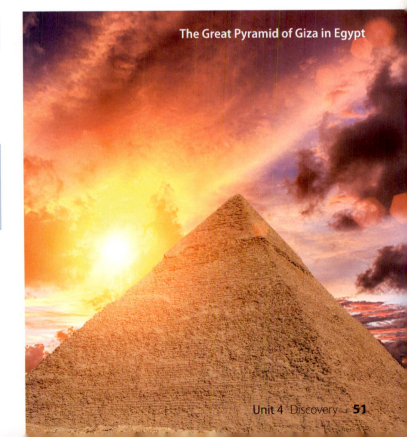

The Great Pyramid of Giza in Egypt

4D The Boiling River of the Amazon

" There remains so much to explore. We live in an incredible world. So go out. Be curious. **"**

ANDRÉS RUZO

Read about Andrés Ruzo and get ready to watch his TED Talk. ▶ **4.0**

AUTHENTIC LISTENING SKILLS

Engaging the listener's attention

Good speakers often engage their listeners' attention by using expressions that focus on interesting or significant information that is coming next. For example, "You'll never guess what happened then," "To my delight / disappointment," "The strange thing is that…" and "What impressed me was that…"

1 Look at the Authentic Listening Skills box. Then listen to two extracts from the TED Talk. Underline the expressions that focus attention on what is coming next. 🎧 **28**

1 But here's the thing: the data is showing that the boiling river exists independent of volcanism. It's neither magmatic or volcanic in origin, and again, over 700 kilometers away from the nearest volcanic center.

2 The river flowed hot and fast. I followed it upriver and was led by, actually, the shaman's apprentice to the most sacred site on the river. And this is what's bizarre. It starts off as a cold stream.

2 Complete the extract from the talk. 🎧 **29**

I asked for tea. I was handed a mug, a tea bag, and, well, pointed towards the river. (1) _____ , the water was clean and had a pleasant taste, which is a little weird for geothermal systems. (2) _____ that the locals had always known about this place, and that I was by no means the first outsider to see it.

WATCH

3 Work in pairs. Discuss the questions.

1 What is the temperature of:
boiling water?   a cup of coffee?   a swimming pool?
2 What do you think could cause a river to boil?

4 Watch Part 1 of the talk. Choose the correct option. ▶ **4.1**

1 Spanish conquistadors arrived in Peru looking for *riches / a new civilization / a mythical river.*
2 The Incas told them they would find a city *made of gold / full of mythical creatures.*
3 They found *riches / strange creatures / a boiling river.*
4 When he was a PhD student, Andrés *read about / remembered* the legend of the boiling river.
5 Other scientists and politicians told him it was *possible / impossible* that the river existed.
6 *His uncle / His aunt / The shaman's wife* had swum in the river.

5 Watch Part 2 of the talk. Label Andrés's actions 1–8 in the order you hear about them. ▶ **4.2**

_____ He saw a stone shaped like a giant serpent.
_____ He heard a loud noise.
_____ He received the shaman's blessing to study the river.
_____ He set off expecting to find a warm stream.
_____ He drank tea made from the river water.
_____ He measured the temperature of the river.
_____ He saw vapor rising from the trees.
_____ He saw a shaman standing above the river.

6 Work in pairs. Discuss the questions.

1 Andrés says about the shaman, "To my tremendous relief—I was freaking out to be honest with you—a smile began to snake across his face, and he just laughed." Why do you think he was so relieved?

2 The shaman allowed Andrés to study the river on the condition that he poured the water back into the ground afterwards. Why do you think this was so important to the shaman?

7 Watch Part 3 of the talk. Are the sentences *true* or *false*? ▶ 4.3

1 Andrés regularly does fieldwork in Peru.
2 His research has not always been easy.
3 The hot water rises from cracks under the Earth's surface.
4 The river temperature fluctuates between hot and cold.
5 The water is probably heated by volcanoes.
6 There are very few similar rivers in the world.
7 More research is needed to fully understand the phenomenon.

8 Watch Part 4 of the talk. Which two ideas do you think Andrés mainly wants to convey? ▶ 4.4

a It is not possible to know everything about the world.
b Researchers find out information, but people need to decide what it means.
c Science has allowed us to make amazing discoveries about the Earth.
d There are still many wonderful things in the world to be discovered.

9 VOCABULARY IN CONTEXT

a Watch the clips from the TED Talk. Choose the correct meaning of the words and phrases. ▶ 4.5

b Complete the sentences with your own words. Then discuss in pairs.

1 When I said that _____ , I was only *kidding*!
2 Despite my *skepticism*, _____ .
3 If you set out on a journey, you should *ensure* that _____ .

10 CHOOSE Choose one of the following activities.

- What characteristics do you need to be a scientific researcher? Do you think you could do the kind of work that Andrés does? What would be the rewards and difficulties? Discuss in groups.

- Research a legend or unsolved mystery from your own culture. Present your research to a partner.

- Andrés describes how different people might understand the significance of the boiling river. Choose one person and write a short newspaper article about the boiling river from the point of view of that person.

CHALLENGE

Andrés says, "Go out. Be curious." Think about an interesting discovery you have made recently—about the world, your country, your town, or your neighborhood. It could be at school, on TV, on the internet, in a book, or in a conversation. Share your discovery with a partner.

4E Breakthroughs

SPEAKING

1 Work in pairs. Look at the list of discoveries, inventions, and technological breakthroughs. Put them in the order they were invented or discovered.

_____ the wheel
_____ electricity
_____ streaming music
_____ paper
_____ the personal computer
_____ the steam engine

_____ the first vaccination
_____ the internet
_____ writing
_____ the television
_____ the internal combustion engine
_____ gravity

2 Listen to three people discussing another important breakthrough. Answer the questions. 🎧 30

1 What are they describing?
2 What are the benefits of it?
3 Has it created any problems or unwelcome side effects?
4 What could happen in the future?

3 Look again at the inventions and discoveries in Activity 1. Choose one of them and answer questions 2 and 3 in Activity 2.

4 Look at the Useful language box. Listen again. Which of the phrases in the Useful language box do you hear? 🎧 30

5 Work in groups. Discuss your ideas from Activity 3. Use expressions in the Useful language box to explain the benefits and ask for and give clarification. Try to agree on which breakthrough has brought the greatest benefit to humanity.

WRITING Discussion essay

6 Look at the question. What information would you need to answer it? Which of these sources would help you find out more?

Is Earth the only planet that has life?

an internet article	a blog	a science teacher
a newspaper article	Wikipedia	a friend or family member
a TV show	a science textbook	a scientific journal

Useful language

Describing benefits

Thanks to X, we can…

X enables people to…

Without X, we'd have to…

Without X, we wouldn't be able to…

Before X was invented, people had to…. Now they can…

Asking for clarification

What do you mean exactly?

What exactly do you mean by… ?

I'm not clear on / about what you're saying.

So are you saying that… ?

So am I right in thinking that… ?

Giving clarification

Well, what I mean is…

No, I'm not saying that exactly.

No, what I'm saying is…

Yes, exactly.

Yes, kind of.

Yes, in a way.

The first steam locomotive was operated in 1804.

7 Read about reliable information. Based on this criteria, are the sources in Activity 6 very reliable, fairly reliable, or possibly unreliable? Give reasons for your opinions.

> Reliable information is true, up-to-date, and accurate. That means:
> - you know and can trust who provided the information.
> - the information is based on research that has been reviewed by experts.
> - the source is not biased (i.e., wanting to convince you of their own opinion).

8 **WRITING SKILL** Hedging

a Read four opinions. Which opinion looks different? Why?
1 People claim that the lost city of Atlantis still exists under the ocean.
2 UFOs do not exist.
3 There is little doubt that we will learn more about black holes in the near future.
4 According to many experts, dinosaurs died out because an asteroid hit the Earth.

b Look at the Writing strategies box. Underline the hedging expressions in Activity 8a.

9 Work in pairs. Use some of the expressions in the Writing strategies box to give your views on the statements in Activity 8a. Then rewrite these sentences using hedging expressions.

1 Fire was humanity's first major discovery.
2 The wheel was discovered 6,000 years ago.
3 The internet was the greatest invention of the twentieth century.
4 Animal migration is one of the great mysteries of nature.

10 Read the essay on page 150. Underline the hedging expressions.

11 Look at the essay again. Find examples of:
- a strong topic sentence stating the situation.
- questions and unsolved mysteries.
- research that has been carried out.
- different theories or beliefs.
- the writer's own opinion.

12 Research and write an essay on one of these questions. Remember to include examples of the features in Activity 11.

Why do rivers boil?

How can remote sensing help archeologists?

What are the practical benefits of artificial satellites?

Writing strategies

Hedging

In factual essays, it is sometimes useful to say how sure or unsure you are about a statement and what your opinion is based on. This is called hedging. Use a range of modal verbs or expressions such as these:

It is generally agreed / widely believed that…

It is often claimed / generally assumed that…

According to most experts / Sarah Parcak, …

Many scientists believe that…

Many experts argue that…

In my view / It seems to me that…

The evidence suggests / There is evidence that…

It is possible / conceivable that…

IN THIS UNIT, YOU...

- talk about the qualities of role models, emphasizing their abilities and achievements.

- read about volunteering.

- learn about two charity challenges.

- watch a TED Talk about how to be a global citizen.

- write a formal letter.

5A Role Models

VOCABULARY Character adjectives

1 MY PERSPECTIVE

Work in pairs. Look at the photo and read the caption. Then read the definition of a role model. Discuss the questions.

A role model is someone you look up to. Your role model may be a famous person who has achieved great things or someone you know personally who has given you encouragement or support. Role models have a positive influence by setting a good example and inspiring or encouraging you to do your best.

1 Do you think it is necessary or helpful to have a role model? Why?
2 Do you have a role model? Who is it? How do they match the description?
3 Which people in your country are good or bad role models for young people?

2 Match these adjectives with the descriptions. Which of these adjectives have a positive or negative meaning? Which are neutral?

apathetic	courageous	idealistic	materialistic
modest	outspoken	single-minded	trustworthy

1 Jun works hard to succeed and doesn't let anyone distract her from her goals.
2 Daniel lacks the motivation or energy to do anything.
3 You can rely on Maiko to keep her word.
4 Sabine values money and possessions above everything else.
5 Kai Shen is never proud and doesn't think he's better than other people.
6 Paula says what she thinks, even if her opinions are not popular.
7 Ahmed does not allow danger or risk to stop him from acting or speaking.
8 Bruno always believes that good things can and will happen.

3 Work in pairs. Form the opposite of the adjectives by adding a prefix: *in-*, *un-*, *ir-*, *im-*, or *dis-*. Write more character adjectives that have the same prefixes.

ambitious	mature	realistic	respectful
responsible	satisfied	supportive	tolerant

trustworthy - *un*trustworthy   modest - *im*modest

4 Complete these sentences with adjectives from Activities 2 and 3 (or their opposites) or other character adjectives. Explain your ideas to a partner.

1 The problem with society today is that most people are too _____ and not _____ enough.
2 The older generation says my generation is _____ .
3 As people get older, they tend to become more _____ .
4 Young people today are more _____ than their parents were at the same age.
5 I think I am very _____ , but I would like to be more _____ .
6 The key to happiness is to be _____ .
7 I really like people who are _____ .
8 I dislike people who are _____ .

This is a stained glass window of Nelson Mandela (born 1918, died 2013) in Soweto, South Africa. Mandela was an icon of leadership and humanity and was a role model for millions of people around the world.

LISTENING

5 You are going to listen to a speech about someone's role model, Malala Yousafzai. What do you know about Malala?

6 Listen to the speech. What adjectives does the speaker use to describe Malala? Are any the same as yours?
🎧 **31**

7 Listen again. Are the sentences *true*, *false*, or is the information *not given*? 🎧 **31**

 1 Malala campaigns for more educational opportunities for girls.
 2 She was not allowed to go to school.
 3 Her father shares her passion for education.
 4 She wrote a blog without revealing her identity.
 5 She was not seriously hurt in the attack.
 6 Malala was in the hospital for six months.
 7 Malala shared her Nobel Peace Prize.
 8 The Malala Foundation puts pressure on world leaders.
 9 Malala was angry with her attackers.
 10 Malala was named after her father.

8 Work in pairs. Discuss the questions.

 1 The name *Malala* means "sad" and "courageous." In what ways are these appropriate descriptions of Malala?
 2 Look again at the definition of a role model on page 57. How was Malala's father a good role model for her?
 3 In what ways is Malala a good role model? What do you think is her greatest achievement?

GRAMMAR Inversion

9 Look at the sentences from the speech in the Grammar box. Notice the inverted word order in bold. Underline the word or words that introduce the inversion.

Inversion
a *Not only **has she co-founded** the Malala Foundation…, but she has also continued to… speak out and challenge world leaders about girls' education.*
b *Little **did he realize** that his own daughter would one day become such a courageous heroine herself.*
c *Malala received death threats, as **did her father**, but…*
d *… so passionate **were they** about the right to education that they continued to speak out.*
e *Only after Malala was attacked **did the law change**.*
f *I am not against anyone. Neither **am I** here to speak in terms of personal revenge.*

10 Choose the correct options to complete the rules about inversion.

 1 In most sentences using inversion, the auxiliary verb or verb *to be* comes *before / after* the subject.
 2 With inversion in the present and simple past, the *main verb / auxiliary* "do" comes before the subject.
 3 Sentences using inversion are *more / less* emphatic.

Check your answers on page 136. Do Activities 1 and 2.

Malala Yousafzai, raised in Pakistan but now living in the UK, is a campaigner for girls' education.

11 Choose the correct options to complete the sentences.

1 Never before *a 17-year-old has won / has a 17-year-old won* a Nobel Prize.
2 Malala was a passionate advocate of girls' education, *as her father was / as was her father*.
3 So difficult *it was / was it* for girls to go to school that Malala *decided / did decide* to start blogging.
4 Only when *her identity was revealed / was her identity revealed*, *she faced / did she face* real danger from her enemies.
5 So badly *was she hurt / she was hurt* that *did she need / she needed* hospitalization.
6 Malala did not stop speaking out about education, nor *she stopped / did she stop* campaigning.

12 Put the words in the sentence beginnings (1–6) in the correct order. Then match them with the sentence endings (a–f).

1 imagine / did / Malala / little
2 had / Nobel / no / the / she / Prize / sooner / won
3 attacked / not / was / Malala / until
4 her / to / she / so / goals / is / achieve / determined
5 a / much / teenage / done / rarely / girl / so / has
6 has / her / not / published / she / only / autobiography

a to achieve global change.
b that one day she would win the Nobel Peace Prize.
c that she has even challenged the president of the US.
d that she used the money to fund a girls' school.
e but she has also had a movie made about her life.
f did the law change in Pakistan.

13 Work in pairs. Complete the sentences to give advice on how to be a good friend. Then explain your ideas to another pair.

1 Under no circumstances should you _____ .
2 Only by _____ can you _____ .
3 Not until _____ .
4 Only when _____ .

14 Prepare to give a short presentation about a good friend. Use the grammar in this lesson and character adjectives. Make notes on:

- your relationship to the person.
- her/his life story.
- her/his character, with examples.
- why she/he is a good friend.

15 Work in groups. Give your presentations. Listeners should think of three questions to ask at the end of each presentation.

16 MY PERSPECTIVE

Work in pairs. In Activity 1 you discussed whether it was helpful to have a role model. How has your opinion changed?

5B Making a Difference

VOCABULARY BUILDING

Collocations

Collocations are groups of words that often appear together. Using collocations can make speech sound more natural.

1 Two of the options collocate with the noun in each sentence. Delete the option that does not collocate with the noun.

1 How can we all *play our* / ~~give~~ / *do our* part in making the world a better place?
2 There are many ways to *perform* / *bring about* / *contribute to* change locally and globally.
3 Volunteering can *do* / *make* / *have* a significant impact on people in local communities.
4 We also need to *address* / *reduce* / *tackle* global issues like hunger and poverty.
5 Charities *make* / *launch* / *run* campaigns to raise money for people affected by man-made and natural disasters.
6 Campaign groups can do a lot to *increase* / *raise* / *rise* awareness of global issues.

2 Complete the sentences using words from Activity 1 and your own ideas. Then compare your ideas in pairs.

1 The key challenge we need to _____ …
2 We should all _____ part in…
3 My school could _____ a campaign to _____ awareness of…
4 If we could…, it would _____ an impact on…

READING

3 Work in pairs. Discuss the questions.

1 Do you think the world is becoming a kinder or less kind place? What evidence supports your opinion?
2 What do you think "Think globally, act locally" means?
3 What are "random acts of kindness"? Give examples.

4 Read the article. Keep the questions from Activity 3 in mind as you read. What ways of making the world a better place are mentioned?

5 Work in pairs. Find these words and phrases in the article and try to guess their meaning. Use the context to help you. Then check your ideas in a dictionary.

1 coverage (line 1)
2 criteria (line 8)
3 a good cause (line 24)
4 win-win (line 32)
5 altruistic (line 35)
6 not your thing (line 44)
7 get down (line 60)
8 grass-roots (line 64)

6 Read the article again. Are the sentences *true* or *false*, or is the information *not given*? Find evidence for the true or false answers.

1 The World Giving Index has gathered data for five years.
2 More and more people worldwide are taking part in volunteer activities.
3 Myanmar is the kindest country according to the World Giving Index criteria.
4 More young people volunteer in the US than in other countries.
5 Five percent of young people worldwide do volunteer work.
6 Volunteering has a positive effect on the volunteers.
7 RAKtivists take part in altruistic activities.
8 Online groups have a mainly educational purpose.

CRITICAL THINKING Faults in arguments

There are many ways that a writer can have a flawed argument. Sometimes it is deliberate, in order to produce a response (e.g., in advertisements), but often it is not on purpose. A common issue is drawing an illogical conclusion from a situation or fact (e.g., *A lot of people in my school volunteer, which demonstrates that young people are altruistic*).

7 Work in pairs. Answer the questions.

1 Look at this sentence from the article. Why is ending **a** a more logical conclusion than ending **b**?

   By socializing with people from different social and cultural backgrounds, you can learn more about people who are different from yourself,

   a *and in this way help to break down social barriers.*
   b *and in this way enjoy volunteering even more.*

2 Complete the article with the more logical conclusions to each numbered paragraph (1–3).

   1a This demonstrates how the desire to help people is an innate part of what it means to be human.
   1b This demonstrates how people are often inspired to behave altruistically to people experiencing adversity.
   2a For all these reasons, there is evidence that volunteering can give you an advantage in college admissions or job interviews.
   2b In this way, you will be able to get a better job after volunteering.
   3a RAKtivism is therefore a highly effective way of raising awareness and contributing to positive social change.
   3b So there is no excuse for thinking there is nothing you can do to help.

8 MY PERSPECTIVE

Do you volunteer? Do you know anyone who does? If you don't, what type of volunteer activity interests you most? Why?

Volunteers painting
a wall together

A kinder world?

🎧 32 With more and more coverage of local and global disasters in the media, you'd be forgiven for thinking that the world is becoming a more violent and heartless place. But according to the World Giving Index,
5 an annual survey of charitable acts in 140 countries around the world, people across the globe are actually getting kinder. The survey measures kindness according to three criteria: donating money to charity; helping a stranger in need; and volunteering time to an organization.
10 Participation in all these areas, relative to the population as a whole, increased across the world in 2016 for the fifth year in a row, with Myanmar topping the list, followed by the US and Australia. One of the most encouraging statistics is that more than half of the global population
15 said they had helped a stranger—and the proportion was even higher in war-torn areas and places experiencing natural disasters, like Nepal, which suffered a devastating earthquake in 2015. (1) _____

Another interesting result from the survey is that it is
20 young people who tend to be the most active in their local communities. The largest group of people doing volunteer work was people between the ages of fifteen and twenty-nine, with one in five giving up their time for a good cause. And according to a survey reported on the
25 website *DoSomething.org*, more than half of teenagers and young adults in the US volunteered in 2011. The most popular activity was fundraising, but young people also tend to prefer direct forms of action that involve helping people or animals in need, such as working with
30 the homeless, the disabled, and the elderly, or with food banks or programs for younger children.

Volunteering is a win-win situation. Research shows that it can be a hugely valuable and rewarding experience for both the volunteers and the communities they support,
35 and that people who take part in such altruistic activities report a greater sense of purpose and meaning in their lives. By socializing with people from different social and cultural backgrounds, you can learn more about people who are different from yourself. This helps to
40 break down social barriers. Plus volunteering provides a great opportunity to learn new skills and boost your employment prospects, so it looks good on a résumé. (2) _____

If volunteering is not your thing, there are other ways of
45 making a positive impact. You could become an activist in a local or online group to campaign for local or global change; or you could become a RAKtivist. RAKtivist is short for "Random Acts of Kindness activist." Random acts of kindness are kind and selfless actions performed
50 to help or cheer up a stranger, just to make them happier. The student who writes Post-it notes to classmates to brighten their day; the jogger who spends ten minutes picking up litter in the local park; the customer who compliments the waiter on his cheerful
55 service; the person who starts collecting money for a good cause—they are all RAKtivists. The website *RandomActsofKindness.org* lists hundreds of ways you can lift someone's spirits with your actions as much as your words. (3) _____

60 It can be easy to get down when looking at all the huge challenges that confront humanity, but the saying "Think globally, act locally" urges people to consider the health of the entire planet and to take action in small ways at a grass-roots level in their own communities. In this way,
65 everybody has the potential to change the world. Why not start today?

A group of people participate in the ALS Ice Bucket Challenge in Hangzhou, Zhejiang, China.

5C Ice Buckets and Rice Buckets

GRAMMAR Cleft sentences

1 Work in pairs. Discuss the questions.

1 Look at the photo of the Ice Bucket Challenge. Have you heard about it? How does it raise money for charity?
2 Read *Ice Bucket Challenge* and check your ideas. Do you think it is a good idea? What would you have done if you had been challenged to take part?

Ice Bucket Challenge

The Ice Bucket Challenge has been described as "the world's largest social media phenomenon." The idea was simple. People were filmed having a bucket of water and ice poured over them in return for donations to a charity and the chance to nominate others to do the same. It was Pete Frates, a former US baseball player, who started the challenge in 2011, after he was diagnosed with ALS (a disease that affects nerve cells in the brain and spine). He invited friends in the US to take the challenge to raise money for an ALS charity. But it was in mid-2014, when the Ice Bucket Challenge went viral*, that the challenge really took off. The ALS Association reportedly received over 40 million dollars in donations. It is because of this success that the challenge has been used by other charities to encourage donations.

went viral *spread rapidly through social media and email*

It cleft sentences
Cleft sentences are a way of changing the word order in a sentence to emphasize certain information.

1a *It was Pete Frates, a former US baseball player, who started the challenge.*
1b *Pete Frates, a former US baseball player, started the challenge.*
2a *It is because of this success that the challenge has been used by other charities.*
2b *The challenge has been used by other charities because of this success.*

2 Look at the Grammar box. Answer the questions.

1 How many main clauses are there in the **a** sentences, and how many in the **b** sentences?
2 How does each **a** sentence begin?
3 What is the most important information in sentence **1a** and in sentence **2a**?
4 Is the most important information at the beginning or the end of the **a** sentences?

Check your answers on page 136. Do Activity 3.

3 Work in pairs. Rewrite the sentences to highlight the information in bold.

Over 40 million dollars have been raised **thanks to the Ice Bucket Challenge**.
It is thanks to the Ice Bucket Challenge that over 40 million dollars have been raised.

1 The Ice Bucket Challenge started **in the US**.
2 Pete Frates wanted to help **a medical charity**.
3 Pete Frates was diagnosed with ALS **in 2011**.
4 **Social media** publicized the challenge.
5 The challenge really took off **at that point**.
6 Some people have been critical **because of the lighthearted nature of the challenge**.

4 PRONUNCIATION Contrastive stress

a Listen to two short exchanges. Answer the questions.
🎧 **33**

> **A** The first challenge took place in 2014.
> **B** <u>I think you're mistaken.</u> *It was* <u>actually</u> *in 2011 that the first challenge took place.*

> **A** Pete Frates played basketball.
> **B** <u>Uh, no. I think you'll see</u> *that it was baseball that he played,* <u>actually</u>.

1 Which word or words carry the main stress in the parts of the sentences in italics?
2 Why are those words stressed?
3 Listen and repeat the exchanges.

b Work in pairs. Make similar exchanges, correcting the information in bold. Use the underlined words and phrases in Activity 4a.

1 A bucket of **ice** is poured over people.
2 Pete Frates invited **politicians** to take the challenge.
3 He wanted to support a **cancer charity**.
4 The ALS Association received **14 million dollars**.

5 Read about the Rice Bucket Challenge. How is it different from the Ice Bucket Challenge?

Rice Bucket Challenge

It was Manju Latha Kalanidhi, an Indian journalist, who came up with the idea for the Rice Bucket Challenge. What worried her about the Ice Bucket Challenge was that it wasted water, a precious resource in many parts of the world. She thought that it would be more useful to provide food, another precious resource, for those in need. What people were asked to do was to donate a bucket of rice to somebody in need. Soon after posting the challenge on social media, the page had 7,000 likes, and a month later the Twitter hashtag #ricebucketchallenge had been tweeted 11,000 times.

What cleft sentences

a *What worried her about the Ice Bucket Challenge was that it wasted water.*
b *What people were asked to do was donate a bucket of rice to somebody in need.*

6 Look at the sentences from *Rice Bucket Challenge* in the Grammar box. Answer the questions.

1 How do the sentences start?
2 How many clauses are there in the sentences?
3 Where is the important information?

Check your answers on page 136. Do Activity 4.

Manju Latha Kalanidhi is the founder of the Rice Bucket Challenge.

7 Match the two parts of the sentences.

1 What is different about the Rice Bucket Challenge _____
2 What both challenges illustrate _____
3 What the Rice Bucket Challenge highlights _____
4 What Manju Latha Kalanidhi suggested doing _____
5 What she did _____
6 What both challenges do _____
7 What people put in the bucket _____
8 What inspired Manju Latha Kalanidhi _____

a is help people in need.
b was rice.
c is the scarcity of food.
d is the global power of social media.
e was post her idea on social media.
f was giving food to the poor.
g was the Ice Bucket Challenge.
h is that people do not donate money.

8 Finish the sentences. Then read your sentences in groups. Do you have the same ideas?

1 What I love / What worries me about social media is…
2 What charities should do to raise awareness is…
3 What concerns people about giving to charities is…
4 What inspires me about… is the way…

9 CHOOSE Choose one of the following activities.

- Work in pairs. Plan another challenge to raise money for a charity. Then present it to another pair. Use cleft sentences to explain your ideas.

- Write a short paragraph about charities that answers these questions: *What inspires people to raise money for charities? What worries people about donating to charities?*

- Have a whole-class discussion on the topic *The government should provide for the sick and needy in society, not charities.* Use cleft sentences.

5D What does it mean to be a citizen of the world?

" They are ultimately global issues, and they can ultimately only be solved by global citizens demanding global solutions from their leaders. **"**

HUGH EVANS

Read about Hugh Evans and get ready to watch his TED Talk. ▶ **5.0**

AUTHENTIC LISTENING SKILLS

Rhetorical questions

Speakers sometimes announce what is coming next by asking a rhetorical question (a question they don't expect an answer to) and then answering it themselves. This can introduce a new topic or section to the talk.

1 Look at the Authentic Listening Skills box. Listen and read the first rhetorical question from the TED Talk. What do you expect the speaker to talk about next? Listen and check your idea. 🎧 **34**

But how did we actually go about recruiting and engaging those global citizens?

2 Complete the extracts from the talk with the questions. Then listen and check. 🎧 **35**

a So where are we?
b But have we achieved our mission?
c How will that achieve anything?

Now, maybe that doesn't sound like a lot to you. (1) _____ Well, it achieved a lot because she wasn't alone.
(2) _____ We run this amazing festival, we've scored some big policy wins, and citizens are signing up all over the world. (3) _____ No. We have such a long way to go.

WATCH

3 Work in pairs. What kind of citizen do you identify as? Rank the descriptions in the correct order for you (1 = most; 4 = least). Say why.

_____ as a member of your local community
_____ as a citizen of your town, city, or region
_____ as a citizen of your country
_____ as a global citizen

4 Watch Part 1 of the talk. Choose the correct options to complete the sentences. ▶ **5.1**

1 Davinia is unusual because she *works selflessly for other people / became a politician at a very young age.*
2 She *donated / raised* money for girls' education.
3 Global citizens are defined by *their actions / their beliefs and their actions.*
4 Working with others worldwide is *the best way / the only way* to solve the world's problems.

5 Watch Part 2 of the talk. Are the sentences *true* or *false*? ▶ **5.2**

1 As a boy, Hugh was not interested in social issues.
2 Sonny Boy's family was rich.
3 The family slept together in a tiny room.
4 Meeting Sonny Boy made Hugh aware of inequalities.
5 Hugh says that governments did not cause Sonny Boy's problems.
6 He believes money can solve the problems.
7 He says that communities cannot find their own solutions to their problems.
8 Hugh decided to start a movement when he got back to Australia.

6 Watch Part 3 of the talk. Complete the sentences. ▶ 5.3

1 According to research, _____ of people who are concerned about the world's problems have taken action to change them.

2 Hugh wanted to encourage _____ of people in _____ countries to become global citizens.

3 Hugh found that many different kinds of people were concerned about the same _____ .

4 Hugh organized the Global Citizen Music Festival at the same time as the _____ .

5 People earned tickets for the festival by _____ on a global issue.

6 Last year, _____ people in New York were able to get tickets to the festival.

7 Members of Global Citizen come from _____ countries, and last year _____ people joined every week.

8 Davinia and _____ other people raised enough money to encourage donations from the US government.

7 Watch Part 4 of the talk. ▶ 5.4

1 What does Hugh mean by these statements?
   a *Those of us who look beyond our borders are on the right side of history.*
   b *We have such a long way to go.*

2 Label the future hopes in the order that Hugh mentions them. Global Citizen will:
   _____ be recruited from every country in the world.
   _____ become more determined.
   _____ make sure that world leaders achieve new goals.
   _____ increase in numbers.
   _____ work to eradicate illnesses.

8 VOCABULARY IN CONTEXT

a Watch the clips from the TED Talk. Choose the correct meaning of the words and phrases. ▶ 5.5

b Complete the sentences in your own words. Then compare your sentences in pairs.
   1 I didn't *sleep a wink* the day before / after _____ .
   2 I wonder why some people find it so hard to _____ . After all, it's *not rocket science.*
   3 I'm not a _____ person. *Far from it.* I'm actually very _____ .

CHALLENGE

Work in pairs. Discuss the questions.

1 Which of these words would you use to describe Hugh's ambitions for Global Citizen? Why?
   a idealistic   **b** realistic   **c** ambitious   **d** achievable

2 "Think globally, act locally." What can you do at a local level to change the world?

---

9 MY PERSPECTIVE

Work in pairs. Do you think younger people have a more global outlook than older people? Why? What are the advantages of thinking globally?

5E Changes

SPEAKING

1 Match verbs in column A with nouns in column B to make collocations about ways to change society or your community.

A	B
1 collect	a blog
2 put on	a petition
3 sign	a charity run
4 go on	money
5 write	a concert
6 hold	a volunteer group
7 boycott	a demonstration
8 join	money
9 take part in	a product
10 donate	a fund-raising sale

2 Work in pairs. Discuss the questions.

   1 Have you ever done any of the things in Activity 1?

   2 If so, when and why? Did you achieve your goal?

   3 If you have not done any of these things, why not?

3 Listen to a conversation between two friends. Answer the questions. 🎧 36

   1 What things does the girl try to persuade the boy to do? Does she succeed?

   2 What three excuses does the boy make?

   3 What points does she make to convince him?

4 Listen again to either the girl or the boy. Which of the phrases in the Useful language box do you hear? Then compare in pairs. 🎧 36

5 Work in pairs. Choose two or three of the ideas and make short dialogs.

climb a mountain	get a part-time job	go on a day trip	help a neighbor
join a gym	prepare a special meal	watch a sport	

   A *Why don't we have a barbecue tomorrow to celebrate the end of the semester?*

   B *I'm afraid I'm busy. I have to finish a project.*

   A *Oh, come on. You could easily do it later. It'll be fun.*

   B *Oh, fine.*

6 Work in pairs. You are going to try to persuade other people to take action to improve the local community. Complete these steps.

1 Think of a change you would like to make in one of these areas:
- **Your school**: e.g., provide a new sports field, better food in the cafeteria, more after-school activities / clubs, or a recycling program.
- **Your local community**: e.g., improve or add a facility (e.g., the local youth club), raise awareness of an issue (e.g., homelessness), or introduce a new system (e.g., keeping the streets clean).

2 Decide what you will do. Use the ideas in Activity 1 to help you.
3 Think of three reasons to help persuade other people to join you.

7 Work in groups. Try to persuade other people to join you.

WRITING A formal letter

8 Work in pairs. Read the letter on page 151. Answer the questions.

1 What is the writer concerned about? Why?
2 What does she want the politician to do?

9 **WRITING SKILL** Making a point

Read the letter again. Answer the questions.

1 Notice how the writer uses the "EPIC" format to make her point. Divide the letter into sections.
   E **Engage** attention
   P State the **problem**
   I **Inform** about solutions
   C **Call** for action

2 What facts and statistics does the writer mention?
3 What adjectives does she use to create an emotional response?
4 Does she use short or long sentences?
5 Find examples of optimistic statements. How could these persuade the reader to take action?

10 Write a letter to a leader urging him/her to take action on a national or global issue (e.g., education, climate change, disease, the environment, or poverty).

- Begin with *Dear Mr. / Ms. (last name)* and end with *Yours sincerely*.
- Begin with *Dear Sir / Madam* if you don't know the person's name.
- Use the "EPIC" format.
- Use inversions and cleft sentences.

Making a point

E   Engage attention

Use short sentences and strong adjectives to engage the reader's emotions.

I am writing to / in connection with / in response to…

P   State the problem

Support your statements with facts.

A key challenge that we face is…

Not only is this…, but it is also…

I   Inform about solutions

State clearly what action you want him/her to take. Make optimistic statements.

What we need to do is…

What I suggest doing is…

Only by…ing can we…

C   Call for action

I urge you to… / I call on you to…

This is our chance to…

Together, we can…

The New York City Marathon is a popular race for people running for charity.

6 Education

The Green School in Bali believes that "Everyone must act in a way which promotes the dignity, health, and safety of others."

IN THIS UNIT, YOU...

- talk about school rules and why they are important.
- read about a fascinating experiment in changing teaching methods.
- learn about Bangladeshi boat schools.
- watch a TED Talk about an inspirational teacher who fixed a broken school.
- write an opinion essay about the internet.

6A Play by the Rules

VOCABULARY School rules

1 Work in pairs. Look at the photo and read the caption. Give three examples of how you think students would be expected to act at the Green School. Do you agree with the quote?

2 Work in pairs. Discuss the questions.

1 Why do schools have rules or codes of conduct?
2 How are they set up? Should students have any say in what the rules are?

3 Match the excerpts from the Green School's Code of Conduct about expected behavior (1–5) with the rules below (a–e).

1 Students are expected to respect the rights, needs, and feelings of others. In return, they can expect such consideration to be shown to them.
2 It is everyone's right to have a safe, clean, and comfortable place to work.
3 Courtesy is an important part of our daily lives. It costs nothing but shows our respect for each other and makes life more pleasant for everyone.
4 Absence of even one day will cause students to miss lessons and lose out on essential teaching.
5 Students are responsible for their personal appearance and are expected to take pride in it.

a No **inappropriate** clothing. _____
b No **vandalism**. _____
c Don't **bully** other students and don't **show disrespect** to anyone. _____
d No **offensive** language or **disruptive** behavior in class. _____
e Don't **skip class**, and **be punctual**. _____

4 Read the **consequences of** not following a code of conduct. Are they fair? How can they help students improve their behavior?

The school will **give** a range of **punishments** if students misbehave. Students who are not punctual will **be given a warning**. With regard to truancy, students who skip classes will **be given a detention** after school, where they will do extra homework so they don't fall behind with schoolwork. If the student's conduct does not improve, the school may **take away some privileges**; for example, they will not be allowed to leave the school at lunchtime. In cases of more severe **misbehavior**, different punishments will be applied. If students bully or disrespect staff or other students, we take a **mediation approach** in which students and staff discuss the effects of their behavior on other people. If their behavior does not improve, they will be **suspended** from school, either temporarily or permanently. With everyone's cooperation, the rules will not need **enforcing**, but they will ensure that we can all live and work happily together.

5 Work in pairs. Explain the difference between the options in bold.

1 The school promotes caring and positive relationships. We will **suspend / take a mediation approach with** students who **bully / show disrespect**.
2 Students learn best in a calm, friendly environment. It is disruptive to the class if students make **offensive / inappropriate** comments.
3 You need to be in class in order to learn. Students who **are not on time / skip class** are given a **detention / warning**.

LISTENING

6 Work in groups. Discuss the questions.

1 What type of behavior is expected at your school?
2 What punishments are given if students misbehave? Which are the most effective / appropriate? Why?

7 Listen to a podcast about school rules around the world. Note the punishments you hear. 🎧 **37**

8 Listen again. Choose the correct options to complete the sentences. 🎧 **37**

1 In the school in Mexico, phones can *sometimes / never* be used in class.
2 In the school in Thailand, *students got away with / punishments were given for* lateness.
3 In the school in South Korea, punishments were *very serious / relatively lenient*.
4 In the school in Brazil, students may be suspended for *serious / minor* misbehavior.
5 The Japanese high school had a *strict / lenient* attitude toward students' appearance.
6 In the school in Colorado, US, the students' behavior *improved / got worse*.
7 In the Argentinian school, the students *were punished for / got away with* speaking Spanish.

9 Listen again. Which of the students (1–7) mention the following? 🎧 **37**

a a punishment that benefits the school
b different rules for elementary and high schools
c a regret about the past
d people discussing problems together
e a public punishment
f a popular punishment
g an unnecessary worry

10 MY PERSPECTIVE

Work in pairs. Discuss the questions.

1 Which of the schools is most similar to your school?
2 Which one would you most like to attend?

GRAMMAR Modals of permission and obligation

11 Work in pairs. Look at the extracts from the podcast in the Grammar box. Which other ways can you think of to express the words in bold in each context?

Modals of permission and obligation

a *In some schools in Mexico you're allowed to use phones… in class.*
b *But in my school, you can't use them at all, except for emergencies.*
c *We're supposed to leave them in our lockers.*
d *… shouting "I must be punctual" or "I must not be late."*
e *… students who break the rules have to do jobs like cleaning the classrooms.*
f *At Japanese elementary schools, children usually don't have to wear a uniform.*

12 Complete these sentences from the podcast with the past forms of the modals and expressions in parentheses. Then listen and check your answers. 🎧 **38**

1 … students who arrived late _____ (must / run) around the school several times…

2 We _____ (not be allowed / wear) make-up…

3 … and the boys _____ (not can / have) long hair…

4 … we _____ (be supposed / answer) them in English, but nobody did.

13 Work in pairs. Look at sentences *a* and *b* in each pair. Is there a difference in meaning? Discuss the difference if there is one.

1 a We **must not use** our phones at all during school hours.
b We **couldn't use** our phones at all during school hours.

2 a The girls **couldn't wear** pants to school.
b The girls **didn't have to wear** pants to school.

3 a You **didn't have to write** a 2,000-word essay this time.
b You **weren't supposed to write** a 2,000-word essay this time.

4 a If we're late three times in a row, we **have to see** the principal.
b If we're late three times in a row, we **must see** the principal.

5 a We **aren't supposed to bring** any phones into the class.
b We **shouldn't bring** any phones into the class.

Check your answers on page 138. Do Activities 1–3.

14 Read the paragraphs from a college guidebook for students. Identify parts where a modal verb or expression from Activities 12–13 can be used. Rewrite the paragraphs from the students' point of view.

Assignments

You are expected to turn in your assignments on time and with a high standard of legibility. Typed assignments are preferable; handwritten is acceptable in certain situations, but it is necessary to request your professor's approval. It is also necessary to request an extension from your professor if you are unable to turn in a piece of work on time. If you disagree with any grade given to you, it is necessary to discuss it with your professor.

We have to turn in our assignments on time and…

Exams

You are forbidden to take books, mobile devices, or other aids into the exam. Students who arrive more than five minutes late may not be allowed to take the exam. Students are obligated to remain in the exam room for the first half hour, after which time they are allowed to hand in their exam and leave.

15 Work in groups. Discuss the rules relating to these areas at your school. Do you think they are fair? Rewrite some of the rules to make them more fair in your opinion. Justify your new rules.

bullying	electronic devices
food and drink	homework
other areas	punctuality
speaking in class	truancy
uniform and appearance	

Students in school uniforms in Havana, Cuba

6B Culture Shock!

VOCABULARY BUILDING

Nouns and prepositions

Some nouns, as well as some verbs and adjectives, are normally followed by the same preposition (e.g., *have admiration for someone, have a talent for something, have a reason for doing something*). When you learn new vocabulary, make a note of the prepositions it is used with.

1 Match each group of nouns with a preposition that the words are all commonly used with.

between	for	in	on	to

a approach   attitude   challenge   damage   threat
b need   punishment   respect   responsibility   talent
c advice   ban   focus   influence   impact
d change   decrease   improvement   increase   rise
e clash   comparison   conflict   difference   gap

2 Complete the sentences with nouns from Activity 1. There may be more than one possible answer.

1 Although teachers have a significant _____ on how well students learn, in the end students should take _____ for their own learning.
2 The huge _____ in the use of computers in recent years presents a significant _____ to older people.
3 There is a _____ for a radical _____ in teaching methods for certain subjects.
4 There is sometimes a _____ between students' abilities and their parents' expectations.
5 If schools establish a _____ on smartphone use, it could lead to an _____ in concentration.

3 MY PERSPECTIVE

Work in pairs. Do you agree with the statements in Activity 2? Why?

READING

4 Read a review of a television show called *Are our kids tough enough? Chinese School*. Answer the questions.

1 Who are the kids referred to in the title of the TV show? Why do they need to be "tough"?
2 What exactly was the experiment, and what was the reason for it?
3 What is the reviewer's opinion of the show?

5 Work in pairs. Find differences between the British and Chinese educational systems in these areas that are mentioned or suggested in the review.

1 talking in class
2 the teacher's authority
3 educational achievement in math and science
4 the length of the school day
5 class size
6 attitudes toward competition
7 hobbies and extracurricular activities
8 concentration and paying attention
9 teaching methods

6 Choose the best meaning for these words and phrases in the text.

1 talk back (line 9)
  a argue   **b** reply
2 insights into (line 11)
  a new understandings of   **b** descriptions of
3 counterparts (line 24)
  a rivals   **b** people in a similar situation
4 let off steam (line 35)
  a release tension   **b** be allowed to play
5 a far cry from (line 52)
  a very different from   **b** separate from
6 thrive (line 58)
  a succeed and be happy   **b** compete

7 Work in pairs. How do you think the experiment ended? Why?

CRITICAL THINKING Evaluating an experiment

8 Read about the results of the Chinese school experiment. Compare them with your ideas in Activity 7.

After four weeks, the two groups were tested in science, math, and Mandarin, and the group taught by the Chinese method had higher scores in all subjects.

9 Read some comments* about the experiment. Do you think they are true? How could the experiment be improved to get a better result?

1 Of course the students using the Chinese method got better scores. They had many more hours of teaching.
2 I wonder what was in the tests. Did they test knowledge or understanding?
3 They probably got higher scores because they were on television. They wanted to show off in front of their friends.

*The comments were created for this activity.

Are our kids tough enough? Chinese School

39 "This is why you learn less than Chinese students. You slow the teachers down. We have to wait until you stop talking." Miss Yang's class of British teenagers stares at her with a mixture of bewilderment and amusement. "You can't
5 say that. That's so rude," retorts 13-year-old Sophie. "Please be quiet," says Miss Yang. Such a challenge to a teacher's authority would be unthinkable back in China, where respect for the teacher is absolute, students do as they are told, and it would not occur to students to talk back.

10 The first episode of the BBC's *Are our kids tough enough? Chinese School* was full of such entertaining insights into the clash between two very distinct educational cultures. Part innovative educational experiment, part reality TV*, the four-part series will follow the progress of a class of relatively
15 well-behaved 13- to 14-year-olds in a successful British comprehensive school* who are to be taught math, science, and Mandarin by highly-experienced and qualified Chinese teachers using traditional Chinese teaching methods. At the end of the four-week period, the students will have been
20 exposed to very different teaching styles than their peers, who they will be tested against. This is in the context of an increasingly competitive employment market in which British schoolchildren are three years behind their Chinese counterparts in math and science. Will it be possible for their
25 academic performance to be improved by a drastic change in teaching methods and educational principles?

There were some shocks in store for the British children. Not only did they have to attend classes for twelve hours a day, almost double the length of their normal school day, but they
30 were also taught in a class with fifty students, as opposed to the normal UK maximum class size of thirty. The day started at 7:00 a.m. with a two-hour mandatory PE session which entailed running several laps around the sports field, and which turned out to be the most popular class—a chance to
35 let off steam and have fun. But there was also a competitive element, with students being timed, tested, and ranked.

This proved disheartening to Joe, who excelled academically but finished last. It was also a contrast from the system they were used to, in which they competed not
40 against each other, but against themselves.

This was followed by ten grueling hours of classes until seven p.m., when the students were allowed to go home for two hours of mandatory homework to review what they had learned. Unlike British schoolchildren, Chinese students
45 do not normally have time for hobbies or extracurricular activities*; their focus is often on achieving the high test scores, which allows them to get a place at a top university. This also instills in them the ability to concentrate and pay attention, a skill that the British children evidently lacked.
50 British children yawned their way through hours of lessons in which the teacher taught from the board at a fast pace, expecting them to absorb information. This was a far cry from the discovery-style learning the class is used to, which involves figuring things out for themselves, questioning
55 what they are taught, and learning from their mistakes.

The show raised as many questions as it answered. Is there such a thing as an ideal teaching method? Can students thrive in an educational system from a country whose assumptions and norms differ so radically from
60 their own? Having been exposed to a different way of learning, would the students prefer to be taught using the new teaching methods? How would the Chinese teachers cope with extremely disrespectful students? And would the experiment work the other way around, with Chinese
65 students taught by British teachers? It will be fascinating to see the results after four weeks.

reality TV *a TV show about the real lives of ordinary people*
comprehensive school *a UK school that does not pick students based on their ability*
extracurricular activities *activities held at school after classes finish*

Students sit in the classroom of a solar-powered boat school in Bangladesh.

6C Education Initiatives

GRAMMAR Passive -ing forms and infinitives

1 Work in pairs. List four things you can remember about the Chinese school experiment.

Passive -ing forms and infinitives

1 ... *a class of relatively well-behaved 13- to 14-year-olds... who are* **to be taught** *math, science, and Mandarin by highly-experienced and qualified Chinese teachers...*

2 *At the end of the four-week period, the students will* **have been exposed** *to very different teaching styles than their peers, who they will* **be tested** *against.*

3 *Will it be possible for their academic performance* **to be improved** *by a drastic change in teaching methods and educational principles?*

4 *But there was also a competitive element, with students* **being timed, tested, and ranked.**

5 **Having been exposed** *to a different way of learning, would the students prefer* **to be taught** *using the new teaching methods?*

6 *And would the experiment work the other way around, with Chinese students* **taught** *by British teachers?*

2 Look at the examples in the Grammar box from the review on page 73. Circle examples of the passive gerund (-*ing* form). Underline examples of the passive infinitive.

3 Work in pairs. Look at the examples in the Grammar box again. Answer the questions.

1 Look at the sentences containing an infinitive. Why is the infinitive without *to* (base form) used? Why is the infinitive with *to* used?
2 How do you express the passive infinitive in the past?
3 Look at the examples of the passive -*ing* form. Why is the -*ing* form used?
4 The verb *be* is missing from sentence 6. Rewrite the sentence with the full passive form.
5 Why does the writer use the passive in each sentence?
6 Which sentences include the agent of the passive verb? Why?

Check your answers on page 138. Do Activities 4 and 5.

4 Read about a school in China. Put the verbs in the correct passive or active form.

A private school in China is taking its students back to traditional ways of learning, which involve (1) _____ (learn) the ancient art of calligraphy, or decorative handwriting, and (2) _____ (study) ancient Chinese texts rather than (3) _____ (teach) math or science. After (4) _____ (show) how to form the Chinese characters used in calligraphy, the students are then expected (5) _____ (memorize) long passages from Chinese philosophy. The teachers believe that (6) _____ (educate) in such traditional ways enables the students (7) _____ (develop) better concentration skills. Despite these methods (8) _____ (consider) old-fashioned by many, students appear to enjoy (9) _____ (challenge) in this way. The teachers hope their ideas will (10) _____ (adopt) by mainstream schools in the future.

5 Work in pairs. What do you think of the idea of the school in Activity 4? Could something similar work in your country? Why?

6 Choose the correct options to complete the article about a different type of school.

The Boat Schools of Bangladesh

Every day during the rainy season, Anna Akter, a nine-year-old student in Bangladesh's remote Natore district, waits by the river to (1) *being picked / be picked* up by the boat that has become her school for the duration of the annual monsoon floods. Then, (2) *having been picked up / being picked up* from different riverside stops, Anna and the other children are taught their usual material before (3) *being dropped / to be dropped* off at the end of the day. These "floating schools" mean that, instead of (4) *be prevented / being prevented* from going to class because the roads have been flooded with water, Anna and hundreds of children like her can (5) *be educated / to be educated* on the boat, without their education (6) *being interrupted / be interrupted*.

Up to two thirds of rural Bangladesh is hit by annual flooding, a situation that may (7) *have been made / having been made* worse by the effects of climate change. In 2007, for example, it was estimated that around 1.5 million people were affected by floods. As a result, every year many of the country's schools have (8) *to be closed / be closed* temporarily. The founder of the Boat Schools, Mohammed Rezwan, was lucky enough (9) *being taken / to be taken* to school in his family's boat as a child, but he remembers many of his classmates (10) *having been forced / have been forced* to stay at home. As a result, he launched the Floating Schools initiative with his own money in 2002. It was the first such program (11) *to be launched / having been launched*, but its success has led to floating schools (12) *being introduced / to be introduced* in other flood-prone countries, including Cambodia, Nigeria, the Philippines, Vietnam, and Zambia.

7 Work in pairs. Read the article again. How do Floating Schools improve children's education?

8 MY PERSPECTIVE

Work in groups. Discuss the three educational initiatives you have read about: a Chinese school in the UK, traditional learning, and floating schools. Which did you find most interesting? Why?

9 Make brief notes to answer each question. Then discuss your answers in groups.

  1 Which subjects should students be encouraged to study these days?
  2 What can you remember being told when you first started learning English?
  3 Is there anything you regret not learning when you were younger? What?
  4 When your parents, or other older members of the family, buy a new phone, do they need to be taught how to use it? What do you do to help them?
  5 Do you like being challenged? By what?

10 CHOOSE

Choose one of the following activities.

- Think of your favorite lesson from last week. Work in pairs. Explain why you liked it and what you learned.

- Work in pairs. Think of another interesting type of school—either one you know or one you research on the internet. Write a short essay about it. Then share the essays in class and vote on the most interesting one.

- Research teaching methods used when your parents and / or grandparents went to school. Report back to the class in a later lesson.

A teacher leads the class in a well-equipped classroom in a Bangladeshi boat school.

LINDA CLIATT-WAYMAN

Read about Linda Cliatt-Wayman and get ready to watch her TED Talk. ▶ **6.0**

AUTHENTIC LISTENING SKILLS

Deducing the meaning of unknown words

It is often possible to guess the meaning of new words that you hear, especially when someone is speaking slowly. You can do this by using the context and your knowledge of other words and word-building. Often you can guess the spelling, too, even if you have never heard the word before. You can then look the word up in a dictionary.

1 Look at the Authentic Listening Skills box. Then listen to two extracts from the TED Talk. Complete what Linda says with one word in each space. 🎧 **40**

1 I graduated from Philadelphia public schools, and I went on to teach special education for 20 years in a low-income, low-performing school in North Philadelphia, where crime is _____ and deep poverty is among the highest in the nation.

2 After things were quickly under control, I immediately called a meeting in the school's _____ to introduce myself as the school's new principal.

2 Work in pairs. Compare the words you wrote, and see if you can figure out their meanings. Use a dictionary to check your ideas.

3 Listen to two more excerpts. Write down any words that you do not recognize. 🎧 **41**

4 Work in pairs. Compare the words you wrote down and see if you can figure out their meanings. Use a dictionary if you need to.

WATCH

5 Work in pairs. Discuss the questions.

1 Which of these might you expect to find in a "broken school"? Use your dictionary if you need to. Can you think of other things?

affluence	assaults	bullying	creativity
high exam scores		high morale	illiteracy
juvenile delinquency		truancy	vandalism

2 If you were in charge of a "broken school," which of these areas would be your top priority to fix? Why? Would you choose any other areas to tackle?

behavior	morale	school environment	test scores

3 Imagine it is your first day in charge of a "broken school." How would you spend it? Why?

6 Watch Part 1 of the talk. Are the statements *true* or *false*? ▶ **6.1**

1 Linda had never been to Philadelphia before becoming principal.
2 She spoke to the school on her first day as principal.
3 She was not used to working in schools with social problems.
4 Ashley interrupted Linda's lecture to challenge her.
5 Ashley's words helped Linda understand her own school days.
6 She met Ashley again at Strawberry Mansion School.

7 Watch Part 2 of the talk. Number Linda's actions in the order she describes them. ▶ 6.2

a throw away unwanted equipment
b appoint an excellent team
c redecorate and clean the school
d give students safe lockers

8 Watch Part 3 of the talk. What problems among the students does Linda mention? How did Linda and her team improve the students' performance? ▶ 6.3

1 poor attendance   5 violence
2 bullying   6 problems with learning
3 poverty   7 vandalism
4 difficult home life 8 poor academic
                         achievement

9 Watch Part 4 of the talk. Match the sentence beginnings with the endings. ▶ 6.4

1 Linda holds regular "town hall" meetings at school so that _____
2 She is strict about discipline so that _____
3 It is important to give students a "real school" so that _____
4 Teachers should remember students are sometimes scared so that _____

a her students respect her and they can work together better.
b communication can be improved.
c they can provide them with hope for the future.
d they can do well in life after school.

10 **VOCABULARY IN CONTEXT**

a Watch the clips from the TED Talk. Choose the correct meaning of the words and phrases. ▶ 6.5

b Complete the sentences in your own words. Then compare in pairs.
1 I hope that one day I'll be able to _____ , but I still have *a very long way to go*.
2 *Fast forwarding* to _____ (time / date), I'll probably be _____ .
3 Something that's often *on my mind* lately is _____ .

11 Work in pairs. Discuss the questions.

1 Which of these words describe Linda's leadership style?

approachable	authoritarian	compassionate
democratic	empathic	imaginative
inspirational	tough	

2 Linda described the improvements made at her school. What do you think were the three most important factors in achieving these?
3 Would you like to have a principal like Linda? Would her approach work in your school? Why?

12 Which of the ideas you discussed in Activity 5 were mentioned in the talk? Have you changed your mind about any of your ideas as a result of watching the talk?

CHALLENGE

Work in pairs. Can you remember Linda's three slogans? If you could create three slogans for your school, what would they be? Why did you choose them?

6E Testing Times

SPEAKING

1 Work in pairs. Discuss the questions.

1 What do you think the difference is between tests and continuous assessment?
2 Which do you prefer?
3 Can you think of other types of testing?

2 Listen to two students discussing tests and continuous assessment. Complete the table. 🎧 **42**

	in favor of tests	against tests	arguments used
Mateo			
Sofía			

3 Listen again. Which expressions from the Useful language box do you hear? 🎧 **42**

4 Listen again. Write down the expressions for agreeing and disagreeing that you hear. What others do you know? 🎧 **42**

5 PRONUNCIATION Rise-fall-rise intonation

a Look at the expressions for partially agreeing in the Useful language box. Then listen and underline the word(s) with the main stress. Notice the rise-fall-rise intonation at the end. 🎧 **43**

b Listen again and repeat the intonation. 🎧 **43**

6 Work in groups. Discuss two or three of these opinions.

1 In my opinion, schools should do more to develop children's creativity.
2 Frankly, I think that studying literature is a waste of time.
3 I don't think people should have to wear a school uniform.
4 I personally feel that it should be mandatory to study computer skills starting at the age of five.
5 My view is that speaking English fluently is more important than learning grammar rules.

Students take their examination in an exam hall at Dongguan University of Technology in south China's Guangdong province.

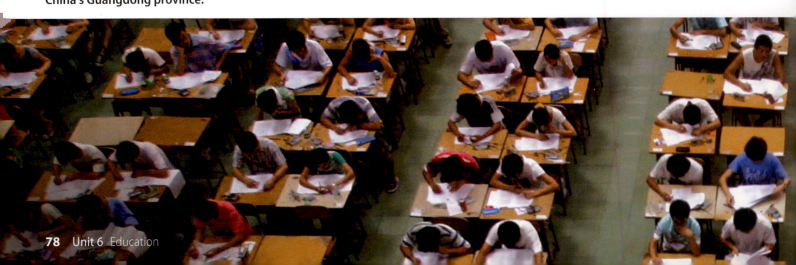

WRITING An opinion essay

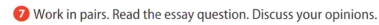

7 Work in pairs. Read the essay question. Discuss your opinions.

Some people believe that the main goal of schools is to prepare students for work. Others say that personal development is a more important focus. What is your opinion? Support your ideas with arguments and examples from your own experience.

8 Read the essay on page 151. Answer the questions.

   1 In the writer's view, what is the key goal of schools?
   2 Does the writer mention your ideas?
   3 What other ideas are mentioned?

9 Work in pairs. Answer the questions.

   1 In paragraph 1, which two opposing views are introduced? What background information is given?
   2 In paragraph 2, what two arguments are mentioned for seeing education as preparation for work?
   3 In paragraph 3, what other purposes of education are mentioned?
   4 In paragraph 4, what is the writer's personal view and what justification is mentioned?

10 **WRITING SKILL** Avoiding repetition

   a Work in pairs. Read the essay on page 151 again. Find at least two different words and phrases which have a similar meaning to the words below.
a aim	**c** get a job	**e** be a good citizen
b most important	**d** enable	**f** do well at school

   b Read two opinions about the internet. Which one do you agree with more? Why?

   Some people <u>think</u> that the internet <u>enhances</u> people's lives because they can <u>get</u> all the information <u>they need</u> for their lives and studies. Others <u>maintain</u> we have <u>far too much</u> information nowadays.

   c Match the underlined words and phrases with those with a similar meaning (a–f).
a access	**c** improves	**e** necessary
b an excessive amount of	**d** say	**f** consider

   d Which alternatives are more formal, and which more informal? Can you think of other alternatives?

11 You are going to write an essay discussing the opinions in Activity 10b. Make notes for a four-paragraph essay. Support your ideas with arguments and examples from your own experience.

12 Write your essay. Use phrases from the Useful language box. Avoid repetition.

Useful language

Discussing an opposing opinion
On the one hand, it is true that…
It is definitely true that…
It is probably true to say that…
There are strong arguments for the idea that…

Expressing a personal opinion
On the other hand,…
However, …
It seems to me that…
I would question whether…
I would argue that…
It is my (personal) view that…
I strongly believe that…

Concluding
To conclude, …
To sum up, …
All in all, …
In conclusion, …

7 Moving Forward

IN THIS UNIT, YOU...

- talk about ways of commuting to school.

- read about innovative designs inspired by nature.

- learn about sustainable cities.

- watch a TED Talk about transportation systems of the future.

- write a report.

Subway trains in Tokyo, Japan, get so crowded that people are hired as "pushers" to make sure everyone fits.

7A Getting There

VOCABULARY Everyday commutes

1 Look at the photo. Is public transportation busy where you live? Could a scene like this happen?

2 Complete the text about getting to school with these words and phrases.

breakdowns	carpool	commute	commuters	commuting
congested	congestion	connection	drop them off	exhaust
shuttle service	smog	stuck	subway	

Some trips to school can be as simple as walking ten minutes down the road, but, increasingly in our urbanized world, the daily (1) _____ is taking longer and uses several methods of transportation, making it more complicated.

In Tokyo, Japan, students regularly take the train, bus, or (2) _____ to get to school, and (3) _____ can be as young as six. Their journeys can easily be an hour or more and can include several types of transportation. Although public transportation in Japan is reliable, (4) _____ can happen, so the youngest kids have yellow flaps on their backpacks so that adults know to look out for them if they miss a (5) _____ or appear lost.

In UK towns and cities, the trip to school is usually by school buses or public transportation (i.e., trains, buses, and the Tube in London), though a lot of parents take younger kids by car and (6) _____ at school. This adds to the volume of rush-hour traffic and can result in vehicles getting (7) _____ in gridlock. One way of helping the problem may be to (8) _____—several people traveling to school in a single car. Another may be encouraging students to bike or walk to school. While that may ease the (9) _____ , students will then be among the cars and therefore breathing in (10) _____ .

If you live in Istanbul, Turkey, (11) _____ to school can involve changing continents! Crossing the Bosporus, a waterway in the city, means going from Asia to Europe or vice versa. In a city known to be badly (12) _____ , the ferry (13) _____ is the most pleasant means of avoiding the (14) _____ that can occur in parts of the city, and it has connections to the city's bus and subway services.

3 Work in pairs. Answer the questions.

1 Find the three forms of *commute*. What parts of speech are they?
2 Look at these groups of words from the text. Do the words in each group have the same meaning? If not, what is the difference?
   a commute (n), crossing (n), trip (n)   **d** congestion, gridlock, rush hour
   b transportation, vehicles   **e** subway, Tube
   c exhaust (n), smog

4 MY PERSPECTIVE

Work in groups. Discuss the questions about your commute to school.

1 How do you commute to school? Is it expensive? Is it tiring?
2 How far do you travel and how long does it take you?
3 What are the advantages and disadvantages of your commute?

LISTENING

5 Listen to a radio show about commuting in cities. Identify the problems mentioned for each city. 🎧 **44**

	Mexico City	Istanbul
air pollution		
the city's location		
shortage of public transportation		
the number of traffic lanes		
congestion at rush hour		
lack of incentive to use public transportation		
overcrowded public transportation		

6 Listen again. Complete the sentences. 🎧 **44**

1 There is air pollution in Mexico City because the smog _____ .
2 Gloria's father commutes from his home _____ to the business district.
3 He regularly spends _____ a day commuting.
4 The population of Mexico City is more than _____ .
5 Mexico City has experimented with _____ .
6 Mexico City may soon have a new _____ system.
7 Many streets in Istanbul are too _____ for cars.
8 People need to use bridges to get from _____ .
9 In heavy traffic, motorists often _____ lanes and _____ their horns.
10 Istanbul has a large new _____ and will soon have more _____ .

7 Work in pairs. Do you think these solutions relate to Mexico City, Istanbul, or both?

1 They're planning to introduce more ferries to ease the congestion.
2 They've improved emissions testing for vehicles.
3 They've increased the number of bus lanes.
4 They're looking into building a fourth bridge.
5 They're introducing a bike-sharing program.

GRAMMAR Ellipsis and substitution

8 Work in pairs. Look at the sentences from the radio show in the Grammar box. Answer the questions about the words in bold.

1 In sentences a–e, which words are omitted?
2 In sentences f–j, which words do the underlined words replace?

Ellipsis and substitution

a *It's infuriating.* **Yes, it must be.**
b *Could you move closer to the center?* **We'd really like to.**
c *You can imagine how heavy the traffic gets during rush hour.* **I definitely can.**
d *Hasn't the government widened the roads?* **Well, maybe they could have,** *but no.*
e *Has the government come up with any solutions?* **They have, but we need more.**
f *Why not use public transportation instead?* **He's tried** <u>doing that</u>.
g *Are things any better where you are?* **I'm afraid** <u>not</u>.
h *We have a similar problem to* **the** <u>one</u> *Gloria talked about.*
i *Do you get to school by car?* **I** <u>don't</u>, *but lots of my friends* <u>do</u>.
j *I hope that'll help.* **I hope** <u>so</u>, *too.*

Check your answers on page 140. Do Activities 1–3.

9 Choose the best answer in each response to the questions below.

1 What is public transportation like where you live?
  a It's better than it used to.
  b It's better than it used to be.

2 Do towns and cities have enough bike lanes?
  a Well, there are some, but not enough.
  b Well, there are some ones, but not enough.

3 Are towns and cities likely to introduce bike-sharing programs?
  a I don't know, but I definitely hope to.
  b I don't know, but I definitely hope so.

4 Do drivers usually obey the rules of the road?
  a Well, most drivers do obey, but some don't obey.
  b Well, most drivers do, but some don't.

5 Does the government need to build more sidewalks in rural areas?
  a Walking in the country can be dangerous… so yes, they really need to.
  b Walking in the country can be dangerous… so yes, they really need.

6 Has your country introduced strict regulations for private drivers and taxis?
  a They must, but I don't know the details.
  b They must have, but I don't know the details.

10 MY PERSPECTIVE

Work in pairs. Discuss the questions in Activity 9.

Ferries at Eminonu with the Topkapi Palace in the background in Istanbul, Turkey

11 Rewrite the underlined phrases to use ellipsis or substitution.

Dad's a civil engineer, and he travels a lot for his job. His company had been saying they would send him abroad, and last year they (1) finally sent him abroad—to Thailand. I'd always wanted to visit Bangkok, so at last I was finally able (2) to visit Bangkok. I'd heard that public transportation in Bangkok could be really busy, and (3) it was really busy! *Tuk-tuks* (three-wheeled taxis) are great. They're disappearing, but I got a ride in (4) a tuk-tuk once; but they're too dangerous for the school commute. I would have loved to commute on the Skytrain—an elevated railway—but that's mainly for the business districts, so (5) I couldn't use it.

12 Work in pairs. Write questions for these answers. Then ask another pair your questions. Answer using ellipsis and/or substitution.

1 Can you ride a bike?

1 No, I wish I could.
2 I might, some day.
3 No, never, but I'd like to.
4 No, but I will be very soon.
5 I don't, but I have a friend who does.
6 Because I was told to.
7 I wouldn't have if I'd known.
8 I definitely am!
9 I should have, but I didn't have time.

7B Nature's Algorithms

VOCABULARY BUILDING

Verb suffixes

Many verbs in English have the suffixes *-ize*, *-ify*, *-ate*, or *-en*. Examples: *civilize, minimize; clarify, identify; estimate, operate; harden, weaken.*

1 Complete the words with *-ize, -ify,* or *-ate.*

circul_____	collabor_____	communic_____
imit_____	innov_____	just_____
maxim_____	memor_____	priorit_____
pur_____	regul_____	replic_____
subsid_____	un_____	util_____

2 Add the suffixes *-ize, -ify, -ate,* or *-en* to these words to form verbs. You may need to change the part of speech.

electric	formula	long	origin
simple	stable	strong	urban

3 Complete the sentences with a verb from Activities 1 or 2 in the correct form. There may be more than one possible answer.

1 There are many ways in which we design technology to _____ the natural world in some way.
2 The doctors needed to _____ the patient's heart rate in order to do the operation.
3 Many species of insects _____ in groups to work more effectively.
4 Increasing online crime has _____ efforts from IT experts everywhere to improve online security.
5 Sometimes new transportation ideas are too complex and need to be _____ .

READING

4 Work in pairs. You are going to read an article about biomimicry. Can you think of any connections between these pairs?

a bullet train—a kingfisher's beak
a car windshield—a butterfly's wing
a drone—a moth
a sailboat—a shark
traffic—a swarm of ants

5 Read the article and check your answers. What other examples of biomimicry are mentioned?

6 Work in pairs. Read the article again. Choose the best subtitle for each paragraph and say why it is best. There is one subtitle you do not need.

a A field of study uniting experts
b A smart way to save money and electricity
c An improvement inspired by a hobby
d Designing new roads for the future
e Flying machines designed to copy nature
f Working together to prevent gridlock

7 Underline the evidence in the article for these statements.

1 Natural systems and organisms have evolved over a long period of time.
2 The designer of the bullet train decided to rethink the shape of the engine.
3 Modern flying machines cannot completely avoid risks in the natural environment.
4 Smart energy grids copy the way bees communicate with each other.
5 Smart traffic solutions require drivers to have a new mindset.

CRITICAL THINKING Understanding connotation

Writers can create a positive or negative impression with the words they use. Some words (e.g., *relaxed, young*) have **positive connotations** (they suggest positive ideas), while others (e.g., *lazy, immature*) have **negative connotations**.

8 Work in pairs. Answer the questions.

1 Find words and phrases with positive or negative connotations in paragraph 1.
2 What impression of biomimicry is the writer trying to convey with their word choice? Is it successful?
3 Find words in these sentences that convey a positive or negative impression of biomimicry.
   a Biomimicry seeks sustainable solutions by imitating nature's tried-and-true patterns and strategies.
   b The so-called benefits remain unconvincing.
   c The Biomimicry Institute empowers people to create nature-inspired solutions for a healthy planet.
   d Butterfly wings are undoubtedly beautiful, but nature also has a darker and more competitive side.
   e Biomimicry will catalyze a new era in design and business that benefits both people and the planet.

9 MY PERSPECTIVE

What do you think of the parallels made in the text between the natural world and human innovation? Think about ways in which the natural world might have inspired the following: flight, underwater exploration, clothing, building materials, societies.

Designers can use vapor during wind-tunnel tests to show how aerodynamic a car is.

Biological blueprints

45 What do a Japanese bullet train and a kingfisher have in common? The answer lies in the exciting and rapidly emerging discipline called *biomimicry*. Literally meaning "imitation of life" or "copying nature,"
5 biomimicry looks to the natural world for solutions to human challenges. Increasingly, creative minds from such diverse fields as biology, architecture, engineering, and medicine are studying processes that nature has developed and streamlined over billions of
10 years and replicating them in innovative products and technologies. These include Olympic-winning sailboats and swimsuits whose surfaces mimic a shark's skin; solar cells based on the structure of a leaf; building materials inspired by bones and eggshells; and non-
15 reflective, energy-efficient windshields inspired by butterflies' wings. The questions behind such innovations are "How would nature solve this?" or "What blueprint already exists in the natural world?"

But back to the bullet train. The first train was, as the
20 name suggests, shaped like a bullet, with a rounded engine at the front. But when it entered tunnels, it created a pressure wave that resulted in a huge sonic boom, like a clap of thunder, as the train emerged at the other end. The train's designer, an engineer who
25 also happened to be an avid birdwatcher, went back to the drawing board. Observing how a kingfisher was able to move smoothly between the air and the water with minimum turbulence, he remodeled the nose of the engine using the shape of the kingfisher's beak. The
30 result? Today's super-streamlined bullet train, which travels at higher speeds than the original prototype and uses less energy.

Designs inspired by nature are not new. Da Vinci's drawings of helicopters and parachutes are clearly based
35 on observations from nature, and the Wright brothers created their first aircraft by studying the flight of birds. But in recent years, teams of engineers and researchers worldwide have been studying the characteristics of winged creatures to come up with designs for even
40 more complex vehicles, including robotic drones (unmanned aircraft) the size of hummingbirds, moths, or even tiny bees. These vehicles are programmed to avoid obstacles and to stabilize themselves after a collision, but they face the same threats as actual
45 insects, which include being eaten, caught in a spider's web, or even squashed by pedestrians.

Urban planners are also drawing inspiration from the biological world to come up with smart energy and transportation solutions. A problem with complex
50 human infrastructure, such as the electrical grid, is that its various parts don't talk to each other or monitor the whole grid. In bee colonies, by contrast, individuals can sense what jobs need to be done and do them instinctively without central organization. By identifying
55 the unifying pattern, or algorithm, underlying the bees' system, energy companies can design interconnected components that communicate with each other, thus maximizing efficiency and reducing costs.

Researchers have also discovered an exemplary case of
60 perfect traffic in nature: there is never congestion on ant tracks. Like bees, ants continuously communicate by touch and by the release of pheromones, or chemical signals, which give them an overview of the movements of the swarm as a whole. Could cars use such "swarm
65 intelligence" in the future to communicate with each other and reduce traffic? In purely technical terms it is a possibility. But radical new systems like these can only function if people are prepared to think collaboratively, and that may take some time.

7C Sustainable Cities

GRAMMAR Nominalization

1 Work in pairs. Read the text in the Grammar box about the challenges of urbanization. What do you think the other problems are? What sustainable solutions might there be?

Nominalization

A *The rapid growth of our cities has led to an increase in the world's urban population. UN predictions suggest that by 2050, about two-thirds of the world's population will be living in cities, creating a shortage of living space and other problems. Therefore, there is a desperate need to find sustainable solutions to these problems of urbanization.*

---

2 Text A in the Grammar box contains the same facts as Text B below, but they are expressed differently. Look at the underlined sections of Text B. How are they different from Text A?

B Our cities are (1) <u>growing rapidly</u>, and so the world's urban population (2) <u>has increased</u>. (3) <u>The UN has predicted</u> that by 2050, about two-thirds of the world's population will be living in cities, and there (4) <u>won't be enough</u> living space. So, (5) <u>we desperately need</u> to find sustainable (6) <u>ways of solving the problems</u> which will be created because so many (7) <u>people will be living in urban areas</u>.

3 Answer the questions about the two texts.

1 How are the adverb + verb combinations in Text B expressed in Text A?
2 How many clauses does each text contain?
3 Which text has more nouns? Which has more verbs?
4 Which text is more formal and impersonal?

Check your answers on page 140. Do Activities 4–6.

4 PRONUNCIATION Words with two stress patterns

a Where do you think the main stress is in the words in bold?
  1 The population of urban areas will **increase**.
  2 There will be an **increase** in the population of urban areas.

b Listen and check. Then choose the correct options to complete the rule. 🎧 46
  Some two-syllable words are stressed on the (1) *first / second* syllable when they are verbs and on the (2) *first / second* syllable when they are nouns.

c Listen to five pairs of sentences. Underline the stressed syllable and write N (noun) or V (verb). 🎧 47

	a	b	
1	decrease	decrease	_____
2	imports	imports	_____
3	record	record	_____
4	present	present	_____
5	suspect	suspect	_____

The rapid-transit system in Curitiba, Brazil, connects express buses that get around the city quickly. Its popularity has decreased traffic and helped reduce pollution.

5 Work in pairs. Complete the text about sustainable cities with these nominalizations.

change	conservation	contribution
cost	creation	decrease
disruption	improvements	need
reduction		

Transportation

In light of the widespread problems with traffic jams, there is an urgent need for a radical (1) _____ in the way people travel. We need sustainable cities. First of all, sustainable cities support the (2) _____ of communities in which amenities are built close together, so there is a reduced (3) _____ for commuting far. Other measures include (4) _____ to existing public transportation systems. For example, the Brazilian city of Curitiba, rather than accepting the huge (5) _____ of constructing a whole new subway system and the severe (6) _____ to the lives of the city's residents, decided to improve and speed up the public bus network by making it more like a subway system, with raised platforms, longer buses, and pre-paid tickets.

Energy use

An important aim of sustainable cities is to achieve a (7) _____ in the city's carbon footprint. The use of renewable energy and the introduction of energy (8) _____ measures can produce a massive (9) _____ in CO_2 emissions. Waste recycling can also make an important (10) _____ to energy production.

6 Complete the cause-and-effect sentences (1–6) by nominalizing these phrases.

it improves air quality	sea levels rise
they get healthier	they get more independent
~~they pollute the air~~	we invest in renewable energy

1 _Air pollution_ is largely due to vehicle emissions.
2 A reduction in car ownership could result in _____ .

3 _____ in young people could result from encouragement to walk to school.
4 Lowering the driving age to 16 could lead to _____ for young people.
5 _____ would bring about less reliance on fossil fuels.
6 Failure to tackle climate change could cause _____ .

7 Work in pairs. Read about another way of improving energy efficiency. Rewrite the text using nominalizations and verbs expressing cause and effect from Activity 6. Then compare your ideas with another pair.

More and more people are becoming interested in the idea of smart sidewalks, and they are investing more money into research. People can recycle old tires to create small electromagnetic tiles. When people walk on them, they produce energy, which can be used to power small appliances. Smart sidewalks are being installed in places such as shopping centers, concert venues, sports venues, and airports, and one day this could provide more of our energy.

8 Had you heard of smart sidewalks before? Where else do you think they could be installed to produce energy?

9 MY PERSPECTIVE

Work in groups. Discuss the initiatives from this lesson that you find most interesting, giving your reasons.

10 CHOOSE

Choose one of the following activities.

• Research how different towns around the world are becoming more sustainable. Write a report on an initiative that you find interesting.

• Work in pairs. Write a paragraph for how a town or city in your country could become more sustainable. Then read your paragraph and explain your ideas in groups.

• Work in pairs. Find four or five interesting facts in this unit. Write a multiple-choice question about each one. Then work with another pair to ask and answer your questions.

The Van Gogh–Roosegaarde bicycle path in the Netherlands is made from thousands of stones poured into concrete and covered in a material that allows them to absorb energy during daylight and glow after dark.

> ❝ Our current way of thinking is not working. For our transportation to flow, we need a new source of inspiration. ❞

WANIS KABBAJ

Read about Wanis Kabbaj and get ready to watch his TED Talk. ▶ **7.0**

AUTHENTIC LISTENING SKILLS

Predicting what comes next

When people listen to a speaker, they constantly make and update predictions about what the speaker might say next. It is often possible to do this by noticing the words he or she uses, especially if they are stressed. This makes it easier to follow the flow of ideas.

1 Look at the Authentic Listening Skills box. Then read the first sentence from the TED Talk. Decide which of the topics Wanis is most likely to talk about next. Listen and check your answer. 🎧 **48**

One of my greatest pleasures in life is, I have to admit, a bit special.

a the speaker's life
b a description of the pleasure
c why the pleasure is special

2 Work in pairs. Read and listen to three more sentences from the talk. Predict what Wanis might talk about after these sentences. Use the stressed words in bold to help. 🎧 **49**

1 *Some cities are calmly industrious, like Dusseldorf or Louisville.*
2 *For decades, our **remedy** for **congestion** was simple.*
3 *But if you look at our cities, **yes**, we have some underground subway systems and some tunnels and bridges, and also some helicopters in the sky. **But** …*

3 Listen and check your ideas. 🎧 **50**

WATCH

4 Work in pairs. What do you know about driverless cars? What could be the advantages and disadvantages?

5 Watch Part 1 of the talk. Choose the correct options to complete these sentences. ▶ **7.1**

1 Wanis sees cities as "living beings" because
   a they are full of people.
   b the roads remind him of a human body.
   c they are lively and energetic places.
2 Wanis's main complaint about traffic is that
   a there are too many vehicles on the road.
   b people make too many unnecessary trips.
   c people waste too much time traveling slowly.
3 Wanis says that a program of expanding or building new roads
   a can never solve the problem of traffic jams.
   b is only possible outside cities.
   c is possible in some cities, but not others.

6 Watch Part 2 of the talk. Are these statements *true* or *false*? ▶ **7.2**

1 Wanis was first inspired by the vascular system when he was sick.
2 The body contains 16,000 miles of blood vessels.
3 Wanis believes more vehicles should travel in the air and underground.
4 The Chinese bus can travel above congested streets.
5 Commuters in Tel Aviv and Abu Dhabi are traveling in detachable pods.
6 Businesses are interested in the potential of urban flying vehicles.

7 Watch Part 3 of the talk. Complete the statements with numbers or a percentage. ▶ 7.3

1 Almost _____ of traffic in cities is caused by drivers looking for somewhere to park.
2 _____ of cars in cities contain only one passenger.
3 Every time our heart beats, it pushes _____ of red blood cells around the body.
4 More than _____ of the oxygen capacity of our blood cells is used efficiently.

8 Complete the summary.

The train Wanis describes does not need to stop because the cars (1) _____ and turn into (2) _____ buses. Then a section of the bus (3) _____ and (4) _____ to your house.

9 Watch Part 4 of the talk. Choose the correct options. ▶ 7.4

1 It is *easy / difficult* for driverless cars to learn traffic rules.
2 Driverless cities *would still need / would not need* traffic lights and traffic lanes.
3 Cars would drive *faster than / at the same speed as* they do now.
4 Cars would move according to *new rules / changing algorithms*.
5 Driverless cars *will flow freely / will not need robotic control*.
6 Wanis believes these developments could happen *now / in the near future*.

10 **VOCABULARY IN CONTEXT**

a Watch the clips from the TED Talk. Choose the correct meaning of the words and phrases. ▶ 7.5

b Think of an example of each of the following. Then compare your examples in pairs.
1 an *"aha" moment* you have had
2 something that has been an *eye-opener* for you
3 how a city can be *car-centric* or *people-centric*
4 an *attribute* of a healthy transportation system

CHALLENGE

Work in pairs. Imagine you have to design a transportation strategy for a sustainable city. Which three features would you prioritize? Which three would you not include? Make notes on your reasons for each.

- build more bike lanes and paths
- build tunnels and overpasses
- encourage carpooling
- encourage working from home
- only allow parking outside the city center
- expand the subway system
- encourage delivery by drones
- invest in driverless cars
- subsidize all public transportation
- widen existing roads

Now work in groups. Try to agree on a plan to include five different features.

---

11 **MY PERSPECTIVE**

Discuss in pairs. Would you want to travel in a driverless car? Why?

7E Opinion Poll

SPEAKING

1 Work in pairs. Compare the length of different trips from your home to school, the city center, and other places in your town or city.

It's a twenty-minute walk.
It's a ten-minute bus ride.
It's a three-hour drive.

2 Listen to the survey on a local bus system. Number the questions in the order you hear them. (The wording may be different.) 🎧 51

_____ Do you use the bus system?
_____ Why is that?
_____ How could local authorities improve the bus service?
_____ What is the bus fare to the city center?
_____ How do you normally travel?
_____ If the buses ran more frequently, would you use them more often?
_____ How often do you take the bus?
_____ If the city council subsidized the bus service, would you use it more often?

3 Listen to the interview again. Is the interviewee positive or negative about the local bus system? What indicates this? 🎧 51

4 Look at the Asking for information section of the Useful language box. Use these expressions to make the questions in Activity 2 more polite. Then listen again and check. What do you notice about the word order in indirect questions? 🎧 51

5 Work in pairs. Ask and answer the questions in Activity 2 about your own town or city. Use some indirect questions.

6 Work in pairs. Choose one of these topics and write six to eight questions about your town or city. Then ask different class members the questions and write down their answers. (You will use them later to write a report.) Use the expressions in the Useful language box.

traffic near your school / home / in the city center
conditions for cyclists / pedestrians
public transportation (e.g., buses, subway, shuttles, ferries)

Useful language

Introducing a survey

I'm conducting / carrying out a survey on…

Would you mind answering a few questions?

Asking for information

I wonder if I could / Can I ask…?

I'd like to know…

Do you happen to know / Do you have any idea…?

Giving information

I'd say… / I think… / I have a feeling…

Not offhand. / Not off the top of my head.

As far as I know / remember, …

On average, … / Generally speaking, …

Sorry, I have no no idea. / don't have a clue.

School buses in Zhengzhou, the capital of central China's Henan Province

WRITING A report

7 Are there green spaces where you live? How are they used?

8 Work in pairs. Read the report on page 152. What questions do you think the interviewers asked?

9 Work in pairs. Which of these is <u>not</u> a feature of a report? Find examples of the others in the report.

1 a title and subheadings	**5** a formal style
2 a statement of purpose	**6** recommendations
3 the background of the report	**7** personal opinions
4 figures and statistics	**8** nominalizations

10 Find phrases in the report to express the number of students with a particular opinion (e.g., *almost half*).

11 A survey asked students about a bike path to school from the town center. Complete the text with expressions of quantity from Activity 10.

	always	usually	sometimes	occasionally	never
Do you bike to school?	35%	19%	9%	11%	26%
Do you use the bike path?	90%	8%	2%	0%	0%

We surveyed the students about biking to school and found that (1) _____ biked to school at least occasionally. (2) _____ always or usually biked, and (3) _____ said that they sometimes or occasionally did. When asked if they used the bike path, (4) _____ used it all the time while (5) _____ used it most of the time. (6) _____ said they had no or little interest in using the path at all.

12 **WRITING SKILL** Expressions of approval and disapproval

Work in pairs. Find three ways of expressing approval and three of expressing disapproval in the report on page 152. Can you think of any other ways of writing about people's (dis)approval of something?

13 Work in pairs. Plan a report based on the findings of the survey you conducted in Activity 6. Then write the report using the features from Activities 9–12 and expressions in the Useful language box.

Useful language

Explaining the purpose

This report has been written to provide information on…

The purpose of this report is to inform the public about…

The purpose of the survey / investigation was to determine…

Explaining findings

It was found that…

The key finding is that…

Most of the people interviewed feel that / find…

Most respondents said that / reported…

A number of people commented on…

With regard to / Regarding…

In terms of…

Overall, it appears / would appear that…

8 The Real Me

IN THIS UNIT, YOU...

- talk about teenage stereotypes.
- read about Ms. Marvel, the teenage comic superhero.
- learn about how sleep patterns change in adolescence.
- listen to a TED Talk about how the teenage brain is wired.
- write an essay comparing advantages and disadvantages.

Teens in South Africa practice iSbhujwa, a type of local dance, for a competition.

8A A typical teenager?

VOCABULARY Teenage stereotypes

1 Do you think teenagers have typical characteristics and behaviors? Why? If yes, how would you describe them?

2 Take the quiz. Does it mention your ideas? Compare your answers in pairs.

---

1 How much are you **influenced by** your **peers**?
  a I very often give in to **peer pressure**.
  b I **follow the crowd** with some things but sometimes **do my own thing**.
  c I don't pay attention to what other people do.
2 How self-conscious are you?
  a I **couldn't care less about** what other people think of me.
  b I'm aware of how I **come across** but not very worried.
  c What people think of me is very important.
3 What is your attitude toward authority?
  a I never question what other people tell me to do.
  b I obey the rules, but I like to talk about them and know why they exist.
  c I'm the typical rebellious teenager!
4 How moody are you?
  a I'm usually very even-tempered.
  b I'm always cheerful and in a good mood.
  c My moods tend to go up and down a lot.
5 What is your attitude toward risk?
  a I avoid danger, but I sometimes take calculated risks.
  b Risky activities **give me a thrill**.
  c I prefer to **play it safe** and avoid taking risks.
6 How impulsive are you?
  a I often do things without thinking of the consequences.
  b I always have a lot of self-control.
  c I generally **weigh the pros and cons** before acting.

---

3 Work in pairs. Complete the sentences with the correct form of the words or phrases in bold in the quiz. Do you agree with them?

1 Teenagers usually compare themselves with their _____ .
2 There's a lot of _____ to wear fashionable clothes.
3 People who _____ as self-confident are usually less confident deep down.
4 Teenagers tend to be more _____ their friends than by their parents.
5 People who don't _____ when it comes to fashion tend to stand out.
6 Regardless of their own interests, parents should allow kids to _____ in their free time.
7 People who _____ about what other people think are in danger of becoming arrogant.
8 When making a decision, you'll have a better idea of what to do if you _____ .
9 You'll never learn from new experiences if you always _____ and avoid danger.
10 People tend to do extreme sports because the danger _____ .

4 Find six character adjectives in the quiz. Do they have a positive or negative meaning, or could they be either? Use a dictionary if necessary. Then describe people you know using the adjectives.

LISTENING

5 Listen to a radio show where a psychologist and a teenager talk about the teenage years. According to the speakers, are the statements *true*, *false*, or *not given*? 🎧 52

1 Teenagers tend to be the same all over the world.
2 The concept of a "teenager" is a modern invention.
3 Laura is always influenced by her peers.
4 Laura looks more self-confident than she feels.
5 There are cultural differences in attitudes to authority.
6 Many teenagers enjoy volunteering and helping others.
7 Laura prefers to avoid taking risks.
8 Laura had a difficult experience while changing trains.

6 Look at the quiz on page 93. Listen again. Find the answers that best describe a "typical teenager." For which question is it hard to generalize about a typical teenager? 🎧 52

7 MY PERSPECTIVE

Work in pairs. Discuss the questions.

1 How much do you think teenagers in your country fit the stereotypes described?
2 How are teenagers in your country portrayed in the media? Are they ever unfairly criticized?
3 What would you say to point out the positive contributions of teenagers?

GRAMMAR Adverbials

8 Look at the sentences from the radio show in the Grammar box. Underline the adverbs and adverbials. Then answer the questions.

Adverbials

Adverbials consist of one word or expressions of two or more words. They modify the meaning of a sentence or part of a sentence.

a I *definitely* like to follow the fashion.
b *Interestingly*, that depends a lot on the culture.
c I *probably* wouldn't wear anything that made me stand out.
d Teenagers will *often* engage in risky activities.
e I *really* like traveling.
f *In fact*, I have my own taste in music.
g I planned it *carefully*.
h Teenagers will have their ups and downs *from time to time*.
i *Maybe* that's another myth?
j Teenagers also *tend to* be very self-conscious.

1 What do the underlined adverbs and adverbials express: addition, attitude, degree, frequency, manner, or level of certainty?

Teenagers shopping in Hiroshima, Japan

Teenagers shopping in Poznan, Poland

2 Choose the correct option to complete the rules.

a Adverbs expressing an attitude (e.g., **apparently**, **frankly**), **perhaps**, and **maybe** tend to be used *at the beginning / in the middle / at the end* of a clause.

b Longer adverbials and adverbs of manner tend to be used *at the beginning / in the middle / at the end* of a clause.

c Frequency adverbs, adverbs of degree, and others such as **probably**, **also**, and **just** tend to be used *at the beginning / in the middle / at the end* of a clause.

3 Which sentence expresses a stronger negative idea?

a *I really don't like speaking in public.*

b *I don't really like taking risks.*

Check your answers on page 142. Do Activities 1 and 2.

9 PRONUNCIATION *really*

a Listen to the sentences from the radio show. Underline the words that carry the main stress. 🎧 **53**

1 I really like traveling.
2 I really don't like speaking in public.
3 I don't really like taking risks.

b Listen again and repeat the sentences. 🎧 **53**

c Work in pairs. Talk about things you (don't) like, (don't) enjoy, or (don't) want to do. Use *really* and the correct stress in your sentences.

10 Work in pairs. Decide where to put the adverbials in parentheses in the sentences. More than one position may be possible. Then discuss if the statements are true for you.

1 I'd enjoy backpacking around the world. (probably / very much)
2 I wouldn't enjoy extreme sports like rock climbing. (definitely / at all)
3 I might try to overcome an irrational fear I have. (possibly / some day)
4 To make a balanced decision, I try to weigh the pros and cons. (just / carefully)
5 I ask my parents and friends for guidance. (also / most of the time)
6 I do my homework every night; I have more time for my family and friends. (as a result / usually / very quickly)

11 Complete the sentences with your own opinions. Then read them to a partner and explain your ideas.

1 Interestingly, most people in my family…
2 Basically, teenagers are…
3 Strangely enough, I have never…
4 To tell the truth, I would never risk…
5 Honestly, I don't imagine…
6 Apparently, most teenagers…

Teenagers shopping in Dubai, UAE

LOUIS VUITTON

Teenagers shopping in São Paulo, Brazil

8B Teenage Superheroes

VOCABULARY BUILDING

Binomial expressions

Binomial expressions are pairs of words used together, joined by *and*. The words always appear in the same order. (For example, *peace and quiet, black and white, fish and chips*). It would sound awkward to say *quiet and peace*.

1 Work in pairs. Complete the binomial expressions with these words. Then guess what they mean.

clear	downs	ends	figures	foremost
order	sound	sweet	tear	tribulations

1 first and _____
2 odds and _____
3 short and _____
4 trials and _____
5 safe and _____
6 facts and _____
7 law and _____
8 wear and _____
9 ups and _____
10 loud and _____

2 Put these pairs of words into the correct order with *and*.

1 gentlemen / ladies
2 black / white
3 address / name
4 salt / vinegar
5 lightning / thunder
6 there / here
7 bed / breakfast
8 forth / back

3 Complete the sentences with expressions from Activity 1.

1 Their parents were relieved when the children turned up _____ .
2 We don't have much time, so let's keep this _____ .
3 He supported his argument with interesting _____ .
4 They had their _____ , but overall they had a good relationship.
5 The insurance policy doesn't cover _____ to the equipment.

READING

4 Work in pairs. Discuss the question.

Do you know any of these superheroes? Do you know any others? What are their characteristics?

Batman   Captain America   Flash   Wonder Woman   X-Men

5 Read the article about Ms. Marvel. Which of these features of superheroes are described?

a backstory	a desire to help
a secret identity	a special costume
confidence in their own abilities	extraordinary powers

6 Work in pairs. Find these words and phrases in the article and try to guess their meaning using the context to help you. Then check your ideas in a dictionary.

Paragraph 1	groundbreaking, skyrocketed
Paragraph 2	phase, reconcile
Paragraph 3	distinctive, alien
Paragraph 4	coming-of-age, overwhelming
Paragraph 5	misfit, worthy

7 Work in pairs. Answer the questions.

1 In what way is Kamala "torn between two worlds"?
2 How does Kamala's idea of what she wants out of life change?
3 How does Kamala's story reflect "every teenager's coming-of-age crisis"?
4 What is Kamala's "dual identity" and how does she "come to terms" with it?
5 What makes the book different, according to Wilson?
6 What are the similarities between Ms. Marvel and Sana Amanat?
7 What do "misfits" and superheroes have in common?
8 In what way can Ms. Marvel be "a comfort and a joyful inspiration"?

8 MY PERSPECTIVE

Work in pairs. Discuss the questions.

1 Would you like to read a Ms. Marvel comic? Why?
2 Sana says "This character is a celebration!" What do you think she means?
3 What is the value of comic superheroes to teenagers?

CRITICAL THINKING   Evaluating evidence

When writers make arguments, read carefully to see what facts they give as evidence to support them. Then you can decide how much you can trust their opinions and claims.

9 Work in pairs. Answer the questions.

1 Which of the facts support the statement from the article? How strong is the evidence? How could you check it?

   The Ms. Marvel phenomenon has skyrocketed to success.

   a The first series has consistently appeared on the *New York Times* Bestseller List.
   b The first series had seven reprintings in the first year.
   c Even boys and men have become huge fans.

2 Find evidence in the article for these claims. How strong is the evidence?

   a Kamala's "dual identity" becomes her strength. (line 41)
   b That's what makes this book different. (line 47)
   c She is first and foremost a real girl. (line 56)

Ms. Marvel
Teenage comic superhero

🎧 **54** Meet Ms. Marvel—the first female Muslim-American superhero to have her own comic book series. Ever since her first appearance in 2014, the groundbreaking Ms. Marvel phenomenon has skyrocketed to success. The
5 first series has consistently* appeared on the *New York Times* Bestseller List, and it had seven reprintings in the first year alone. Even boys and men have become huge fans, with one naming her "our new Spiderman."

So who is Ms. Marvel? We first meet her as Kamala Khan, an
10 ordinary 16-year-old high school student from New Jersey in the US and the daughter of Pakistani-American immigrants. Though respectful of her heritage, she has always felt different from her more conservative parents and feels torn between two worlds. She is going through a rebellious phase
15 and struggles to reconcile being an American teenager with the demands and expectations of her parents, whom she loves but who drive her crazy, and her peers, who don't really understand what her home life is like.

Kamala is a big fan of superheroes, and her role model is
20 Carol Danvers, the original Ms. Marvel. In the first issue, Kamala has a vision of Carol asking her what she wants out of life. Kamala immediately replies, "I want to be you." All of a sudden, she finds herself transformed into Ms. Marvel, with amazing superhuman powers that allow her to change her
25 body shape and lengthen her arms and legs at will. However, as time goes on, Kamala realizes that merely looking like her hero was not what she wanted after all. She goes on to adopt her own distinctive costume, and to use her superhuman powers first to rescue a friend from drowning, and then to
30 defend New Jersey from enemy alien invaders.

Ms. Marvel is the co-creation of Sana Amanat, Director of Content and Character Development at Marvel Comics, and writer G. Willow Wilson. For Wilson, Kamala's story reflects every teenager's coming-of-age crisis. "She's so
35 young—only 16—that the normal trials and tribulations of being in high school are still very much a part of her life, even as she's becoming something different and amazing." As she grapples with* her overwhelming new powers and gradually comes to terms with her new identity, Kamala
40 realizes that it is possible to be both herself and a superhero at the same time. Wilson believes that this "dual identity" becomes her strength and makes her tough and vulnerable simultaneously. "When you try to straddle* two worlds, one of the first things you learn is that instead of defending
45 good people from bad people, you have to spend a lot of time defending good people from each other. It's both illuminating and emotionally brutal. That's what makes this book different."

Amanat, like Kamala, struggled to find her place in society.
50 The daughter of Pakistani-American immigrants, she felt like a misfit growing up in an overwhelmingly white suburban neighborhood in New Jersey. As a fan of X-Men, she discovered the power of storytelling and the "otherness" of comic superheroes to work through her own identity crisis.
55 For Amanat, Kamala is so valuable in our storytelling culture because she is first and foremost a real girl. "I wanted her to feel accessible to everyone—to be a comfort and a joyful inspiration to women of all colors and backgrounds who are struggling with high school, insecurities, identity, and growth.
60 We wanted to help girls see they are normal and worthy, no matter what they look like or where they come from. This character is a celebration!"

consistently *continuing without change*
grapples with *tries hard to understand*
straddle *be on both sides of something*

A young man naps at the Temple of Heaven in Beijing, China.

8C A Good Night's Sleep

GRAMMAR Expressing habitual actions and states

1 Work in pairs. Discuss the questions.

1 How many hours of sleep do you average a night?
2 Has this changed since you became a teenager? If so, how and why?

2 Read a post and response on a teenage health-advice website. Then answer the questions in pairs.

Problem I'm worried that I'm not getting enough sleep lately. This never used to cause me problems on such a regular basis! When I started high school, I would always go to bed at ten and sleep like a log until the alarm went off at six the next morning. I was doing well at school and getting good grades. Now I tend to not feel sleepy until after midnight. So I'll stay up texting friends or playing computer games. On an average night, I won't fall asleep until around one or two. This means that I feel sleepy and moody the next morning. I'm always losing concentration, and I even fall asleep in classes. I'm not used to feeling like this, and I'm concerned about the effect it's having on my schoolwork and homelife.

Advice I just checked this, and what you're describing is completely normal. We usually follow the pattern of being awake during the day when it's light and asleep at night when it's dark. During adolescence, there's a tendency for this pattern to shift because the body starts to produce melatonin (a hormone that makes you feel sleepy) later at night. It means that teenagers have a natural tendency to fall asleep later, and wake up later than they did as children. Generally speaking, teenagers need about nine hours of sleep. If they don't get enough, it can have a negative impact on their mood and life. But don't worry—there are solutions!

1 Have you experienced this problem with sleep?
2 What new facts did you learn?
3 Can you think of any solutions? What are they?

3 Look at the Grammar box. Then find more examples of expressing habits or regular actions in the post and response in Activity 2.

Expressing habitual actions and states

In addition to using the simple present and simple past tenses, there are many different ways to talk about present and past habits in English.

a *This **never used to cause** me problems on such a regular basis!*
b *I **would always go** to bed at ten…*
c *I **tend to not feel** sleepy until after midnight.*
d *I'**ll stay up texting** my friends.*

4 Choose the correct options to complete the rules. Use the post and response in Activity 2 to help you.

Use:
- *used to* and *would* (*always*) + infinitive to describe repeated actions in the past. We don't use (1) *used to / would* to describe states in the past.
- the present continuous with *always* or *forever* to describe (2) *a frequent / an occasional* action.

- *will* or *won't* + the base form for repeated actions in the (3) *future / present*.
- *be used to* + the *-ing* form to describe actions that we are (4) *accustomed / unaccustomed* to.
- the verb *tend (not)* + infinitive for (5) *states and repeated actions / states but not repeated actions*.

Check your answers on page 142. Do Activities 3–5.

5 Work in pairs. Is there a difference in meaning between the two options? If there is, explain the difference.

1 I *would / used to* go to bed at 9:00 p.m. when I was a kid.
2 Most people *tend to not / don't usually* fall asleep quickly after they've been using a computer.
3 I *used to take / am used to taking* a nap in the afternoon.
4 My mother *will often get up / often gets up* before anyone else in the house.
5 *I always oversleep. / I'm always oversleeping.*
6 Most people *usually wake up / are used to waking up* with an alarm clock.
7 I *never used to / didn't use to* stay up all night.
8 *Teenagers have a tendency / There is a tendency for teenagers* to stay in bed late on weekends.

6 Work in pairs. Make the sentences in Activity 5 true for you.

7 Work in pairs. Look at the tips for improving sleep habits. Can you suggest others? Discuss if these are true for you.

Tips for a good night's sleep
Here are some ideas that those of us in the medical profession tend to suggest to teenagers with sleep problems:

- Have a regular bedtime and stick to it.
- Exercise regularly during the day.
- Listen to relaxing music before you go to bed.
- Avoid having too much caffeine.
- Don't watch horror or action movies before you go to bed.
- Don't use electronic devices right before bedtime.

8 Work in pairs. Choose some of the statements and use them to describe yourself.

When I was a child, my parents would make me eat vegetables. I used to refuse. But I've gotten used to eating them now, and I actually like them a lot.

1 I didn't use to like them, but now I do.
2 I always do that. It drives my parents crazy.
3 I'm getting used to doing it, but it's hard.
4 I'll often do that at night, but I never used to.
5 I wasn't used to doing that.

9 CHOOSE

Choose one of the following activities.

- Work in pairs. Choose one or two of the ideas in Activity 5 or Activity 7 and write questions to find out about the past and present habits of classmates. Then ask your classmates and report on the class's habits.

- Write a blog post about a problem you have with sleep, getting up, or other routine activity, like studying or getting enough exercise. Then exchange your post with a classmate and write a reply.

- Work in groups. Compare your past and present habits in one or more of these areas.

playing video games	playing sports	reading
spending and saving money	watching TV	

Experts say that using electronic devices like tablets can harm sleep patterns.

8D The Mysterious Workings of the Adolescent Brain

> " The adolescent brain undergoes really quite profound development, and this has implications for education. "

SARAH-JAYNE BLAKEMORE

Read about Sarah-Jayne Blakemore and get ready to watch her TED Talk. ▶ 8.0

AUTHENTIC LISTENING SKILLS

Preparing to listen

Before you listen to a talk about a new or complex topic, think about what you are going to listen to. You can do this by using clues (e.g., the title or description of the talk) and by researching the topic beforehand. This lets you focus more on general listening and not just on the complex ideas.

1 Look at the Authentic Listening Skills box. Then read the descriptions of parts of the brain. What else do you know about the human brain?

The *prefrontal cortex* is an area at the front of the brain connected with higher-level thinking.

Gray matter is a substance existing throughout the brain that consists mainly of neurons (cells that carry messages to, from, and within the brain).

The *limbic system* is a complex system of nerves in the brain that is connected to instinct and emotion.

2 Read the title of the TED Talk, the quotation, and the definitions in Activity 1. Which of these topics do you expect the speaker to mention? What might she say about them? Can you predict any others?

- The structure of the brain
- How scientists study the brain
- How adults learn
- How adolescents think and feel
- How adolescents learn

WATCH

3 Watch Part 1 of the talk. Choose the correct option, according to Sarah-Jayne. ▶ 8.1

1 In the past, people thought that the brain changed mainly in *childhood / adolescence*.

2 Nowadays, we have *better equipment / more funding* to study the brain.

3 Structural MRI helps scientists study how the brain *is formed / works*.

4 Functional MRI can reveal how the brain *works in different situations / develops*.

4 Watch Part 2 of the talk. Are the statements *true* or *false*? ▶ 8.2

1 Before the photo was taken, Michael Owen had just scored a goal.

2 Most of the fans in the photo root for Owen's team.

3 The photo shows that people often react without thinking.

4 Sarah-Jayne's experiments compare how adults and adolescents understand the thoughts and feelings of others.

5 Teens and adults think in similar ways in social situations.

5 Watch Part 3 of the talk. Choose the correct option. ▶ 8.3

In the first experiment, …

1 the man behind the shelves (the director) can see *all / some* of the objects.

2 the participant can see *all / some* of the objects.

3 the *director / participant* is asked to move some objects.

4 the participant has to *think about / ask about* which objects the director can see.

In the control experiment, …

5 there is *no / a different* director.

6 participants *have to / do not have to* move objects.

7 participants have to *think about the director's perspective / remember a rule.*

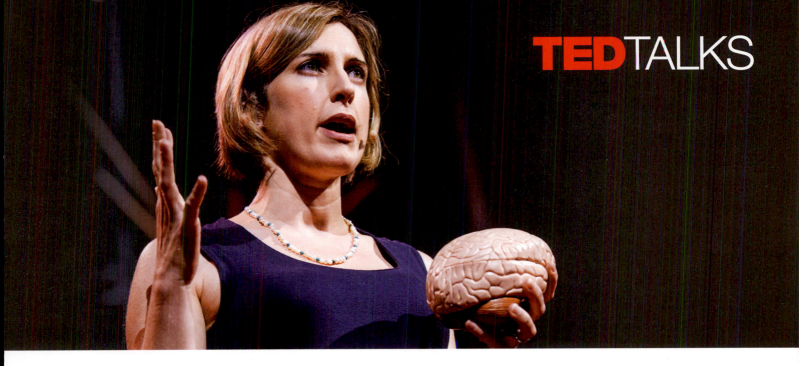

The results

8 All participants make more errors when there is *a director* / *no director*.

9 Children get *better* / *worse* at doing both tasks as they grow older.

10 In adolescence, the ability to see another person's perspective is *fully developed* / *still developing*.

6 Watch Part 4 of the talk. Answer the questions. ▶ 8.4

1 Which of these stereotypical teenage characteristics are mentioned?

desire to be liked by friends		indecision
moodiness	risk-taking	self-consciousness

2 What are the results (a–c) of the brain features (1–3)?

1 a hypersensitive limbic system _____
2 an underdeveloped prefrontal cortex _____
3 the brain is still malleable _____

a The teenage years are a great opportunity for learning and creativity.
b Teens find it more difficult to control their impulses.
c Teens get a rewarding feeling from risk-taking.

7 VOCABULARY IN CONTEXT

a Watch the clips from the TED Talk. Choose the correct meaning of the words and phrases. ▶ 8.5

b Think of examples of the following things. Then compare your ideas with a partner.
1 things you have *radically changed* your views on
2 errors you are particularly *prone to* making in English
3 activities that give you *a kick*
4 an activity you need to do carefully, with *split-second* timing

8 MY PERSPECTIVE

Work in pairs. Choose two statements you agree with and say why.

Neuroscience should be a mandatory subject for adolescents and young adults in school.

Environment and upbringing are more important than genetics in developing a person's character.

Knowing that my brain is still developing makes me more careful about things like diet, sleep, and hobbies.

Teenagers' tendency to take risks should be seen as a positive trait.

CHALLENGE

Work in pairs. Discuss the questions.

1 Sarah-Jayne describes the development of social intelligence as the ability to understand how other people are thinking and feeling. What things do you think can help you interpret this?

2 Practice saying the sentences to demonstrate some of the states in the box. Can your partner guess your mood? Use ideas from question 1 to convey your feelings. Then continue some of the conversations.

astonished	bored	delighted
embarrassed	furious	nervous
puzzled	suspicious	upset

a This isn't mine. Someone else must've left it here.
b I just found out my test score.
c We're spending our vacation at the beach again.
d I'm going climbing tomorrow.
e You're looking very sharp today.
f I've never done anything like this before.

8E Looking on the Bright Side

Useful language

Showing understanding

What a drag / a pain.

You must have been so frustrated.

How upsetting / annoying!

I'm not surprised you feel upset / irritated.

That's totally understandable.

Offering encouragement

Well, at least…

(Look) on the bright side, …

It might not be as bad as you think.

Offering help

I'm more than happy to…, if that would help.

I could…, if that's helpful.

Let me know if you need a hand with…

Would you like me to…?

Is there anything I can do to help?

SPEAKING

1 Work in pairs. Talk about a time when you had a problem and someone offered you help or encouragement. Were they able to see things from your perspective? Did they offer you any comforting "words of wisdom"?

2 Listen to two conversations in which a friend tries to help with a problem. Answer the questions about each conversation. 🎧 55

  1 What is the problem?
  2 How does the friend offer to help?

3 **PRONUNCIATION** Intonation to show understanding

Listen to the expressions for showing understanding. Which word or words carry the main stress? Do the expressions end with a falling or a rising tone? Listen again and repeat. 🎧 56

4 Look at the Useful language box. Work in pairs. Listen to five people describing problems. Respond using expressions for offering understanding or encouragement. 🎧 57

5 Work in pairs. Choose two of the situations and make up conversations. Find out more information, show understanding, and offer encouragement and help.

  • I'm finding it hard to choose a college course.
  • I can't seem to get to school on time these days. I keep oversleeping.
  • I feel stressed out about the test next week.
  • My friend keeps texting me late at night. It's really annoying!!
  • It's Lucia's birthday tomorrow, and I haven't gotten her anything yet.

WRITING An essay comparing advantages and disadvantages

6 Work in pairs. Read the essay question. Discuss your views on the options.

What are the advantages and disadvantages of the different options for getting advice on how to solve a problem? Which do you think is the best? Why?

Talking to your parents   *Posting a question on an online forum*

Talking to a friend   *Talking to a professional (e.g., a teacher or doctor)*

7 Read the essay on page 152. Does the writer mention the points you discussed? What other points are mentioned?

8 Work in pairs. Find expressions in the essay that describe advantages and disadvantages. Then write a paragraph about one of the other options in Activity 6. Use expressions from the Useful language box.

9 **WRITING SKILL** Interpreting essay questions

When you write an essay, it is important to read and analyze the question carefully.

1 Read the question at least twice.

2 Look for instruction words (e.g., *explain*) and topic words (e.g., *advice*).

3 Decide what you must include and what you can include if you want.

4 Decide what is an appropriate style.

5 Check the word count and any other instructions.

Work in pairs. Read the essay question. Interpret it using the guidelines (1–5).

You have read an online article about the best living arrangement for college students. Four of the options are mentioned below, along with some of the readers' comments. Write an essay discussing the advantages and disadvantages of two of the options (1–4). You should explain which one you think is the best option. Give reasons to support your answer. You may refer to the opinions of other readers, but you should use your own words. Write your answer in 220–260 words in the appropriate style.

1 living at home with your parents   *saves a lot of money*
2 sharing an apartment   *roommates could be messy*
3 living in college dorms   *could be noisy*
4 living alone in a studio   *peace and quiet, good for studying*

10 You are going to write an essay comparing advantages and disadvantages. Make notes for a plan with four paragraphs.

11 Write your essay. Use expressions from the Useful language box.

Useful language

Introducing advantages and disadvantages

What are the benefits of… ?

There are pros and cons to…

There are many advantages to…

However, it also has some disadvantages / drawbacks.

One possible advantage / disadvantage of… is…

The main advantage / disadvantage of… is…

This has the (possible) advantage / disadvantage of…

Another plus is…

One major drawback is…

The advantages outweigh the disadvantages.

Listing points

First of all, … / First and foremost, …

Moreover, … / In addition, …

Another benefit…

Most importantly…

Finally / Lastly / Last but not least…

Many college students choose to live in cities or on a college campus because it allows them to be around other people who share their interests.

9 A Healthy Life

IN THIS UNIT, YOU...

- talk about how to stay healthy.

- read about the secrets of living a long and happy life.

- learn about different forms of preventive medicine.

- watch a TED Talk about how a teenager's invention helped his grandfather.

- write a proposal about making positive connections with the elderly.

People around the world participate in activities to feel healthier and connect with others. These people are doing group yoga in a park in Vilnius, Lithuania.

9A How to Stay Well

VOCABULARY Health and fitness

1 Look at the photo and read the caption. What are five ways you stay fit and healthy?

2 Work in pairs. Complete the tips for staying healthy with these words and phrases. Which of your ideas from Activity 1 are mentioned?

alert	beneficial effect	carbohydrates	detrimental effect
enhance	in moderation	intake	nutrients
nutritious	obesity	protein	refined sugar
relieve stress	sedentary lifestyle	unprocessed	well-being

Have a balanced diet. You can get all the essential (1) _____ the body needs if your diet contains foods rich in (2) _____ (e.g., fish, beans, dairy products), (3) _____ (e.g., bread, potatoes, pasta), non-saturated fats, and plenty of fruit and vegetables.

Eat (4) _____ . Overeating will make you put on weight and can lead to (5) _____ .

Eat naturally. Cut down on processed foods and food containing (6) _____ and choose (7) _____ foods such as whole grain bread and brown rice, which are more (8) _____ .

Reduce your salt (9) _____ . Too much salt can have a (10) _____ on your health and is associated with high blood pressure and heart disease.

Drink plenty of water. Staying hydrated can have a (11) _____ on your energy level and also keeps your organs and skin healthy.

Stay active and get exercise. Studies suggest that a (12) _____ (e.g., spending long periods sitting in front of the computer or television) is related to a number of illnesses later in life. Staying active is also good for your heart.

Get enough sleep. A good night's sleep can (13) _____ your mood and help you stay (14) _____ throughout the day.

Relax. Activities such as yoga or meditation or taking deep breaths can (15) _____ when you feel under pressure and help you refocus.

Practice the art of appreciation. Not only is "an attitude of gratitude" good for the people around you, but it can also increase your own emotional (16) _____ .

3 Work in pairs. Write six more tips like the ones in Activity 2. Use these words.

bright colors	junk food	kindness	laugh	smile	sunscreen

4 Complete the sentences. Then work in pairs. Compare and give reasons for your answers.

1 I should reduce my intake of _____ and eat / drink more _____ .
2 If I _____ , it will be beneficial for my well-being.
3 A nutritious meal I had recently was _____ .
4 _____ can have a detrimental effect on the health of young children.
5 People who have a sedentary lifestyle should _____ .
6 Foods such as _____ are full of nutrients.

LISTENING

5 Work in pairs. Discuss the questions, giving reasons for your opinions.

_____ Is drinking coffee bad for you? _____
_____ Is it OK to skip breakfast? _____
_____ Should you exercise every day? _____
_____ Is chocolate really a superfood? _____
_____ Can exercise improve your mood? _____

6 Listen to a radio show in which an expert responds to the questions in Activity 5. Number the questions in the order you hear them. Is the answer to each one *yes*, *no*, or *it depends*? 🎧 58

7 Work in pairs. Match the topics with the statements. More than one answer may be possible. Then listen again and check your ideas. 🎧 58

a skipping breakfast
b drinking coffee
c getting exercise
d eating chocolate

1 It might prevent an illness that affects the elderly.
2 It can be done in moderation.
3 It can make you feel less stressed.
4 You may end up with a less healthy alternative.
5 It has both beneficial and detrimental effects.
6 It could lead to problems at school.
7 It has a range of benefits for the body.
8 Variety is recommended.

8 MY PERSPECTIVE

Work in pairs. Say how much you agree with the statements and why.

1 It's hard to know what is healthy because experts' advice keeps changing.
2 It's too hard to make healthy lifestyle choices because of peer pressure.

GRAMMAR Relative clauses with prepositions

9 Match the sentences with the extracts from the radio show in the Grammar box. There are some differences between 1–3 and a–c. Why do you think they are different?

1 It can also contain sugar and fat, which can both make you put on weight.
2 Exercise can relax you, wake you up, and give you confidence, which are all really important.
3 Find an activity you're interested in.

Relative clauses with prepositions

a *Ideally, young people should find an activity in which they are interested…*
b *… physical activity can relieve stress… make you feel more alert and confident, all of which are obviously important.*
c *… it also contains sugar and fat, both of which contribute to weight gain…*

10 Work in pairs. Look at the sentences in Activity 9 and in the Grammar box. Answer the questions.

1 Which sentences contain defining relative clauses? Which contain non-defining clauses?
2 In which two positions can we put a preposition in a relative clause? Why?
3 Some of the relative clauses contain a word expressing quantity. What are these words, and what positions do they appear in?

Check your answers on page 144. Do Activities 1 and 2.

11 Read the advice to teenagers. Then rewrite it in a less formal way to email to a friend.

1 It is vital to eat breakfast every day. Try to have some cereal, fruit, yogurt, or eggs, all of which contain essential nutrients for your health.
Make sure you eat breakfast every day. Have some…
cereal, fruit, yogurt, or eggs, which are all nutritious.

2 It is essential to do some physical activity each day from which you obtain some enjoyment.
You need to get some exercise everyday, …

3 It is advisable to focus more on school subjects and activities at which you are talented.
You should focus more on subjects and activities…

4 It is a sensible idea to develop a wide circle of friends with whom you can relax and be yourself.
Why don't you make some good friends…

12 Complete the article with these relative expressions.

all of whom	both of which	half of whom
in which	many of which	some of which
the most common of which		where

According to World Health Organization (WHO) estimates, physical inactivity accounts for 3.2 million deaths globally, (1) _____ could be prevented by more active lifestyles. Other studies have shown that inactivity is a major factor in many illnesses, (2) _____ are cancer, diabetes, stroke, and heart disease. Globally, around 31 percent of adults were not active enough in 2008. Furthermore, studies have established a link between activity and dementia. A study at the University of Illinois looked at a number of older adults, (3) _____ engaged in moderate aerobic exercise. Brain scans showed that brain volume increased in this half of the group, unlike in the control half.

The countries (4) _____ people are the least active are higher income countries; inactivity is linked to insufficient exercise in free time and a sedentary lifestyle, (5) _____ are more widespread in the developed world. The WHO makes specific recommendations for children aged between five and seventeen, (6) _____ should do at least 60 minutes of moderate to intense physical activity daily. The organization suggests a number of ways (7) _____ children can get exercise, including games, sports, and household chores, (8) _____ can be easily included in a more active daily routine.

13 MY PERSPECTIVE

Work in pairs. What do you think about the advice given in this lesson? What surprised you the most? Will it make you change your habits at all? Why?

A group of friends practice parkour in Gaza City while bystanders watch.

9B Live Long and Prosper

VOCABULARY BUILDING

Adjective suffixes -able and -ible

Many adjectives in English contain the suffixes -able or -ible, which mean "can be done" (e.g., *sustainable, affordable, accessible*). Adjectives ending with -able usually have a corresponding verb (e.g., *enjoy—enjoyable, afford—affordable*), but adjectives ending in -ible often do not (e.g., *horrible, visible*).

1 Choose the correct options to complete the definitions.

1 Edible mushrooms can be *cooked / eaten*.
2 Legible handwriting can be *appreciated / read*.
3 A feasible project can be *completed / explained*.
4 An audible comment can be *laughed at / heard*.
5 An accessible building can be easily *constructed / reached*.
6 A plausible excuse can be *believed / forgiven*.

2 Match the adjectives (1–10) with the nouns (a–j). Use a dictionary if you need to. More than one alternative may be possible.

1	achievable __a__	a	goal
2	curable _____	b	battery
3	disposable _____	c	bottle
4	inflatable _____	d	coat
5	memorable _____	e	disease
6	preventable _____	f	energy
7	rechargeable _____	g	error
8	recyclable _____	h	trip
9	renewable _____	i	life jacket
10	machine-washable _____	j	razor

READING

3 Work in pairs. Look at the photo. How old do you think these people are? Can you think of any "secrets" to living a long life?

4 Read the article and check your ideas. Which statement best summarizes the article?

1 A healthy diet can increase your life expectancy.
2 Longevity (a long life) is associated with both lifestyle and diet.
3 People living on islands tend to have a healthier lifestyle.

5 Work in pairs. Are the statements *true*, *false*, or *not stated*?

1 People live longer than average in Ikaria and Okinawa.
2 Most people in Ikaria and Okinawa live to be 100.

3 People in Ikaria and Okinawa do not suffer from chronic illnesses.
4 The lifestyle of Ikarians has been influenced by the island's location.
5 Many Ikarians have a vegetarian diet.
6 In Ikaria, all generations work together to fund and organize local festivals.
7 Okinawans have the highest life expectancy in the world.
8 There is a higher ratio of fast food restaurants in Okinawa than in the rest of Japan.
9 Younger Okinawans have a lower life expectancy than their elders.

6 Work in pairs. Find evidence in the article to support these conclusions.

1 Be active in your daily life.
2 Have a sense of purpose.
3 Take time to relax.
4 Belong to a community.
5 Value family life.
6 Eat a plant-based diet.
7 Don't overeat.

7 MY PERSPECTIVE

Work in pairs. Discuss the questions.

1 Do you want to live to be a centenarian? Why?
2 In what ways is the lifestyle of people in Ikaria and Okinawa similar or different from that of your community?
3 Which aspects of life in Ikaria and Okinawa do you think are the most important for good health? Why?

CRITICAL THINKING Checking facts

Some websites and publications contain information that is inaccurate, out of date, or false. Check information carefully from more than one source before accepting it as true. Use this checklist.

- Who is the writer? What experience or qualifications do they have?
- What can you find out about the purpose of the website or publication?
- Does the writer present only one side of the issue or multiple perspectives?
- Does the writer state where they got their information? Can you check it?
- When was the article written? Has the information been updated?

8 Find three claims in the article that you would like to investigate. Then investigate them on two or three websites using the checklist to determine the reliability and credibility of the source.

Vasili and Eleftheria
enjoy a long life in Ikaria.

THE HEALTHIEST PLACES IN THE WORLD?

🎧 **59** We know that our genes determine only about a quarter of our life expectancy. So how do we account for the rest? People have tried to find the secrets to a long and healthy life for thousands of years. In recent years,
5 however, demographers* around the world may have finally found some promising clues. What they discovered were regions around the world where life expectancy is considerably higher than the norm and where there is a high proportion of centenarians*. These places also tend
10 to have a lower rate of preventable chronic illnesses that commonly kill people in the developed world, such as heart disease, cancer, and diabetes.

Ikaria is a small Greek island whose inhabitants live eight years longer than the world average and
15 have considerably lower dementia rates. Its relative geographical and cultural isolation and low numbers of tourists mean that, so far at least, Ikaria has remained largely unaffected by a Western way of life. Islanders live on a variant of the Mediterranean diet—rich in olive
20 oil and vegetables and low in meat and dairy products (apart from goat's milk). Researchers at the University of Athens, in Greece, also point out the health benefits of the local greens and herbs that are a part of the Ikarian diet. Their vegetables are picked wild or home-grown,
25 and they also drink green herbal tea sweetened with locally produced honey rather than a lot of coffee.

Sociability and a slow pace of life are key factors in the health of the community. Ikarians tend to wake up naturally, work in the garden, have a late lunch, take a
30 nap, and visit neighbors after sunset. At local festivals in which everyone—teenagers, parents, the elderly, young children—takes part, they combine their money to buy food and drink and give what is left over to the poor. The one old people's home on the island is only used by
35 those who have lost all their family. "It would shame us to put an old person in a home," said one resident. And as another put it, "Ikaria isn't a *me* place. It's an *us* place."

Okinawa, Japan, consists of 161 small islands some
40 1,300 km (808 miles) south of Tokyo. Researchers, like the ones at the Okinawa Centenarian Study, have found that elderly people here have the longest life expectancy in Japan, which is the world's longest-lived country. Okinawans use small plates to reduce meal portions.
45 Their diet is low in meat, fish, and dairy products but rich in other forms of protein such as beans and tofu* and also includes a high proportion of plants such as seaweed and sweet potatoes. In terms of social life, each resident is assigned at birth to a *moai*—a small social
50 network whose members are responsible for one another throughout their lives. There is no word for retirement in the Okinawan language. Instead, Okinawans' lives are governed by another principle called *ikigai*, which roughly translates as "the reason why you wake up in
55 the morning." Demographers who have visited the island have encountered an 85-year-old whose lifelong passion was his work as a fisherman, an 84-year-old training for a decathlon, a 102-year-old karate grand master, and a 102-year-old woman whose greatest joy was her great-
60 great-great-granddaughter.

However, the famed longevity of Okinawans is now under threat as a generation that grew up eating a Western diet is now reaching middle age. Japan's first fast food restaurant opened in Okinawa in 1963, and
65 it now has more fast food restaurants per person than anywhere else in the country. Today, almost 30 percent of Okinawan men die before reaching 65, and nearly half of men in their forties are obese. In the 1995 census, Okinawa had the highest longevity of all 47 prefectures
70 in Japan. By 2000, it was 26th. Could it be that the secret to longevity is to be found with an earlier generation and in a traditional lifestyle?

demographer *a scientist who studies human populations*
centenarians *people one hundred years old or older*
tofu *a form of solid protein made from soy milk*

Healthy food is a key ingredient in preventing illnesses.

9C Prevention as Cure

GRAMMAR Articles

1 Work in pairs. Read the sayings from around the world in the Grammar box. What does each one mean? Do you agree with the idea in each one? Do you have similar sayings in your language?

Articles
a *Prevention is better than cure.*
b *When the heart is at ease, the body is healthy.*
c *From the bitterness of disease man learns the sweetness of health.*
d *The greatest wealth is health.*
e *Laughter is the best medicine.*
f *Diseases of the soul are more dangerous and more numerous than those of the body.*
g *A man too busy to take care of his health is like a mechanic too busy to take care of his tools.*
h *Time, not medicine, cures the sick.*

2 Read these rules about the use of articles. Then find examples of each use in the sayings in the Grammar box.

1 Use a plural noun without an article to refer to a group in general.
2 Use an uncountable noun without an article to refer to the concept in general.
3 Use *the* with an uncountable noun to make it specific, often with a phrase that specifies it.
4 Use *the* with a singular noun in more formal contexts to refer to all examples of the noun.
5 Use *a/an* to refer to a single example of a group.
6 Use *the* with certain adjectives to refer to a group of people.

Check your answers on page 144. Do Activities 3 and 4.

3 Work in pairs. Which of these health nouns can be both countable and uncountable? For those that can be both, is there a difference in meaning?

activity	checkup	cure	diet
exercise	health	illness	life
medicine	scan	well-being	youth

4 Work in pairs, A and B. Student A completes Text A, and Student B completes Text B. Use with *the, a/an,* or — (no article).

A Preventive medicine

(1) _____ preventive medicine, or (2) _____ preventive healthcare, is not about giving patients (3) _____ cure; it is about enabling (4) _____ people to stay healthy. Many traditional forms of (5) _____ medicine, such as Chinese acupuncture, are based on preventing (6) _____ illness and strengthening (7) _____ immune system. Nowadays it takes the form of giving (8) _____ information on how to live (9) _____ healthy life or (10) _____ advice on exercise and diet. (11) _____ doctors also attempt to detect (12) _____ illness before symptoms emerge, with regular checkups, for example.

B Wearable technology

More and more people are wearing technology to monitor and regulate their own health. (1) _____ wearable fitness trackers, which are worn on (2) _____ wrist like (3) _____ watch, record (4) _____ data on (5) _____ person's activities (e.g., calories burned, steps taken, hours of sleep). This is then transmitted to (6) _____ app on their smartphone. (7) _____ studies have found that in some cases, using (8) _____ wearable technology can lead to (9) _____ increase in (10) _____ physical activity of up to 25 percent and (11) _____ reduction in (12) _____ blood pressure.

5 Tell your partner about what you learned. Which way of preventing illness described in each text do you think is better? Why?

6 Now look at each other's texts. Do you agree with the articles your partner used?

7 Work in pairs. Read about other types of preventive health technology. Add *a/an* or *the* where appropriate. What conditions could these devices help with?

1 This is free, online tool which can help you create daily personalized diet. Just type in information about your age, weight, and health goals.
2 This is wearable electronic device that measures air pollution and gives warning on your smartphone when you should go inside.
3 Research is being conducted in order to develop smart contact lenses that monitor user's blood-sugar level. Lenses then send data to person's smartphone and their doctor.
4 This is small recorder that is inserted under skin to record patient's heart rhythm.

8 Work in groups. Discuss the questions.

1 What are the advantages and disadvantages of the preventive devices described in Activity 7? Which would you be interested in using? Why?
2 What other wearable technology would you like to see? Why? How would it be useful?
3 Do you wear a fitness tracker, or do you know someone who does? If so, how helpful is it? If not, would you like to wear one? Why?

9 CHOOSE

Choose one of the following activities.

- Find reliable information from two or three sources about a type of food or drink that is good or bad for you. Summarize your findings in a short report and read it to the class. Pay attention to article use.

- Work in pairs. Create either a health brochure or a poster for a campaign to promote healthy living for teenagers. Show your brochure or poster to another pair. Pay attention to article use.

- Look at some ingredients that are often promoted as essential for a happy life. Choose the three that you think are the most important, thinking of examples from your own life or the lives of people you know. Work in groups and discuss your ideas.

ability to deal with life's difficulties	awareness
being part of something bigger	exercise
focusing on positive emotions	giving to other people
having a clear purpose	learning new things
self-acceptance	strong relationships

Young runners check their fitness trackers before a run.

KENNETH SHINOZUKA

Read about Kenneth Shinozuka and get ready to watch his TED Talk. ▶ **9.0**

AUTHENTIC LISTENING SKILLS

Understanding fast speech

When you listen to fast speech, listen for key words that can help you understand the gist (main idea). If you are listening to or watching a recording (e.g., online videos or streamed TV or movies), play a short part several times. See if you can understand more each time. Remember that weak forms of common words (e.g., *the, a, an, of, at, to*) are often said very quickly.

1 Look at the Authentic Listening Skills box. Then predict which words complete the extract from the TED Talk.

My family (1) _____ experienced firsthand
(2) _____ struggles (3) _____ caring
(4) _____ Alzheimer's patient. Growing up
(5) _____ family (6) _____ three generations,
I've always been very close (7) _____ my grandfather.

2 Listen and check your ideas. How are the missing words pronounced? 🎧 **60**

3 Listen to three more extracts from the TED Talk. You will hear each section several times. Complete what Kenneth says. Try to guess the words you can't hear. 🎧 **61**

1 As the number of Alzheimer's patients _____ overwhelming societal challenge.
2 When I was _____ suddenly got lost.
3 My aunt _____ the bed.

WATCH

4 Work in pairs. Discuss the questions.

1 What do you know about Alzheimer's disease?
2 What challenges might people who care for those with Alzheimer's face?

5 Watch Part 1 of the talk. Are the sentences *true*, *false*, or *not stated*? ▶ **9.1**

1 Alzheimer's disease is currently the biggest health problem among old people in America.
2 By the middle of this century, there will be twice as many Alzheimer's patients as now.
3 Kenneth's family did not know his grandfather had Alzheimer's until he got lost.
4 His grandfather's illness has gotten worse in the last two years.
5 Kenneth was worried about both his grandfather and his aunt.
6 Kenneth's invention involves sending a signal from a sock to a smartphone.
7 Kenneth wanted his grandfather to be able to sleep better.

6 Watch Part 2 of the talk. Number the statements in the order that Kenneth mentions them. ▶ **9.2**

_____ Kenneth was too young to implement his plan.
_____ An elderly friend was badly hurt in a fall.
_____ Kenneth was inspired to use sensors to help the elderly.
_____ Kenneth designed a system to detect falls.

7 Watch Part 3 of the talk. Match the stage in the invention process with things that Kenneth used. There may be more than one for each stage. ▶ 9.3

1 He created a sensor to put on patients' feet. _____

2 He designed an electric circuit. _____

3 He coded a smartphone app. _____

a YouTube

b a small battery

c ink particles that conduct electricity

d a thin material

e textbooks

f Bluetooth technology

8 Watch Part 4 of the talk. Complete the summary. Then watch again to check your answers. ▶ 9.4

Kenneth designed two different (1) _____ for his device. One was designed to fit inside a (2) _____ , and the other was designed to be worn on the patient's (3) _____ . Since his grandfather started using the device, it has had a 100 percent (4) _____ . Kenneth has tested his invention at residential homes and now hopes to make it into a (5) _____ . He has discovered that not everybody is willing to (6) _____ at night. He is now conducting research into how often patients (7) _____ at night, and how this relates to their (8) _____ during the day. He still remembers how his invention helped him know when his grandfather (9) _____ out of bed, and this has inspired him to use (10) _____ to change people's lives and help them to be healthier.

9 VOCABULARY IN CONTEXT

a Watch the clips from the TED Talk. Choose the correct meaning of the words and phrases. ▶ 9.5

b Think of an example of the following things. Then compare your ideas with a partner.

1 something you have *experienced firsthand* that has taught you a useful lesson about life

2 people who used to *keep an eye on* you

3 an interest that *stems from* shared family activities

4 a skill you have learned from an online *tutorial*

10 MY PERSPECTIVE

Work in pairs. Discuss the questions.

1 In what ways have your grandparents or older relatives helped you and your family throughout your life?

2 What do you do, or what could you do, to improve their quality of life?

CHALLENGE

Work in groups. Read the situation. Discuss the pros and cons of each option. What would you advise your family to do? Why?

Your grandparent lives alone, is getting less mobile and more frail, and finds it hard to do everyday tasks. Your parents work full-time, and there is no spare room in your house. Your grandparent has two more children; one, who is single, lives in a distant city where your grandparent knows no one, and the other, who does not work, is in poor health and has little contact with the family. Your grandparent could:

a come and live with your family.

b live with another relative.

c share living arrangements among the relatives.

d move into a residential care home.

e continue to live at home with specialist help.

9E Stronger Together

WRITING A proposal

Useful language

Introducing the proposal

This proposal is based on a discussion about… / a survey in which…

It outlines / suggests ways in which…

It puts forward suggestions / proposals for…

It concludes by recommending… / making recommendations about…

Making recommendations

There are several steps / measures that could be taken.

It is suggested / recommended that… should…

The school could / might consider doing…

Explaining the reasons for recommendations

If these recommendations are implemented, …

By doing this, … / In this way, …

This would enable people to…

1 How much involvement do elderly people have in your school? How could this be increased? What could the benefits be?

2 Work in pairs. Read the proposal on page 153. Answer the questions.

  1 What concerns did the elderly people express?
  2 What opportunities did they identify?
  3 How do the proposal's suggestions benefit both the elderly and the young?
  4 Is the situation that the writer describes similar in your country?

3 **WRITING SKILL** Impersonal style

> In reports, proposals, and academic writing, it is common to use impersonal structures instead of personal pronouns such as *I*, *we*, or *you*. These include: passive verbs, a gerund (*-ing* form) as subject, *there is / are*, and *it is / would be* + adjective.

  a Find examples of impersonal structures in the proposal on page 153.

  b Rewrite these sentences in a more impersonal style using the words in parentheses.
    1 Perhaps we could schedule regular movie nights. (possible)
    2 We don't have enough volunteers. (a lack)
    3 We should speak clearly and loudly in case they are hard of hearing. (helpful)
    4 If we organized events, they could meet more people. (organizing)
    5 We could devote one day a month to visiting people. (devoted)

4 Choose one of these topics to write a proposal about. Discuss problems with the current situation and make suggestions for improving it. Use phrases from the Useful language box.

  • Providing healthier food at your school cafeteria
  • Creating a buddy system between older and younger students
  • Making the school or local community feel more like an *us* place

SPEAKING Talking about proposals

5 Work in pairs. Look again at the proposal on page 153. Can you think of any potential problems or issues with it?

6 Listen to someone describing and answering questions about the proposal. What three issues or potential problems are mentioned? What solutions are proposed? 🎧 62

7 Listen again. Which expressions from the Useful language box do you hear? How did the speakers respond enthusiastically to suggestions? 🎧 62

8 PRONUNCIATION Intonation in responses

   a Listen to someone responding to proposals. Which word or words are stressed? Does the speaker's voice fall or rise at the end? Why? 🎧 63

     1 That's a great idea!
     2 What a fantastic idea!
     3 I really like the idea of taking them on trips.
     4 That sounds like an excellent way of helping!
     5 It's a good idea in principle, …
     6 Yes, but the problem is…
     7 You'd need to keep in mind that…
     8 It's worth remembering that…

   b Listen to the sentences again. Repeat the intonation. 🎧 63

9 Work in pairs. Use phrases from the Useful language box to respond to these comments on the proposal on page 153.

     1 Some older people may have difficulty hearing.
     2 Some students don't know what to say to older people.
     3 How could students visit older people in their homes?
     4 We'd need to organize a schedule.
     5 Some older people may have difficulty getting up or around.

10 Work in groups. Take turns describing the proposals you wrote in Activity 4. You should respond to each other's ideas and ask questions. Use phrases from the Useful language box. Decide which proposal you like best and why.

Useful language

Summarizing proposals

Basically / In essence what we're aiming to do is…

Our goal is to…

What we're proposing to do, specifically, is…

Our first / second recommendation is…

Responding to proposals

It's a good idea in principle, provided that…

Yes, but the problem is…

You'd need to keep in mind that…

It's worth remembering that…

I wonder how feasible it would be to…

Elderly people being introduced to video games by students.

10 Ideas

IN THIS UNIT, YOU...

- talk about how to express ideas.

- read about the power of photography to change people's perspectives.

- learn about how people respond to new ideas.

- watch a TED Talk about the secret to giving an excellent talk.

- write a review about a performance that changed your perspective.

People line up to speak and ask questions at a TED event in Banff, Canada.

10A Expressing Ideas

VOCABULARY Making your point

1 Work in pairs. Look at the photo and read the caption. When and where do you normally ask questions? Have you ever asked questions in public?

2 Read the quiz about expressing ideas. Match the meanings (1–10) with the words or phrases in bold in the quiz. There are six extra words and phrases. What do these words mean? Use a dictionary if necessary.

1 specialized vocabulary
2 support
3 forget my point
4 exact
5 say again with different words

6 hand or body movements
7 in a few words
8 give more information
9 comparisons explaining something
10 get across

1 How do you make sure your listeners understand you?
  a I **make eye contact** to make sure they haven't tuned me out.
  b I ask questions to make sure they are still with me.
  c I don't. I just keep talking and hope for the best.

2 What do you do to **convey** your ideas to listeners?
  a I speak clearly and **concisely** with examples to **back up** my ideas.
  b I avoid **jargon** and explain any difficult words.
  c I use **analogies** to explain complex ideas.

3 How good are your communication skills?
  a I use **gestures** and **facial expressions** to help get my point across.
  b I vary my intonation to **engage** my listeners' **attention**.
  c I try to be open-minded and listen to others' points of view.

4 How do you react if someone misunderstands or **misinterprets** you?
  a I **rephrase** my answer using simpler and more **precise** words.
  b I **elaborate on** my point with different examples.
  c I tend to freeze, and my **mind goes blank**.

5 What do you do if someone interrupts or makes an irrelevant comment?
  a I try to **stick to the point** and not get distracted.
  b I sometimes panic and **lose my train of thought**.
  c I pause to think of the best way to respond.

3 Work in pairs. Answer the questions in Activity 2 so they are true for you. You can agree with more than one answer. Then compare your answers.

4 Listen to six extracts. Choose the correct statement to describe each extract. 🎧 64

_____ She lost her train of thought.
_____ His mind went blank.
_____ She elaborated on her idea.

_____ He was concise and to the point.
_____ She rephrased her idea.
_____ He used jargon.

5 MY PERSPECTIVE

Work in pairs. Discuss the questions.

1 Has your mind ever gone blank when you were trying to express an idea? What did you do?
2 How can someone convey confidence or a lack of confidence nonverbally?
3 What effect does other people's body language have on you?

LISTENING

6 Work in pairs. You are going to listen to Dr. Emily Grossman talk about how she explains the concept of electricity to students. Study the description of electricity. Label the diagram with the underlined words.

Electricity is a kind of energy caused by the movement of <u>electrons</u>, which are tiny parts of an atom, around a <u>circuit</u>. A circuit is a closed path that allows an electric charge to move from one place to another. One way of creating energy is by attaching a <u>battery</u> to the circuit. The flow of electricity around the circuit is called the <u>current</u>, and the rate of flow is measured in units called *coulombs*. The size of a current depends partly on the voltage of the battery. *Voltage* refers to the amount of power in the electricity flow (and it is measured in units called *joules*).

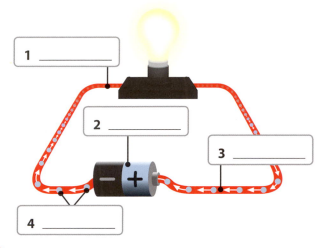

7 Listen to the interview. Answer the questions. 🎧 **65**

1 What three tips for conveying ideas does Emily give?
2 What analogy does Emily use to describe electricity? What do you remember about it?
3 Does she think that analogies are more effective than examples or visuals?

8 Work in pairs. Match the parts of the analogy to the scientific terms. Use a dictionary if necessary. Listen and check your ideas. 🎧 **66**

1 racetrack _____
2 a horse _____
3 hairs _____
4 horses per second _____
5 stable ___*f*___
6 bales of hay _____
7 number of bales of hay _____

a electrons
b circuit
c a coulomb
d current
e voltage
f battery
g joules

9 Listen to the end of the interview again. What types of visuals does Emily mention? Why is each effective? 🎧 **67**

10 Work in pairs. How successful was Emily's analogy for you? Do you feel like you understand electricity more?

GRAMMAR Advanced question types

11 Look at the questions from the interview in the Grammar box. Can you remember the answers?

Question forms

a *How do you think people can get their ideas across most effectively?*
b *Could you tell us how you use analogies to help you explain things?*
c *You do what?*
d *Isn't it hard to think of analogies for some situations?*
e *You think analogies work better than, say, examples or visuals, don't you?*

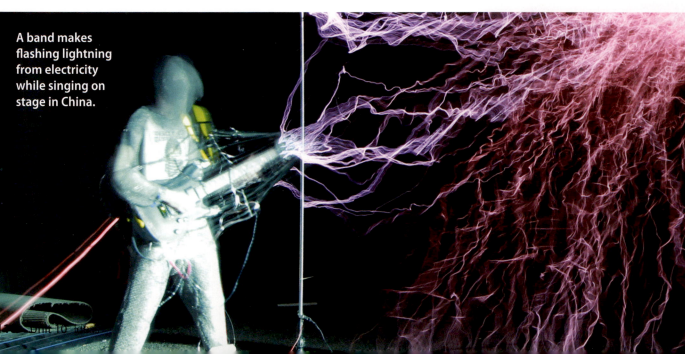

A band makes flashing lightning from electricity while singing on stage in China.

12 Match the questions in the Grammar box with a question type.

1 a tag question _____
2 an echo or reply question _____
3 a negative question _____
4 a polite indirect question _____
5 an indirect opinion question _____

13 Work in groups. What do you know about these question types? Answer the questions.

1 How is the tag question in the Grammar box different from most tag questions? What answer does this expect?
2 What kind of answer do we expect to an echo question?
3 How do we make negative questions? Does the negative question in the Grammar box expect a *yes* or *no* answer?
4 How does the word order change in indirect questions? Do they always have a question mark?
5 Is there anywhere else you could place *do you think* in the indirect opinion question?

Check your answers on page 146. Do Activities 1–3.

14 Complete these questions with one or two words. Then listen to an interview and compare your answers. 🎧 68

1 _____ think that gestures are international?
2 _____ tell us something about differences in the meaning of gestures?
3 So you'd say the biggest issue with using the wrong gesture is causing confusion, _____
4 I'm sorry, _____ considered what?
5 We aren't necessarily conscious of our gestures, though, _____
6 What do _____ the answer is?

15 PRONUNCIATION Question intonation

a Listen to the questions. Does each one end with a rising or falling tone? 🎧 69
b What can a rising tone and a falling tone mean? Match meanings to the questions in Activity 14. You can use some more than once. 🎧 69
_____ I'm surprised by this.
_____ I really want information.
_____ I'm quite sure of this, but I'd like confirmation.
_____ I'm asking for agreement.

16 Listen to the interview again. Take notes on the answers to the questions in Activity 14. 🎧 68

17 Work in pairs. Ask and answer the questions in Activity 14 to recreate the interview.

18 Rewrite the sentences to make one of the question types in Activity 12. Use the words in parentheses.

1 Do you use many gestures when you speak? (Could you?)
2 I'm sorry. I'm not sure I understand what you said exactly. (what?)
3 Why do these gestures help people to understand? (do you think?)
4 It's easier just to rely on speech when we explain something, right? (Isn't?)
5 So, would you use fewer gestures when you talk to someone from another country? (you would)

19 Work in pairs. Make a list of gestures you frequently use when you speak and what they mean. Then discuss your gestures with another pair. Try to use three of the questions from Activity 18 or similar questions.

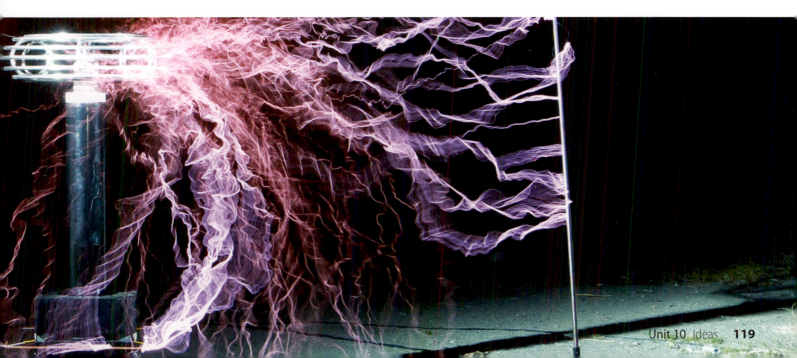

10B Iconic Images

VOCABULARY BUILDING

Adjectives ending in -ful and -less

Some English adjectives end in -ful or -less (e.g., *thankful* – **full of** thanks; *homeless* – **without** a home). Some are paired (e.g., *powerful / powerless*; *hopeful / hopeless*), and some are not. We can say *skillful* (**with** a lot of skill) but not *skillless*, and *jobless* (**without** a job) but not *jobful*.

1 Which of these words can be followed by a) both -*ful* and -*less*, b) only -*ful*, or c) only -*less*?

doubt	event	fear	forget	fruit
heart	meaning	point	regret	tact
taste	thought	waste	worth	

2 Work in pairs. Tell your partner about one of the options.

1 an *eventful / fruitless* journey you have taken
2 a time when you felt *doubtful / regretful*
3 a *fruitful / pointless* discussion you have taken part in
4 a *tactless / meaningful* remark someone made to you
5 someone you know who is *forgetful / thoughtful*
6 a place you know with *tasteful / tasteless* decor

READING

3 Work in pairs. Look at the photo. Answer the questions.

1 What does the photo show?
2 What do you think is special about it?
3 Why do you think it is called "Earthrise"?
4 What thoughts and feelings does the photo inspire in you?

4 Read the article. Check your answers to Activity 3, questions 1–3.

5 Work in pairs. Read the article again. Choose the option that is <u>not</u> indicated in the article.

1 The writer says that photographs can _____
   a show beautiful and poetic images.
   b help us see beyond our normal experiences.
   c change our beliefs and attitudes.

2 The Apollo crew _____
   a was the first to travel around the moon.
   b had been told not to take photographs of the Earth.
   c were surprised by the Earth's beauty.

3 The "Earthrise" photograph _____
   a was the first photo of the Earth taken on the mission.
   b was shot without planning or preparation.
   c showed the Earth as more beautiful than the moon.

4 After seeing the Earth from space, crew members _____
   a turned their attention to the scheduled mission.
   b felt a longing to return to Earth.
   c experienced strong emotions.

5 "Earthrise" has become an iconic image because _____
   a it was widely distributed and viewed.
   b it showed the effects of pollution and loss of resources.
   c it made people think about the planet in a new way.

6 Work in pairs. Answer the questions.

1 Why is "Earthrise" described as "groundbreaking"?
2 What new perspective on the Earth did it give?
3 What is the powerful message that it conveys?
4 Why did it inspire people to protect the planet?
5 What did you find most surprising or inspiring?

CRITICAL THINKING   Understanding quotations

Writers sometimes quote other opinions to back up or elaborate on a point. The words used to introduce the quotation can also persuade readers that the opinion is true. Read carefully and make up your own mind whether or not to agree with an opinion. Use the evidence presented.

7 Work in pairs. Answer the questions.

1 Read the sentences beginning with "According to…" (line 6) and "As National Geographic photographer…" (line 15). Which way of introducing the quotation suggests that the writer agrees with it?

2 Choose the more persuasive option.
   a He *explains / suggests* that "images speak a universal language."
   b She *argues / demonstrates* that "photographs can transport us to other worlds."
   c He *says / points out* that "the best images help us see our lives from a different perspective."

3 Find more quotes by Lovell and Borman in paragraphs 3 and 4. How persuasively are their opinions presented? Do you agree with them? Why?

8 MY PERSPECTIVE

Work in pairs. Tell each other about a photo that is special to you or that you are proud of.

The photo "Earthrise" was taken from the Apollo 8 spacecraft on the morning of December 24, 1968.

EARTHRISE

70 A picture, so the saying goes, is worth a thousand words. But in a world in which millions of photographs are taken and uploaded every minute and we are exposed to a daily avalanche of pictures
5 on our computer screens, what is the value of a single image? According to Martin Barnes, Senior Curator of photographs at the Victoria and Albert Museum in London, "Great photographs are like visual poetry. They neatly capture and express a situation or emotion
10 that transcends the everyday." By capturing a single moment and holding it absolutely still, a photograph can convey a powerful idea in a universal language. But more than that, images can transport us to new places and help us see our lives from a different
15 perspective. As National Geographic photographer Aaron Huey says, "Photography has the power to undo your assumptions about the world."

Nowhere is this more clearly illustrated than in "Earthrise," the groundbreaking picture which, though
20 not the first ever photo of the Earth from space, transformed people's attitudes to a world they had taken for granted up to that point. It all started on the morning of December 21, 1968, when the crew of Apollo 8—Frank Borman, Jim Lovell, and Bill Anders—
25 set out for humanity's first manned mission to orbit the moon. With the excitement of lunar exploration, photographs of Earth were not included at all in the official NASA plans. Yet when, on Christmas Eve, and on their fourth orbit, the crew emerged from behind
30 the moon's dark side, they saw in front of them an astounding sight—an exquisite blue sphere hanging in the blackness of space.

"Look at that picture over there. Here's the Earth coming up. Wow! That is pretty!", exclaimed Anders. It
35 is thought that at this point Borman snapped a black-and-white image of the scene. "Hey, don't take that. It's

not scheduled," Anders joked. He then added, "Hand me that roll of color, quick." After a brief scramble to find the film, Anders shot a color photograph. It
40 showed the Earth as a blue planet, partially covered by white swirling clouds and contrasting starkly with the empty backdrop of space and the dead, gray lunar surface, which Borman described as "a vast, lonely, forbidding expanse of nothing." Looking back on the
45 mission, Anders observed, "I was immediately almost overcome by the thought that here we came all this way to the moon, and yet the most significant thing we're seeing is our own home planet." Borman also said that glimpsing Earth was "the most beautiful,
50 heart-catching sight of my life, one that sent a torrent of nostalgia, of sheer homesickness, surging through me."

The true power of photographs lies in what is done with them after they are created. Within just a few
55 months of the shot being taken, millions of people on Earth had seen the picture, which soon became one of the most iconic images of the century. "Earthrise" gave a new perspective on the planet at a time of great social and political unrest. As Borman
60 remarked, "Raging nationalistic interests, famines, wars, pestilences don't show from that distance. From out there, it really is 'one world.'" Moreover, many people credit the birth of the environmental movement and the first Earth Day celebration in 1970, to this view of
65 the planet from outer space—a view that showed its smallness, fragility, and vulnerability. People realized there was no other sanctuary in the solar system, and so they needed to conserve Earth's resources and protect it from pollution and destruction. Lovell
70 concluded, "It was the most beautiful thing there was to see in all the heavens. People down here don't realize what they have."

Albert Einstein at home

10C Ideas Worth Spreading

GRAMMAR Subordinate and participle clauses

1 Work in pairs. Read about new ideas. Discuss the questions.

New ideas are often met with resistance and criticism, or even rejected, when they are first proposed. For example, when Thomas Edison first had the idea for the electric light bulb, experts in the scientific community couldn't imagine why it would ever work. Even Einstein's theory of relativity was initially ridiculed.

1 Can you think of other ideas (in science, society, or everyday life) that are now widely accepted, but which were initially rejected?
2 What can people do nowadays to gain widespread acceptance of their ideas?

2 Read the text. Could Ignaz Semmelweis have done more to gain acceptance of his idea?

Please wash your hands

Ignaz Semmelweis, known as "the savior of mothers," was a nineteenth-century Hungarian physician. Having worked for a number of years as Director of Maternity Care at Vienna General Hospital, Semmelweis became concerned with the high number of mothers dying at the hospital shortly after childbirth. Since he had noticed that fewer mothers died when giving birth in hospital wards run by midwives,* he wondered if this might be due to infection being spread by doctors who were working with dead bodies before delivering babies. He therefore proposed the radically simple idea that doctors should wash their hands before they delivered babies. Once implemented, this practice drastically reduced the mortality rate. However, his colleagues were offended by his idea, refusing to believe they could be responsible for the deaths of their patients. Not being able to persuade his colleagues, Semmelweis argued with many of them and eventually left the hospital.

Although his hypothesis was supported by the statistical analysis he conducted in the 1840s, Semmelweis did not publish his results until 1861, only a few years before his death in 1865. Later in the century, scientists such as Pasteur and Koch proved the link between germs and disease, leading to the request now repeated every day across the world: "Please wash your hands."

midwives *people trained in helping women give birth*

3 Work in pairs. Look at the examples from the text in the Grammar box. Answer the questions.

Subordinate and participle clauses

a *Having worked for a number of years as Director of Maternity Care, …*

b *… the high number of mothers dying at the hospital…*

c *Since he had noticed that…*

d *… fewer mothers died when giving birth in hospital wards run by midwives, …*

e *… doctors should wash their hands before they delivered babies.*

f *Once implemented, this practice drastically reduced the mortality rate.*

g *…, refusing to believe they could be responsible for the deaths of their patients.*

h *Not being able to persuade his colleagues, …*

1 Which examples are participle clauses? Which are subordinate clauses? What are the differences between them?

2 Which of the participle clauses are active? Which are passive? What is the rule?

3 Which example is negative? How do we make participles negative?

4 Which participle indicates the past?

5 Which ones are reduced relative clauses?

6 The two subordinate clauses express a notion (e.g., purpose, contrast). Which notions do they express? Do the participle clauses express notions?

Check your answers on page 146. Do Activities 4–6.

4 Work in pairs. Delete the incorrect option in the sentence. Why is it incorrect?

1 *Having worked / Worked* as a physician, Semmelweis noticed that many mothers were dying after childbirth.

2 *Offended / Having offended* by his idea, people rejected it as untrue.

3 His colleagues refused to wash their hands, not *realizing / realized* the danger.

4 *Discouraging / Discouraged* by the hostile reception to his views, he left the hospital.

5 *Proved / Being proved / Once proved* by scientific evidence, the link between germs and disease was widely accepted.

5 Complete the text about an innovative businesswoman with the correct form of the verbs in parentheses. There may be more than one correct answer.

Born and (1) _____ (raise) in Monterrey, Mexico, Blanca Treviño is one of Latin America's most well-known business innovators. (2) _____ (study) computer science in Monterrey, she joined Softtek, the Mexican IT company, which, (3) _____ (lead) by Treviño as its President, has become the most prominent IT company in Latin America. The company is now also (4) _____ (enjoy) success in the United States. (5) _____ (promote) both Latin American information technology and women in business, Treviño has become a popular speaker at international conferences. She was also once (6) _____ (feature) in CNN's Leading Women series. Now (7) _____ (know) beyond her home country, Treviño has been identified by several media publications as one of the most influential executives in Latin America.

6 Work in pairs. Student A looks at the A prompts, and Student B looks at the B prompts. Using the prompts and any other information you can find, write "The story of an idea." Then read your story to your partner. What are the similarities and differences?

A discovery of penicillin—Alexander Fleming / returned from vacation / accidentally left dish with bacteria open / green mold growing / bacteria hadn't spread / mold not poisonous / turned into penicillin / saved many lives

B how Cornflakes came about—Dr. John Kellogg / worked in US hospital / patients on strict diets and bland food / Kellogg cooked wheat / left for too long / went stale / not much money for meals / flattened wheat and toasted it / served to patients / proved very popular

7 **CHOOSE** Choose one of the activities below.

- Research a famous "person of ideas" (for example, Gabriel Garcia Marquez, Mary Wollstonecraft, King Sejong, Muhammad Yunus, Ellen Ochoa, or somebody else). Make a poster and include a short description of the person's life and the development of their ideas.

- Write a short story called "A change of mind." Answer these questions. Then read your story to a partner.

  Who had the idea? What was it? Why was it good? How did the person pursue it? What was the final result?

- Work in pairs. Think of an idea that people disagree about nowadays (for example, the use of animals in science). Make notes about the idea. Then discuss it with another pair.

Blanca Treviño, President of Mexican IT company Softtek

AUTHENTIC LISTENING SKILLS

Collaborative listening

Often when you listen, you aren't alone. People naturally discuss what they have just heard because it is common for different members of an audience to hear and remember different things. By comparing notes and ideas, you can find that as a group you understand something better than any one individual.

1 Look at the Authentic Listening Skills box. Then work in groups. Listen to the beginning of the TED Talk. 🎧 **71**

Student A: listen and note any references to ways of giving a TED Talk

Student B: listen and note any references to Chris's experience

Student C: listen and note any information you want

2 Compare your notes. Listen again and check. 🎧 **71**

3 Listen to another extract from the talk without taking notes. Then compare what you heard in your groups. Did you remember the same information? Listen again and check. 🎧 **72**

WATCH

4 Watch Part 1 of the talk. Make notes to answer the questions. ▶ **10.1**

1 What is the danger of trying to follow a fixed formula?
2 What "gift" do successful speakers give their audience?
3 What do Haley's and the listeners' brains have in common?

4 What are the components of the idea in Haley's mind?
5 How is Haley's idea "teleported" into people's minds?
6 How does Chris define "an idea"?

5 Watch Part 2 of the talk. Match the speakers with their topics. Two topics are not used. ▶ **10.2**

1 Sir Ken Robinson _____
2 Elora Hardy _____
3 Chimamanda Adichie _____

a an innovation in construction
b the importance of literature
c understanding cultural complexity
d how to raise stronger children
e how to improve schools

6 Complete the summary. Watch Part 2 again to check your answers. ▶ **10.2**

Chris Anderson says that everyone's mind contains many ideas which are (1) _____ to create an individual (2) _____ . The different (3) _____ of this make people react and see things differently, so they should be very (4) _____ . It is important to convey ideas clearly because they can (5) _____ the way people understand reality and (6) _____ both their behavior and civilization as a whole.

7 Watch Part 3 of the talk. What are the four key ingredients of a good TED Talk? ▶ **10.3**

TEDTALKS

8 Watch Part 3 of the talk again. Choose the correct options to complete ideas from Chris's guidelines. ▶ 10.3

1 You should focus on *a single idea / a few important ideas*.
2 It's helpful to *elaborate on / check that the audience understands* your main idea.
3 You should *present your idea logically / help listeners realize what they don't know*.
4 You should *explain your concepts carefully / build on the audience's current knowledge*.
5 Metaphors can *be very helpful / sometimes be confusing*.
6 It's a good idea to *edit your talk carefully beforehand / rehearse your talk*.
7 An idea worth sharing is *practical for / relevant to* your audience.
8 A good idea is one that *inspires large or small changes / changes everything*.

9 **VOCABULARY IN CONTEXT**

a Watch the clips from the TED Talk. Choose the correct meaning of the words and phrases. ▶ 10.4

b Think of examples of the following things. Then compare your ideas in pairs.
1 the elements that *make up* a good story
2 a piece of news or an event you found *startling*
3 a time when someone *saw through* an excuse you made
4 how you might *bridge the communication gap* when speaking to someone who doesn't speak your language

10 **MY PERSPECTIVE**

Look back at the TED Talks you have seen in this course. Choose your favorite talk. Work in pairs. Explain why you have chosen that talk.

CHALLENGE

Look at the strategies for giving a good presentation. Choose the five you consider to be the most important and think about how to justify your ideas.

- Keep it short and simple.
- Think about your audience.
- Use visual aids (pictures, objects, charts, or slides with key phrases).
- Anticipate questions.
- Rehearse and time your presentation.
- Speak at a normal speed and volume.
- Look at the audience and vary your eye contact.
- Vary your intonation.
- Explain key words.
- Check understanding.
- Relax and be aware of your body language.
- Use gestures to help explain your ideas and connect with the audience.

Work in groups and compare your ideas.

10E Changing Perspectives

SPEAKING

1 Work in pairs. Discuss the questions.

1 Have you ever kept a diary? What did you write about? When did you write it? Do you still write it?
2 What could be the rewards and challenges of keeping a diary?

2 Listen to a talk about keeping a diary. Answer the questions. 🎧 **73**

1 How does the speaker engage the audience's attention and interest?
2 Label the sections of the presentation in the order you hear them.
_____ research on keeping a diary
_____ a life-changing experience
_____ the writer's first diary

3 Work in pairs. Discuss what you can remember about each section. Then listen again to check your ideas and add more information. 🎧 **73**

4 Match the signpost expressions with their uses. You can use one more than once.

1 Turning now to (research), …
2 To elaborate on that, …
3 To expand a little on that…
4 To digress for a moment, …
5 To go back to (my diary), …
6 To summarize, …
7 To illustrate that, …

a to give an example
b to start a new section
c to return to an earlier point
d to repeat the main points
e to talk about an unrelated topic
f to give more information

5 **PRONUNCIATION** Intonation of signpost expressions

Listen to the expressions in Activity 4. Does the speaker's voice go up or down at the end of each one? Listen again and repeat. 🎧 **74**

6 Plan a presentation. Follow this procedure.

1 Think of an experience you've had which has changed your perspective.
2 Decide on the content for your talk and structure it clearly. Use the four suggestions from Chris's TED Talk. Use expressions from the Useful language box.
3 Think of a good opening line.

Useful language

Introducing your presentation

I'm going to talk to you / tell you about…

I want to share with you…

Starting

Put your hands up if…

I want to start by asking…

So, let's start by looking at…

Highlighting important points

Now, …

So, why / what…? Well, …

As you can see, …

The really interesting / strange thing is that…

And / But more than that, …

Finishing

Thank you for listening.

If you have any questions, I'll do my best to answer them.

Are there any questions?

Singer Juan Luis Guerra performs onstage during the 16th Latin GRAMMY Awards in Las Vegas, Nevada.

7 Work in groups. Give your presentations. Ask questions at the end.

WRITING A review

8 Work in pairs. Talk about a concert, play, or sports event you have been to that made an impression on you. What made it special?

9 Read the review of a concert on page 154. How did the concert change the writer's perspective on life and why?

10 **WRITING SKILL** Reference

> Like *the*, you can use *this* or *these* to refer back to something you have just mentioned (e.g., *this* in line 9 refers back to *a new song*). *This*, *these*, and *such / such a(n)* (meaning *of this kind* or *like this*) can also be followed by a summarizing noun (e.g., *these musicians* refer back to the group 440, and *such versatility* refers back to Guerra's musical abilities).

Work in pairs. Complete the sentences with *this*, *these*, or *such* followed by these summarizing adjectives.

classic songs	concert	encore	energy	solos	stage presence

1 I was struck by the young musician's confidence and rapport with the audience. _____ is rare in a performer of his age.

2 After finishing the set, the band returned and played two more songs. _____ lasted over fifteen minutes.

3 The singer left the stage while the drummer and guitarist each played for several minutes. _____ were greeted with loud applause.

4 The band played non-stop for four hours. I don't know where they found _____ .

5 I saw the group live two years ago. _____ was their first gig in this country.

6 The audience was singing along to old favorites. _____ included hits from their first album.

11 Write a review based on the ideas you discussed in Activity 8. Use the expressions in the Useful language box.

REVIEW OF TENSES

Future forms

Use:

- the simple present for scheduled future events.

*The class **starts** next September.*

- the present continuous for definite future arrangements.

*They**'re opening** a new restaurant next month.*

- *be going to* for predictions based on information in the present and definite intentions.

*This math test is **going to be** tough. I didn't study enough.*

- *will/won't* for predictions that are certain or possible, often with *guess, think, hope,* etc. It is also used for predictions based on experience.

*I**'ll have** the chance to learn another instrument.*

*It**'ll be** easier the second time.*

- the future continuous for actions that will be in progress at a point in the future.

*I**'ll be practicing** hard all next summer.*

Note that the choice of future form can be subjective, depending on the attitude of the speaker.

Time expressions referring to the future are often used with these forms (e.g., *tonight, [by] next week/month/year, in five years*).

Present and past tenses

Use:

- the present continuous for changing trends.

*People are **becoming** more aware of the need to stay healthy.*

- the simple past for a series of actions in the past.

*The chance **came up**, so I **grabbed** the opportunity.*

- the past continuous for repeated actions over a temporary period in the past.

*We **were feeding** the neighbor's cat while she was away.*

- the simple present or the present perfect after time words (e.g., *when, after, as soon as, once*).

*As soon as I**'ve finished** my homework…*

- the present perfect and present perfect continuous to express actions starting at a point in the past and continuing to (just before) the present or having an effect on the present.

*I**'ve** always **lived** in a big city.*

*I**'ve been learning** Chinese for the last three years.*

- the past perfect and past perfect continuous to express actions starting at a point in the past and continuing to a more recent past.

*I**'d** never **been** interested in cycling before (that time).*

*My dad **had been working** in the family business (up to that time).*

It is possible to use verbs that are usually considered stative verbs in an active way by using a different tense. This is common when the verb takes a different meaning.

*We **have** a chain of language schools. (have = own—stative verb)*

*I**'ve been having** a good time. (have = experience—action verb)*

Stative verbs can also be used in a continuous form to emphasize the temporary/current nature of the activity. It is more often used in speech.

*They**'re** absolutely **loving** it.*

CONTINUOUS AND PERFECT ASPECTS

Continuous aspect

Continuous forms focus on the temporary nature of an action.

*I **work** in Costa Rica. = on a permanent basis*

*I**'m** currently **working** in Costa Rica. = for a limited period*

The temporary nature of the action is often shown with time adverbs and expressions such as *at the moment, currently,* etc.

The continuous aspect emphasizes duration in contrast with a completed action.

*We**'ve stayed** here a couple of times.*

*We**'ve been staying** with our aunt while our parents are away.*

Perfect aspect

The perfect aspect usually creates a link between two times.

In the case of the past perfect between two actions in the past, one occurs at a time before the other.

*I**'d been studying** law for a year before I came here.*

The continuous and perfect aspects can be used together. In the case of the present perfect, the simple is used to express completed actions and the continuous for ongoing actions.

*I**'ve read** the book for tomorrow's class. (= completed; I won't read any more.)*

*I**'ve been reading** the book for tomorrow's class for three hours now. (= I might read more though.)*

Some verbs can be used in the simple or continuous in the perfect form with no difference in meaning (e.g., *work, live, study*).

1 Choose the best option to complete the sentences.

1 It's always been my dream to study as a ballet dancer, and I think that next summer
   a I'm finally making it happen!
   b I'm finally going to make it happen!

2 I'm applying to a school in Moscow, and hopefully
   a I won't run into too many obstacles.
   b I don't run into too many obstacles.

3 Applications have to be in by early May; the first interviews are in June; and the final selection
   a takes place at the end of August.
   b is taking place at the end of August.

4 Classes start in October, so I'll know in early September if I have a spot, and, if I do,
   a I'm moving to Moscow that month.
   b I'll move to Moscow that month.

2 Are the sentences correct? If not, correct the mistake.

1 It was clear after only a couple of hours that he had taken on too much.

2 As soon as I've achieved my goal of running five miles a day, I start training for a marathon.

3 The recent report shows that more students in the US currently take full-time rather than part-time classes.

4 We arrived at summer camp last week, and so far we've been loving every minute.

5 Large numbers of people are walking or biking to work every day because of the traffic problems.

6 Excuse me. I'm wanting to go to the health center. Is this the right way?

7 This piano piece is really difficult. I'm practicing it for weeks now, and I'm still making mistakes.

8 Let me tell you, if you want to realize your potential here, you weren't trying hard enough up to now.

3 Complete the text with these verb phrases.

completed	do not	going to
had emerged	had initially shown	has become
has progressively	lost	managed to
was pursuing		

Stephen Hawking is a name that few people
(1) _____ instantly recognize, and his life story
(2) _____ even more famous since the release of the
2014 film, *The Theory of Everything*. Born in 1942, Hawking
had an uneventful early life. Although he (3) _____
little academic talent at school, he (4) _____ school
earlier than most students, finishing at the age of 17 to study
physics and chemistry at Oxford. It was while he

(5) _____ his postgraduate studies at Cambridge
that he developed motor neuron disease, a condition where
all muscle control is eventually (6) _____ , and he
became very depressed. Once he (7) _____ from the
depression, Hawking (8) _____ continue his career and
became a brilliant physicist.
Now in his seventies, Hawking continues to contribute to
science, although his condition (9) _____ worsened.
He still works and is not (10) _____ retire from
scientific life yet.

4 Choose the correct response to each question.

1 So, you're without a job at the moment. Is that right?
   a Yes, I'm looking for something new for three months now.
   b Yes, I've been looking for something new for three months now.

2 You lost your job a few months ago. Are you on unemployment?
   a Well, I've only received one payment so far.
   b Well, I've only been receiving one payment so far.

3 Your grandfather worked in local government, didn't he?
   a Yes, he was staying in the same job his entire career.
   b Yes, he stayed in the same job his entire career.

4 Are you earning the minimum wage at your job?
   a Yes, but I only do it for the summer.
   b Yes, but I'm only doing it for the summer.

5 Complete the sentences in each pair. Use the verb in each of the forms given.

1 *work* – simple past/past continuous
   a My mother _____ as a nurse for the first few years of her career, before she had children.
   b My mother _____ as a nurse when she met my father.

2 *try* – present perfect continuous/present continuous
   a Working women _____ to break the glass ceiling since the 1970s.
   b Working women _____ to break the glass ceiling with ever more enthusiasm.

3 *put* – present perfect/present perfect continuous
   a The government _____ training programs in place for many years now.
   b The government _____ a new series of training programs in place.

4 *spend* – present continuous/present perfect continuous
   a Both of us _____ more time at home since the baby was born.
   b Both of us _____ more time at home at the same time.

MODIFYING ADJECTIVES

Adjectives can be modified by using an adverb (e.g., *really, absolutely*) or with adverbial phrases (e.g., *a little, at all*).

*He's a **really slow** reader, and he's **a little distracted** this morning.*

Gradable and ungradable adjectives

Gradable adjectives represent a point on a scale and can be modified to express degrees of a quality (e.g., *interesting, cold, tired, angry, scared, sad*).

They can be made comparative.

*His latest book is **more interesting than** his others.*

Ungradable adjectives express the limit of a quality or scale (e.g., *fascinating, freezing, exhausted, furious, terrified, heartbroken*).

They usually can't be compared.

It's much more freezing in the library today than usual.

Adverbs of degree

Common adverbs that strengthen gradable adjectives are *very, really, so, pretty, extremely*, and *terribly*.

*You should see that movie. It's **extremely funny**.*

Common adverbs that strengthen ungradable adjectives are *really, absolutely, incredibly, so*, and *completely*.

*You must see that movie. It's **absolutely hilarious**!*

Other adverbs can be used with ungradable adjectives, such as *completely, totally*, and *highly*, but these are only used with certain adjectives (e.g., *completely disastrous, totally deaf, highly acclaimed*).

Adverbs and adverbials can also be used to weaken adjectives. With gradable adjectives, *a little, slightly, not very / not all that*, and *somewhat* are usually used.

*It's **a little warm** in here.*

With ungradable adjectives, use *nearly, almost*, or *practically*.

*These two books are **practically identical**.*

Pretty is usually used with gradable adjectives with a negative meaning.

*Her latest book is **pretty disappointing**.*

If used with a positive adjective, it expresses surprise.

*This book is **pretty good**. I didn't enjoy her other books.*

NARRATIVE TENSES AND FUTURE IN THE PAST

Narrative tenses

The simple past is used to talk about a series of completed events that happened in the past. Background actions and those in progress at the time are introduced with the past continuous.

*All our friends **were complaining** about the cost of books, so we **decided** to share our books.*

The past perfect describes actions that took place before the main narrative time of the story. The past perfect describes an action completed before the main narrative, and the past perfect continuous expresses an action that was in progress before the time of the main narrative.

*We **had been wondering** if it was possible for readers to put their thoughts about the book on a website once they **had finished** it.*

The narrative can also be moved with verbs in the *-ing* form after time prepositions and conjunctions of time.

After leaving all the books for others to find, we felt very lighthearted.

After we had left all the books for others to find, we felt very lighthearted.

Future in the past

There are several different ways of expressing a future event from a viewpoint in the past. *Was/were going to* + the base form of a verb is often used (usually when the event did not take place). The past continuous can also be used.

*We **were going to (intending to / hoping to) get** tickets for the book festival this year, but they sold out.*

Expressions such as *was/were about to* + infinitive and *was/were on the point/verge of* + *-ing* can be used when the future event is imminent and may or may not have taken place.

*I **was about to buy** (**was on the verge / point of buying**) the book when I realized I didn't have my wallet.*

Use *would* + base form or *was/were* + base form (more formal) when the future event actually did happen.

*When writing the book, she had no idea that it **would become / was to become** the work that made her name known all over the world.*

Use *was/were* + infinitive if the event did not happen.

*The book launch **was to take place** at the festival in July (but the book wasn't ready in time).*

1 Write these adjectives under the correct heading.

angry	big	boiling	cheap	cold
difficult	disgusting	enormous	exhausted	free
freezing	furious	hot	impossible	priceless
scared	terrified	tired	unpleasant	valuable

Gradable   Ungradable

2 Choose the correct option to complete the sentences.

1 Jo Nesbo's latest thriller is absolutely *interesting / intriguing*, but the ending gets a little *unpleasant / disgusting*.
2 **A** What did you think of that new comedy?
  B I thought it was pretty *funny / hilarious*—I couldn't stop laughing.
3 This first edition of *The Hobbit* is more *valuable / priceless* than I thought.
4 Have you read this book? I found it practically *difficult / impossible* to understand.
5 Gina was absolutely *angry / furious* when her friend told her the ending of the book she was reading.
6 It's very *cheap / free* to go to the local movie theater on Monday evenings, so we go every week, even if we're totally *tired / exhausted*.

3 Complete the paragraph with the verbs in parentheses in the simple past, past continuous, past perfect, or the *-ing* form.

I (1) _____ (start) studying literature at college last month. I didn't know anyone there, so I decided to join a club. One day, after my class (2) _____ (finish), I (3) _____ (walk) past the literature department bulletin board when a small sign (4) _____ (catch) my eye. It (5) _____ (advertise) a book club. What's the point of a book club when you're already studying literature, I thought, but I was intrigued, so I decided to follow up on it. After (6) _____ (call) the phone number on the sign and (7) _____ (talk) to the organizer, we agreed that I'd go to the next meeting, a few days later. It (8) _____ (become) apparent that this was no ordinary book club. Each member (9) _____ (bring) along their choice of book for the following meeting. The one rule was that the choices (10) _____ (must) be books that weren't from the literature classes, so there were biographies, history books, travel books—you name it. It turned out to be the most interesting club I've ever joined!

4 Use the word in parentheses to complete the second sentence so that it means the same as the first. Use no more than five words.

1 We meant to visit the book festival this year as usual, but it was on the weekend of Marta's wedding. (going)
  We _____ the book festival this year as usual, but it was on the weekend of Marta's wedding.
2 You took that book by Paulo Coelho back to the library? I wanted to start reading it tonight! (about)
  You took that book by Paulo Coelho back to the library, but I _____ it.
3 Luis had the pen in his hand, ready to sign the publishing contract when he noticed that there was a spelling mistake in his name. (verge)
  Luis was _____ the contract when he noticed that there was a spelling mistake in his name.
4 I took the Suzanne Collins trilogy on vacation, but I hardly had any time for reading. (thinking)
  I _____ the Suzanne Collins trilogy on vacation, but I hardly had any time for reading.
5 They announced that they would reveal the identity of the new James Bond after the ceremony. (was)
  They announced that the identity of the new James Bond _____ after the ceremony.

5 Choose the correct option to complete the text.

I (1) *was dusting / dusted* my bookshelves about a year ago when I wondered why I (2) *accumulated / had accumulated* so many books. Did I need them? I was (3) *on the verge of / about to* donating some of them, but something stopped me. I (4) *had also been considering / also considered* selling some of them but wondered if there was a better way.

That was when I (5) *had discovered / discovered* BookCrossing. It was set up in 2001, by Americans Ron and Kaori Hornbaker and Bruce and Heather Pedersen after Ron (6) *noticed / was noticing* that, unlike for dollar bills, for example, there was no website dedicated to tracking books throughout their life.

The four then (7) *had come up / came up* with the idea of a website that allowed used books to be distributed and followed, simply by giving each book a unique number that could be tracked online. I joined immediately and started registering my books. After (8) *doing / done* that, I distributed them—to friends, family, strangers on buses, etc.—and then I tracked their locations. Within a few months, my books (9) *had traveled / been traveling* to several different countries and had had many readers. When I started using BookCrossing, I had no idea that it (10) *was becoming / would become* such an interesting part of my life.

FIRST AND SECOND CONDITIONAL

The first conditional is used to describe an event in the result clause that is a real possibility in the future but is dependent on the condition in the *if*-clause. It is often used to express requests, offers, suggestions, and warnings.

If you don't take action now, it could be too late.

Any present form can be used in the *if*-clause and any future form in the result clause.

*If global temperatures **have increased** again this year, carbon emissions **will need** to be further reduced.*

Most modals can be used in the result clause to express differing levels of certainty (e.g., *may, might, should, can, could*).

*If global temperatures **have increased** again this year, carbon emissions **may need to be / should be** further reduced.*

Unless expresses a negative condition and has a similar meaning to *if… not* or *except if…* .

***Unless** we act now, the problem will never be fixed.*

Suppose can be used in speech to introduce the *if*-clause, often with a question.

***Suppose** we lower the price, will that help?*

Note that sometimes the difference between the first conditional and zero conditional comes down to the speaker's point of view. With a sentence like *If you see someone dumping chemicals, please report it immediately*, the speaker may be thinking of any time this happens, in which case it is the zero conditional and *if* is similar to *when*. But if the speaker is thinking about a specific future time when it might happen, it is the first conditional.

The second conditional is used to express an unlikely future event or a hypothetical situation (contrary to known facts) that is dependent on the condition in the *if*-clause. It is often used to express advice, desires, and polite requests.

If we had recycling centers, it would make life much easier!

The simple past or past continuous can be used in the *if*-clause. *Would/might/could* + base form / *be* + *-ing* form can be used in the result clause.

Unlikely event: *If everyone **recycled** more, we **might need** fewer landfills.*

Impossible situation: *If we **weren't filling** landfill sites, we **wouldn't be poisoning** the land.*

Using *could* in the result clause expresses ability.

*If local authorities **provided** the facilities, we **could** all **recycle** more.*

There are alternatives to *if* for conditional sentences. *Provided/On the condition (that)* and *As long as* make the condition necessary for the result to be achieved.

***As long as** everyone helps, the problem might disappear.*

In the second conditional, the event in the result clause can be made less likely by using *was/were* + infinitive in the *if*-clause and more formal by removing *if* and transposing *was/were* and the subject.

*If everyone **were to recycle** more…*

***Were** everyone **to recycle** more…*

THIRD AND MIXED CONDITIONALS, *I WISH / IF ONLY*

The third conditional is used to express a hypothetical (imaginary) past event or situation that is dependent on the condition in the *if*-clause. It is often used to express regret.

If I had bought that new car, I would be spending less on gas.

The past perfect can be used in the *if*-clause with *would/could/might have* + past participle in the result clause.

*If the local authorities **hadn't stopped** the development, the Roman villa **might/could/would have been destroyed**.*

The third conditional can be made more formal by removing *if* and transposing *had* and the subject.

***Had** they **not stopped** the development…*

The condition can be made more necessary with *had it not been for…* + noun.

***Had it not been for** their quick action…*

The two common mixed conditionals are:

- a hypothetical situation in the past with a hypothetical result in the present; the past perfect in the *if*-clause and *would might/could* + base form / *be* + *-ing* form in the result clause.

*If you **hadn't told** her the truth, we **would** still **be talking**.*

- a hypothetical situation in the present with a hypothetical result in the past; a past form in the *if*-clause and *would/might/could* + *have* + past participle in the result clause.

*If UNESCO **didn't exist**, the site **might have been lost**.*

Use *I wish/if only* to express regrets about the past.

***I wish/If only** I had bought the new car…*

Other structures can be used to express regret.

***I should have bought** the new car…*

1 Complete the sentences with the correct form of the verb in parentheses. There may be more than one possible answer.

1 If we want to slow the pace of global warming in the future, we _____ (have to) take action now.
2 We could reduce the effects of climate change if less carbon _____ (be released) into the air.
3 Less carbon _____ (be released) if we were all more aware of our carbon footprint.
4 Renewable energy _____ (be) a serious possibility if the government were prepared to invest in it.
5 Low-lying land will be in danger of severe flooding if sea levels _____ (rise) significantly.

2 Put the words and phrases in the correct order to complete the sentences.

1 *your town / green / suppose / to go / decided*
_____ ?

2 Stores will get lower energy bills *at night / condition / turn / that / the lights / they / on / off / the*
_____ .

3 Also, all the streetlights would be turned off at night to save energy, *dangerous areas / they / unless / potentially / were / in*
_____ .

4 *solar panels / homeowners / on their roofs / should / install*
_____ ,
the city will pay 25% of the costs.

3 Match the *if*-clauses (1–5) with the result clauses (a–e).

1 If the polar ice caps weren't melting, _____
2 If temperatures hadn't risen in some parts of the world, _____
3 If numbers of the spruce bark beetle* hadn't increased because of warm summers, _____
4 If fewer tourists visited the Great Barrier Reef each year, _____
5 If some animal parts weren't believed to cure diseases, _____

spruce bark beetle *an insect that eats spruce trees*

a Alaska would have more spruce trees now.
b fewer species would have been put on the endangered list.
c sea levels wouldn't have risen so quickly over the last century.
d some animal species wouldn't have moved to cooler areas.
e it might not have suffered so much damage.

4 Complete the paragraphs about UNESCO World Heritage Sites using the correct form of the verbs in parentheses to make conditional sentences. Use the texts to help you.

> In 1999, there were plans to enlarge a salt factory in a bay that was a safe home for the Pacific gray whale. UNESCO warned the Mexican government about the potential danger to wildlife, and Mexico refused to give permission to build the factory in 2000. The Whale Sanctuary of El Vizcaíno now also protects seals, sea lions, and four endangered species of sea turtles.

If UNESCO (1) _____ (not warn) the Mexican government about the threats to wildlife, they (2) _____ (give) permission to build the factory, and the Whale Sanctuary (3) _____ (not contain) so many endangered species today. If they (4) _____ (build) the factory, the Pacific gray whale (5) _____ (be) extinct today.

> Dubrovnik, Croatia, suffered serious damage during the Balkan War in 1991. Given the city's historical importance, the Croatian government received assistance—both technical and financial—from UNESCO to help them restore important buildings. Consequently, the city was removed from the World Heritage in Danger list in 1998.

If Dubrovnik (6) _____ (not be considered) such an important historic city, UNESCO (7) _____ (not provide) assistance. If UNESCO (8) _____ (not give) technical advice and financial assistance, the Croatian government (9) _____ (not restore) the buildings, and the heritage of the city (10) _____ (be) in danger today .

5 Complete the second sentence so that it means the same as the first.

1 If I'd accepted the offer to go on the safari, I'd have seen a lot of endangered animals.
I wish I _____ .
2 If only I hadn't thrown away that old coat. I could really use it now!
If I _____ .
3 We overuse fossil fuels, so the global temperature has risen too much.
The global temperature _____ .
4 I regret not taking an ecology class in college.
If _____ .
5 We're changing the biodiversity of the planet because we have caused so many species to disappear.
If so many species hadn't _____ .

MODALS OF DEDUCTION AND PROBABILITY

To express certainty that something is or is not true based on logical deduction from available evidence, use *must* or *can't* + base form / *be* + *-ing* form.

There **must be** more planets in the universe than we are aware of.

Life forms similar to our own **can't exist** in our solar system.

Somewhere in the universe a life form **must be watching** us.

To express present or future possibility, use *may, might,* or *could* + base form / *be* + *-ing* form.

Life **could exist** elsewhere in the universe.

Some countries **might send** people into space again in the future.

Modal verbs can also be used to make logical deductions about the past that express certainty or probability.

A *The US space program **couldn't have been** cheap!*
B *No, it **must have cost** billions of dollars.*
A *Yes, and it **might have cost** more than they estimated.*

Modal adjectives, adverbs, and expressions can also be used to indicate probability.

adjectives: *It is **probable** that humans will go to the Moon again.*

adverbs: *I'd **definitely** be interested in visiting the space station.*

expressions: *It**'s bound to** cost a huge amount. It**'s likely to** be funded by taxes.*

PASSIVE VOICE

The passive is formed the same way in every tense (i.e., a form of the verb *to be* + the past participle).

New discoveries **are being made** all the time.

You**'ll be contacted** as soon as the funding **has been put** in place.

The excavations **had been started** before the final decision **was made**.

The object of the active verb becomes the subject of the passive verb; if the subject of the active verb is included, it is called the agent, and it is introduced with *by*.

The archeology student [subject] *removed the wrong items* [object] *from the tomb.*

The wrong items [subject] *were removed from the tomb (by the archeology student* [agent]*).*

Some verbs have two objects (e.g., *bring, give, lend, offer, show, teach*). Both need to be included in the passive.

The team leader *showed* **the team the ancient vase.**

The team *was shown* **the ancient vase.**

The ancient vase *was shown* **to the team.**

The first passive example is more common.

The passive is used when the agent is obvious, unimportant, or unknown or when the speaker wants to "hide" the subject of the active verb.

I'm afraid I broke this vase while I was digging it up.

I'm afraid this vase was broken while it was being dug up.

Passive reporting structures

The passive is used with verbs such as *say, think, believe, know, consider, estimate, expect,* and *report* to express general beliefs and opinions and to report events. The passive can be used with *it,* followed by a *that*-clause.

It is believed that the Great Wall of China is the world's most visited ancient site.

Or the passive can start with the main focus of the clause and an infinitive clause.

The Great Wall of China is believed to be the world's most visited ancient site.

This structure can be used in the future and the past.

It is estimated that around ten million people **will visit** the Great Wall this year.

Around ten million people **are expected to visit** the Great Wall this year.

It is generally thought that the Great Wall **was built** to keep out Mongolian invaders.

The Great Wall **is generally thought to have been built** to keep out Mongolian invaders.

Information order

It is best to put known information at the beginning of a clause, and the passive is often used in order to achieve this.

The first artificial satellite was Sputnik 1. **It was launched** by the Soviet Union in 1957. (*It* = the satellite = known information)

Compare this with the active equivalent which is less natural.

The first artificial satellite was Sputnik 1. The Soviet Union **launched it** in 1957.

The passive puts the new information in end-focus position to highlight it.

1 Choose the correct option to complete the sentences.

1 The human race has always looked to the stars, so we *might / can't* have always believed that it would be *impossible / possible* to go there one day.

2 We face *a certain / an uncertain* future now, and it is highly *unlikely / likely* that countries will look at exploring other planets.

3 China has really accelerated its space program, and it is *probable / unlikely* that it will land an unmanned vehicle on the Moon soon.

4 The International Space Station shows that it *must / can't* be possible for countries to work together to explore space for the benefit of us all.

5 For most countries, space exploration is *bound / unlikely* to have a positive effect on national identity.

2 Complete the second sentence so that it means the same as the first. Use *must, can't, could, couldn't,* or *might* (+ *have*).

1 It is thought that Marco Polo was born in Venice.
Marco Polo ___*might have been born*___ in Venice.

2 It is likely that the name "Polo" comes from *paulus*, the name of a bird.
The name "Polo" _____ from the name of a bird.

3 His father traveled a lot, so it is virtually impossible that Marco knew him well as a child.
His father traveled a lot, so Marco _____ him well as a child.

4 It is highly likely that Marco worked for Kublai Khan when he was in China.
Marco _____ for Kublai Khan when he was in China.

5 So many different versions of his travels exist that it is almost certain that we don't know the truth.
So many different versions of his travels exist that we _____ the truth.

3 Rewrite the sentences in the passive, including the agent if necessary.

1 The ancient Greek philosopher Aristotle devised the first method of classifying the living world.

2 Ferdinand Magellan could have circumnavigated the Earth before anyone else if soldiers in the Philippines hadn't killed him.

3 People were making fairly accurate maps of the world about 2,000 years ago.

4 We can date the origins of microbiology to the seventeenth century, after Leeuwenhoek discovered techniques for magnifying objects up to 500 times.

5 In the 1960s, Watson and Crick modeled the working of DNA, and we have reached a much greater understanding of disease since then.

4 Rewrite these headlines in two different ways using the verb in parentheses.

1 Damaged space shuttle lands in Antarctica (think)

It is thought that the damaged space shuttle has landed in Antarctica.
The damaged space shuttle is thought to have landed in Antarctica.

2 Missing mountaineer found alive and well in remote mountain hut (report)

3 Number of potential space tourists now over 1,000 (estimate)

4 Archeologist finds new evidence of ancient Mayan settlement (believe)

5 Recent storms cause at least $2 billion in damage to homes and businesses (know)

5 Choose the best option to complete the text.

Krystyna Chojnowska-Liskiewicz is a Polish explorer who was born in Warsaw in 1936. She always loved the ocean and studied shipbuilding at Gdansk University, (1) _____ , whom she later married. She worked at Gdansk Shipyard as a ship designer, and, while she was there, she improved her sailing skills.

Her breakthrough solo circumnavigation of the world in the yacht *Mazurek* started in 1976 and lasted for two years. (2) _____ . Chojnowska-Liskiewicz was not alone in making this attempt; another sailor named Naomi James from New Zealand was trying for the record at the same time, (3) _____ . When Chojnowska-Liskiewicz completed her voyage in April of 1978, she became the first woman to successfully sail around the world alone. (4) _____ .

1 a where a man with a similar affection for the sea attracted her
b where she was attracted to a man with a similar affection for the sea

2 a The yacht had been built by her husband for this journey
b Her husband had built the yacht for this journey

3 a and she completed her voyage not long afterwards
b and her voyage was completed not long afterwards

4 a Others, such as James and Kay Cottee of Australia, would subsequently repeat this feat
b This feat would subsequently be repeated by others, such as James and Kay Cottee of Australia

INVERSION

Inversion is when the order of the subject and verb in a clause changes so that the auxiliary verb comes before the subject, or if the main verb is *be*, a form of *be* comes before the subject. This places greater emphasis on the subject.

be: Not only **was Malala** very brave…

simple present and simple past: *Little* **did anyone** *realize that*…

other tenses: *Never before* **had anyone** *challenged the idea that*…, *Rarely* **have I** *encountered such rudeness*…

modal verbs: *Under no circumstance* **should we** *underestimate*…

Inversion is used after particular grammatical features:

- negative adverbials such as *not only* (… *but*), *no sooner* (… *than*), *under no circumstances*, *in no way*.

No sooner had *I arrived home* **than** *the doorbell rang.*

- adverbs with negative or restrictive meaning (e.g., *little, hardly, scarcely, rarely, seldom, never, neither, nor*).

Little did anyone realize *that her profile would bring such danger.*

- negative or restrictive adverbial clauses, such as *only + when / because / if / after*, and *not + since / until*.

Only if *we listen to people like Malala* **will the world become** *a safer place for girls.*

Note that inversion here comes in the main clause, not after the conjunction.

- comparisons using *as, so,* and *such*.

Malala's parents were very worried about her, **as was** *the entire world.*

Some of Malala's peers didn't attend school. **Such is** *the life of many girls.*

CLEFT SENTENCES

Two of the most common types of cleft sentences are *it*-clefts and *what*-clefts. Both types change one clause into two and emphasize particular information by doing so.

it-cleft sentences

An *it*-cleft takes important information from a simple clause and foregrounds it in a clause starting *It* + a form of *to be*. This is followed by a subordinate clause, usually a relative clause.

Malala's bus was stopped on this road. (important information = on this road)

It was on this road that *Malala's bus was stopped.*

The attackers wanted to target Malala. (important information = Malala)

It was Malala whom *the attackers wanted to target.*

Any part of a clause can be emphasized using *it*-clefts.

Nelson Mandela made his final speech in Johannesburg in 2004.

subject: **It was Nelson Mandela who** *made his final speech in Johannesburg in 2004.*

object: **It was his final speech that** *Nelson Mandela made in Johannesburg in 2004.*

place adverbial: **It was in Johannesburg that / where** *Nelson Mandela made his final speech (in 2004).*

time adverbial: **It was in 2004 that / when** *Nelson Mandela made his final speech (in Johannesburg).*

Note that the adverbs *where* and *when* can be used to begin the subordinate clause after place and time adverbials. This structure is often used to make a connection or a contrast with what was said before.

Alessandro worked at a shelter for homeless people on his trip. It was **there that** *he met Lia and Joe.*

Joe didn't change his political views; it was **Lia who** *did that.*

what-cleft sentences

A *what*-cleft emphasizes important information by creating a new subject for the clause. The subject is a nominal clause starting with *what* (and sometimes *who*). Unlike *it*-clefts, the important information in *what*-clefts is put at the end of the sentence.

The *what*-clause uses the main verb from the original clause, and the important information is introduced with a form of *to be*.

Her passion inspired us all. (important information = her passion)

What *inspired us all* **was her passion.**

The new organization needs some good publicity. (important information = good publicity)

What *the new organization needs* **is some good publicity.**

Note that *what* in these sentences means "the thing(s) that."

What-clefts can be used to emphasize the subject or object of a clause and verb phrases.

subject: *The new fundraising initiative began yesterday.* ⟶ **What** *began yesterday* **was the new fundraising initiative.**

object: *The new fundraising initiative raised a lot of issues.* ⟶ **What** *the new fundraising initiative raised* **was a lot of issues.**

verb phrase: *The initiative needs to raise awareness.* ⟶ **What** *the initiative needs* **is to raise awareness.** */ What the initiative needs to do* **is raise awareness.**

1 Complete the speech with one word in each space.

My friends, it is an honor to stand before you and accept this award for service to the community. Little (1) _____ I expect to find myself in this position. In fact, I imagine it is not (2) _____ me who is surprised to be here, but also all my neighbors who suffered because of my actions as a teenager. I was not a model citizen in my youth, but (3) _____ was I a bad person. I was just bored because I was not able to find a job after finishing school. In fact, (4) _____ until I had to face some of the consequences of my actions (5) _____ I began to appreciate the trouble I was causing people. Once I realized this, in no (6) _____ could I continue to behave as I had, so I decided to focus my energy on doing good deeds for my neighbors—things as simple as shopping for elderly people and helping in their gardens. No sooner (7) _____ I filled my week with these tasks (8) _____ I was offered a job. That was when I started to recruit my unemployed friends to do some of my good deeds. So, I'd like to finish by thanking them for helping out and by thanking you for this award.

2 Complete the sentences with these words and phrases.

as was	no sooner	only after
seldom	under no circumstances	

1 _____ had the politician finished her speech than the audience stood up and clapped.
2 The mayor of the town was nominated for a community award, _____ the deputy mayor.
3 _____ should you listen to that girl; she's a bad influence.
4 _____ he had had several operations did he fully recover from his wounds.
5 _____ have I seen this kind of behavior from someone so young.

3 Write *it*-cleft sentences to emphasize the part of the sentence given in each case.

The Chairman of the Norwegian Nobel Committee awarded Malala the Nobel Peace Prize in Oslo in December of 2014.

1 the Chairman of the Norwegian Nobel Committee
2 Malala
3 the Nobel Peace Prize
4 in Oslo
5 in December of 2014

4 Put the words and phrases in the correct order to make *what*-cleft sentences.

1 us / what / amazed / was / to the group / commitment / his
2 will make / what / difference / big / a / is / social media / having / a / presence
3 charity / needs / this / what / is / to promote / a new face / it
4 all the students / what / surprised / was / the report / tone / negative / the / of
5 principal / what / the / requested / was / the school / to improve / six months
6 what / a higher profile / is / need / we / why / the advertising agency / that's / we've hired

5 Complete the paragraph with the best options. There are three clauses that you do not need.

UNICEF is the United Nations charity that works to help children across the world. (1) _____ that it focuses on to a great extent. Over 59 million children around the world don't go to elementary school, and UNICEF tries to improve the situation for them. (2) _____ , but it also tries to ensure continuing education in conflict and disaster zones. For example, after the earthquake in Nepal in 2014, (3) _____ was build 1,400 temporary schools for the displaced children. (4) _____ had to try to provide continuing education for so many children—both for those in conflict zones and those who have left conflicts behind. (5) _____ is the basic belief that every child has a right to an education, and (6) _____ that it can fulfill its mission.

a what UNICEF did
b It provides textbooks,
c What fuels UNICEF's mission
d only with financial help from people around the world
e It is the education of children in unsafe situations
f Not until recent times with so many conflicts has UNICEF
g Not until recent times with many conflicts did UNICEF
h it is only with financial help from people around the world
i Not only does it provide textbooks,

MODALS OF PERMISSION AND OBLIGATION

Permission is expressed by *can* or *am/is/are allowed to*.
*Girls **can wear** pants, and they**'re allowed to wear** jewelry.*

For the past, use *could* or *was/were allowed to*.
*In elementary school we **could wear** whatever we wanted, and in kindergarten we **were** even **allowed to bring** toys to school.*

May for permission is more formal.
*Visitors **may leave** their belongings in the staff room.*

Obligation can be expressed by *must, have to, need to, should, ought to*, and *be supposed to*. *Must* and *have to* express strong obligation.
*We **have to wear** a uniform, and we **must** always **carry** ID.*

Must is usually more formal than *have to*, but often they are interchangeable.
*We **have to keep** all personal details confidential.*
*You **must show** your ID to get in.*

There is no past form of *must* for obligation, so the past is always expressed by *had to*.
*Every day, we **had to wait** until our parents came to pick us up.*

Need to is used in a similar way to *must* and *have to* but can express a more physical necessity.
*You **need to take** a break every two hours to be productive.*

For less strong obligation *should, ought to*, or *be supposed to* are used. These often suggest that the obligation is not followed.
*We **should/ought to/are supposed to do** our homework during our study period, but we usually just talk.*

For the past, use *was/were supposed to* + base form or *should have* + past participle.
*We **were supposed to study** three times a week.*

Should have can suggest the action didn't happen.
*We **should have studied** three times a week.*

For strong prohibition, use *can't* or *not be allowed to*.
*The students **can't run** in the hallways.*
*We **aren't allowed to use** our phones at school.*

Use *shouldn't* and *not be supposed to* for less strong prohibition and to suggest that sometimes we do the prohibited action.
*We **aren't supposed to leave** early, but sometimes we do.*

For the past, use *couldn't, wasn't/weren't allowed to* or *wasn't/weren't supposed to*.
*We definitely **couldn't leave** the school at lunchtime.*

Shouldn't have + past participle suggests that the action was done.
*You **shouldn't have yelled** at him; you'll get in trouble.*

Use *doesn't/don't have to* or *doesn't/don't need to* when something isn't necessary.
*In the last two years of school, we **don't have to wear** a uniform.*

For the past, use *didn't have to* or *didn't need to* + past participle.
*In elementary school, we **didn't have to/didn't need to carry** any books around; they were all in the classrooms.*

PASSIVE *-ING* FORMS AND INFINITIVE

The present passive *-ing* form and present passive infinitive are formed with a past participle.

-ing form = *being* + past participle: ***Being taught** by a real actor is amazing!*

infinitive = *to be* + past participle: *They don't want **to be given** any credit.*

As with the active voice, the passive *-ing* forms are used after certain verbs and prepositions and in non-finite clauses.
*The important thing is **being recognized** for your work.*

The passive infinitive is used after certain verbs, in adjective constructions, and in infinitive clauses.
***To be voted** "teacher of the year" is a great honor.*

Form the past passive *-ing* form and past passive infinitive with *been* + past participle.

-ing form = *having been* + past participle: *I regret **never having been given** the opportunity to go to college.*

infinitive = *(to) have been* + past participle: *I would like **to have been invited**, but I wasn't.*

Use the past passive *-ing* form and past passive infinitive in the same constructions as in the present.
***Having been exposed** to the hot sun, he got heatstroke.*
*It was impossible not **to have been affected** by the recession.*

1 Choose the two options that are possible in each sentence.

1 The girls in our school aren't very happy with the rule that they *can't / don't have to / aren't allowed to* wear pants.

2 We all understand the dangers of bullying; the principal *wasn't supposed to give / didn't need to give / didn't have to give* us a lecture about it!

3 Punishment *can / may / must* be given after three unexcused school absences if the principal considers it necessary.

4 Disruptive behavior will result in losing privileges. Respect *should / can / needs to* be shown in all areas of school life.

5 The school *can't / shouldn't / isn't allowed to* suspend students without warning.

2 Complete the text with these modal expressions. Use each expression once.

are supposed to	don't have to	don't have to
have to	have to	should
should	shouldn't	

If you're looking for innovative solutions to engage both children and teachers in the learning process, you (1) _____ look any further than Finland, and, in particular, the elementary school run by Jussi Hietava, a teacher and teacher trainer. In this school, neither the students nor the teacher (2) _____ rely on technology to make the school day interesting and fulfilling. Students (3) _____ move around during classes, and they (4) _____ take endless tests and exams or do a lot of homework. However, they currently (5) _____ assess themselves and their peers, offering constructive feedback. They also take outside play breaks of fifteen minutes up to four times a day. Their teachers believe that they (6) _____ take these breaks in order to maximize their learning. Similarly, the teachers are freer than in many schools. Hietava believes that they (7) _____ feel restricted by rules and regulations but (8) _____ feel able to experiment with new styles of teaching and learning.

3 Complete the second sentence so that it means the same as the first. Use the word in parentheses.

1 Fortunately, it wasn't necessary for me to get a master's degree in education to become a teacher. (need)
I _____ a master's degree in education to become a teacher.

2 We obviously weren't supposed to skip school, but we sometimes skipped gym class. (shouldn't)
We obviously _____ school, but sometimes we skipped gym class.

3 It wasn't necessary for the younger children to wear the school uniform. (to)
The younger children _____ the school uniform.

4 We brought all the ingredients for the cooking class, but it wasn't necessary since the class was canceled. (have)
We _____ all the ingredients for the cooking class since the class was canceled.

4 Complete the text with one word in each space. You can repeat words.

Having long (1) _____ considered one of the best education systems in the world, the system in Singapore has also been criticized in the past for being too dependent on formal testing. An initiative to (2) _____ implemented in the next few years will change the system to a broader view of achievement. Exams (3) _____ already been abandoned in elementary schools, with students now (4) _____ encouraged to learn a wider range of skills. While students would have (5) _____ recognized individually for their achievement in the past, the emphasis is now more on group achievement and on students (6) _____ rewarded for overcoming challenges and for improving. The former emphasis on memorization (7) _____ largely been dropped and soon (8) _____ be fully replaced with more applied learning, based on real-life topics and situations.

5 Complete the second sentence so that it means the same as the first. Use a passive form.

1 The school administration may suspend any student who exhibits poor behavior.
Any student who exhibits _____ .

2 Only teaching assistants with a college education can monitor advanced-level classes.
Advanced-level classes _____ .

3 The emphasis on testing young children regularly will be reconsidered next year.
The emphasis on young children _____ .

4 Given this new information, we should have adopted a different approach.
A different approach _____ .

5 Having abandoned the recent trial, the team will now move on to a new project.
The recent trial _____ .

ELLIPSIS AND SUBSTITUTION

Ellipsis

Ellipsis is leaving out an element of a clause because the meaning can be understood without it. This avoids repetition.

These parts of a clause can be omitted in speech and writing.

A repeated noun/pronoun in a second clause starting with *and* or *but* can be omitted. However, it cannot be omitted after a subordinating conjunction (e.g., *because, if, although*).

(< > = words that can be omitted)

I learned to drive and <I> took the test when I was 17.

Adjectives can be omitted after the verb *be*.

They say it's really crowded there. Yes, it is <crowded>.

The main verb can be omitted after auxiliaries and modal verbs.

A *I think they're bringing in traffic reduction measures.*
B *They are <bringing in traffic reduction measures>, but not yet.*
A *They said it would lower pollution, and we're sure that it will <lower pollution>.*

With complex verb phrases (more than one auxiliary), just the main verb or one or more of the auxiliaries can be omitted.

A *The new road should have been completed weeks ago.*
B *Yes, it should have been <completed weeks ago>. / Yes, it should have <been completed weeks ago>. / Yes, it should <have been completed weeks ago>.*

Infinitive clauses can be omitted, ending the sentence with *to*.

A *They expect to increase the number of bus routes next month.*
B *Good. They need to <increase the number of bus routes>.*

Substitution

Substitution replaces one part of a clause with something else.

Like personal pronouns (*he, us, them*, etc.) which substitute for nouns, quantifiers such as *any, both, few,* and *much* are commonly used as pronouns.

*There used to be a lot of smog, but there isn't as **much** now.*

The pronoun *one* is used only with countable nouns and can be made plural.

*We use electric cars, but we still have some gas **ones**.*

An adjective can't be used on its own to substitute for a noun.

My car doesn't meet the emissions standards, so I'll have to buy a new.

After some verbs usually followed by a *that*-clause (e.g., *be afraid, appear, believe, expect, guess, hope, suppose, think*), *so* or *not* can be used to substitute for the clause.

A *Can we drive into this part of the city?*
B *I guess **so**.*

The negative of *be afraid* and *hope* is usually formed with *not* after the verb; most of the other verbs form the negative with auxiliary *do* + *not* + verb, but in more formal contexts verb + *not* can be used.

*It was thought that most teachers wanted on-site parking, but it would appear **not**.*

With the simple present and simple past, the auxiliary *do* is used as a substitute for the main verb.

*Asked if he drove here, he said that he **did**.*

Use *do it/that/so* to substitute a whole clause.

*We didn't use to recycle our old clothes, but at school they encouraged us to **do it / do so**.*

NOMINALIZATION

Nominalization is the creation of nouns, often abstract, from verbs and sometimes adjectives.

*The committee **decided** to close the school, which angered all the students' parents.* ⟶ *The **decision** of the committee to close the school angered all the students' parents.*

*The artist's creation was **perfect**, and critics praised it.* ⟶ *The **perfection** of the artist's creation was praised by critics.*

Nominalization is very common in more formal and academic writing. The focus is more on ideas than actions.

Some verbs convert easily to nouns (e.g., *grow* ⟶ *growth, develop* ⟶ *development*). For others, equivalents are used (e.g., *build* ⟶ *construction, buy* ⟶ *purchase*), although the *-ing* form of the verb can be used (e.g., *build* ⟶ *building*).

It took years to build the new station. ⟶ *The **construction/ building** of the new station lasted a long time.*

Nominalizations can be followed by a prepositional phrase, often *of* + noun.

People are consuming more energy. ⟶ *The **consumption** of energy is rising.*

With widely used concepts, compound nouns are often formed (e.g., *energy consumption, air pollution*).

Nominalization is often used as a way of expressing an idea from a previous sentence in one word.

*More people are biking to work. This **trend** is reducing pollution.*

1 Cross out all of the words that could be left out to avoid repetition.

1 I had been warned that the transportation system in the city was very confusing, and ~~it was very confusing~~.

2 The changes were introduced to encourage people to take public transportation, and, after a few months, it became clear that they had ~~encouraged people to take public transportation~~.

3 A We could bike into town.
B We could bike into town, but where will we leave the bikes?

4 The government first introduced a traffic tax on weekdays, and then they ~~introduced the traffic tax~~ on weekends, too.

2 Read part of a text about the transportation system in Rio de Janeiro during Carnival. Write what the pronouns and verbs in italics are substitutes for.

Once you arrive in Rio, you'll notice that the transportation system (1) *there* is easy to use. You can choose between buses, the subway, taxis, and for (2) *those* brave enough to rent and ride a bike, there are plenty of places to (3) *do so*.

Taking the bus is cheap, but it's smart to use (4) *them* only during the day. Another option is the subway. (5) *It* has only two lines, and you might need to take a shuttle bus to get to your destination. If you intend to use the subway during Carnival, check your routes carefully before you (6) *do*.

1 _____Rio_____ 2 _____ 3 _____
4 _____ 5 _____ 6 _____

3 Read the rest of the text from Activity 2. Replace the underlined words with these substitute phrases.

another	do it	do so	not	one	~~these~~

For a lot of tourists, however, the best way to travel in Rio is by taxi. Unlike in some cities, (1) taxis in Rio are cheap. Remember, though, that during Carnival many streets are closed, so you should give yourself plenty of time. If (2) you don't give yourself plenty of time, you might arrive late. Taxis here have two rates—(3) a rate for daytime and (4) a rate at night. If you're staying in a hotel and can book your taxis through them, you should (5) book your taxis through them, as they will know the best companies.

Rio is wonderful at Carnival time, so if you get the opportunity to visit then, (6) visit!

1 _____these_____ 2 _____ 3 _____
4 _____ 5 _____ 6 _____

4 Rewrite the sentences as nominalization + preposition. Use a dictionary if necessary.

1 Can you clarify the meaning? ⟶ a _____clarification of_____ the meaning

2 They changed plans. ⟶ a _____ plans

3 They created new green spaces. ⟶ the _____ new green spaces

4 The idea originated here. ⟶ the _____ the idea

5 We've integrated all the suggestions. ⟶ the _____ the suggestions

6 He justified the expense. ⟶ his _____ the expense

5 Complete the text with these nominalizations.

commute to	donations	food production
for sale in	the creation of	the cultivation of
the use of	volunteer labor	

The town of Todmorden in West Yorkshire, England, has become known for its "Incredible Edible" project—part of which refers to (1) _____ pieces of abandoned land around the town for (2) _____ vegetables and fruit (3) _____ the town's stores and supermarkets. (4) _____ in Todmorden has become a community project, using (5) _____ and (6) _____ from local businesses. A typical program in the town was (7) _____ the garden in the Health Center parking lot, which focuses on plants with medicinal uses. Even businesspeople on their (8) _____ work can help by pulling weeds out of the garden on the train station platform!

6 Complete the text by making nominalizations from the words in parentheses.

Sustainable cities aim to be as self-sufficient as possible in terms of (1) *resource management / the management of resources* (manage / resources) and (2) _____ (produce / food). They encourage grassroots initiatives such as (3) _____ (create / urban farms), as well as smart solutions such as (4) _____ (monitor) energy use to maximize resource efficiency. Other priorities include (5) _____ (create / jobs), (6) _____ (develop) community-based businesses, (7) _____ (prevent / crime), and (8) _____ (encourage) strong community links, in order to cause (9) _____ (improve) in the quality of life of their inhabitants.

ADVERBIALS

Adverbials are both single-word adverbs (e.g., *quickly, perhaps*) and longer phrases with an adverbial function (e.g., *on time, at the end of the day*).

Adverbials can express different meanings and can appear in different positions in the clause/sentence.

Front position

Adverbials of attitude (e.g., *perhaps, basically, honestly, in fact*) and some time adverbs (e.g., *then, later, suddenly*) are put at the beginning of the sentence.

Honestly, I don't agree.

Then we need to consider the changes happening at this time.

Text connectors of addition, result, contrast, etc., are also put at the beginning (e.g., *in addition, as a result, however*).

*That is one idea. **However**, there are others.*

Some adverbs can also be moved from other positions to the beginning of a sentence to foreground them.

Occasionally, we all do something that we later regret.

Mid position

Adverbs of frequency (e.g., *always, often, rarely*), adverbs of degree (e.g., *very, really, almost*), and adverbs of certainty (e.g., *definitely, probably*) are usually put in the middle of the clause.

*We've **almost** finished the study on risk-taking in teens.*

The adverb comes before the verb in simple tenses, but it follows *be*. In compound tenses, it comes between the auxiliary and the verb.

*He **always agrees** with us / He **is always** in agreement with us / He **has always agreed** with us.*

In the negative, the adverb usually follows the negative auxiliary.

*He **doesn't always** agree / He **isn't always** in agreement / He **hasn't always** agreed.*

Notice the word order with adverbs of certainty in the negative.

*He **definitely** doesn't agree with everything we say.*

*We **probably** wouldn't want to stay up all night.*

Note the difference in meaning with *really* in different positions in negative sentences.

*We **wouldn't really** want to do that. (slight reluctance)*

*We **really wouldn't** want to do that. (strong reluctance)*

While most frequency adverbs can come at the beginning for emphasis, *always* has to be placed with the verb, and negative

adverbs of frequency (*never, hardly, rarely*) need subject-verb inversion if they are placed at the beginning.

End position

Adverbs of manner (e.g., *quickly, carefully, well, fully*) can go before or after the verb + object.

*We planned the experiment **carefully**.*

*We **carefully** planned the experiment.*

Longer adverbial phrases of place and time usually go at the end of the clause, following the order manner, then place, then time.

*We waited **patiently outside the theater for hours**.*

EXPRESSING HABITUAL ACTIONS AND STATES

Use the present and past continuous, often with an adverb such as *always, forever*, or *constantly*, to express habitual actions.

*Mom's **constantly telling** me to sit up straight.*

This form can describe an emotional reaction to a habitual action, often annoyance, but also other emotions (e.g., pleasure).

*The puppy was so sweet; he **was always following** me around.*

Use *will* for present habits and *would* for past habits, sometimes with *always*.

*My younger sister **will keep working** at the restaurant.*

*I **would always borrow** my sister's clothes as a child.*

To suggest annoyance in speech, *will* or *would* can be stressed.

Note that *always* is not used to express habits in the negative because this expresses "sometimes."

*My best friend **wouldn't always invite** me to go with her.* (= sometimes she invited me, but not every time)

Use *used to* + base form to express past habits or states.

*I **used to bite** my nails when I was a child.*

Use *didn't use to* or *never used to* (more emphatic) for the lack of a habit.

*You **never used to take** me to school!*

Note the difference between *used to* + base form and *be/get used to* + *-ing* form. This refers to actions or states that the speaker is or is becoming accustomed to.

*I never used to like it, but now I'**m getting used to living** here.*

Use *tend to* + base form or, more formally, expressions like *have a tendency* + infinitive or *there is a tendency* + infinitive.

*Teenagers **tend to / have a tendency to worry** a lot.*

1 Correct the mistake in each sentence.

1 People often think that when you're a teenager you follow foolishly the crowd without making up your own mind.

2 My brother always disturbs me when I've finished almost my homework.

3 If I had more self-confidence, I wouldn't probably give in to peer pressure.

4 People think I'm rebellious, but that's just because of what I say; I often don't act badly.

5 I totally had misunderstood what was needed for the chemistry assignment last week.

6 I'm completely out of cash at the moment. I bought a really expensive pair of boots last Friday stupidly.

2 Put the words and phrases in the correct order.

1 most teenagers / influenced by / aren't / their peers / easily / in fact

2 people / maybe / better / more openly / if we spoke / would understand us / about our emotions

3 acting / instead of / impulsively / weigh / the pros and cons / carefully / you should

4 definitely / our parents / on Saturday night / to go to / the club / wouldn't want

5 stereotypes / annoy me / thought-through / frankly / badly / really / of the moody teenager

6 sensibly / don't / of their brains / developed / young people / always / as certain aspects / fully / aren't / behave

3 Choose the correct options to complete the post on a teenage health-advice website.

Problem I'm really starting to get concerned about the amount of time I'm spending online, especially on social media sites. Every day after school, (1) *I'll / I'd* go straight to my room and go online and then again after dinner. My parents think I'm doing my homework, but I'm sure my mom suspects something because she (2) *'s always asking / always asks* me if I'm finished. I (3) *'m used to / tend to* follow a lot of people that I don't really know on social media, and I know it isn't good. I (4) *used to tell / 'm always telling* myself "just another ten minutes," but that ten minutes turns into an hour, then two. The worst thing is that I (5) *used to get / 'm used to getting* really good grades at school, and I (6) *will / would* hang out with a great group of friends after school, but now my grades are slipping and my friends (7) *would get / are getting* used to me making excuses and disappearing after school. Mom often asks about my friends, but I (8) *'m used to / 'll* just blow her off by saying we're all busy with the exams coming up. In fact, I really don't know what I'm going to do when the exams come along and my parents see how badly I do. Please help me!

4 Complete the response to the problem with these expressions. There is one you do not need.

always following	getting used to	have a tendency
there is a tendency	used to be	will tend to

Advice Young people can (1) _____ to do things in extremes, but I think you do have a problem. From what you say, you (2) _____ an outgoing and hardworking student, and the fact that this has changed is a cause for concern. Spending a lot of time online in itself may not be such an issue. Your parents may not see it this way because (3) _____ for older people to see online time as wasted time, which isn't necessarily the case. What concerns me more is that you appear to be (4) _____ people you don't know online rather than interacting with friends. I think you should start by talking to your friends about this. They may be (5) _____ you disappearing after school, but my guess would be that they're concerned about you. Ask them what they do online and how they control their time, and see if you can change your habits.

5 Complete the second sentence so that it means the same as the first. Use the word in parentheses.

1 My little brother takes my things without asking! (taking)
My little brother is _____
_____ !

2 Older people tend to spend far less time online than younger people. (tendency)
There _____
_____ .

3 I'm used to communicating with my friends by text. (tend)
I _____
_____ .

4 When my parents were my age, they'd spend hours watching TV. What's the difference? (to)
My parents _____
_____ ?

5 Teenagers tend to need more sleep than adults. (tendency)
Teenagers _____
_____ .

RELATIVE CLAUSES WITH PREPOSITIONS

The use of prepositions with relative clauses is the same in both defining and non-defining relative clauses.

In informal language, the preposition is placed at the end of the relative clause.

Defining: *It's your health **that** smoking has a detrimental effect **on**.*

Non-defining: *For breakfast I have a big bowl of cereal, **which** I add extra nuts and berries **to**.*

In formal language, the preposition is placed at the beginning of the relative clause, in front of the relative pronoun.

Defining: *One has to be aware that it's one's own health **on which** smoking has a detrimental effect.*

Non-defining: *For breakfast, we recommend cereals with high fiber, **to which** extra nuts and berries can be added.*

When *who* comes after a preposition, it can become *whom*.

*There are people **for whom** a sedentary lifestyle is unavoidable.*

Note that prepositions are not used before the relative pronoun *that*.

Some words can be placed before the preposition (usually *of*) in formal, non-defining relative clauses. The most common of these are quantifiers (e.g., *all, several, none, both*).

*Try to eat green leafy vegetables, **most of which** are rich in vitamins and minerals.*

*The patient visited several specialists, **all of whom** were puzzled by her symptoms.*

Note that in less formal contexts the quantifiers may have to be changed.

*I visited a lot of doctors, **who** were **all** puzzled by my symptoms.*

Superlatives are placed before *of which/whom*.

*Berries are a good addition to any diet, **the most nutritious of which** is possibly blueberries.*

There are also a number of useful set phrases following this pattern (e.g., *the majority of which, a number of whom*).

ARTICLES

The indefinite article (*a/an*) is used to introduce a singular countable noun for the first time. It is used to refer to something indefinite (i.e., not specified).

*There's **a pharmacy** in the shopping center.* (any pharmacy, not a specific one)

It can also be used for an example of a group.

An antibiotic is a type of medicine that fights infection.

Note that singular countable nouns are almost always preceded by the indefinite or definite article or another determiner.

The definite article (*the*) precedes a singular countable noun when both speaker and listener know which one it is.

*Go to **the pharmacy** in the shopping center. It's open late.*

Here, *pharmacy* is made specific by the prepositional phrase that follows it. It could also be specified by a relative clause or a previous mention.

*He works in **the pharmacy** that opened last year.*

*A new doctor started at the clinic last week. **The doctor** is a specialist in heart disease.*

The definite article is also used when it is assumed that the listener knows "which one" the speaker is talking about.

*It would be a good idea to take **the medicine**, wouldn't it?*

In relatively formal contexts, the definite article can be used to refer to a single object that represents the whole group or class of the object or a species.

*Exercise is good for **the heart**.* (i.e., all hearts)

***The tiger** has been hunted for decades.*

The + adjective is also used to refer to some groups of people.

***The sick** and **the elderly** are the most vulnerable groups in society.*

The zero article (i.e., no article) is used with plural nouns when referring to the group in general and uncountable nouns when referring to the concept in general.

*Humans' immune systems can fight off most minor **illnesses**.*

***Health care** is high on the agenda of most governments these days.*

When either a plural noun or an uncountable noun is made specific by a relative clause or a prepositional phrase, use the definite article.

***The minor illnesses that we all suffer in childhood** can be prevented by vaccinations.*

***The health of people living into old age** is a hot topic for governments these days.*

There are many fixed uses of articles. Some illnesses take the indefinite article (e.g., *a heart attack, a cold*), while others don't take an article (e.g., *diabetes*).

The possessive adjective (*my, his*, etc.) is usually used with parts of the body.

*I broke **my wrist**.*

1 Complete the text using one or two words in each blank.

The human body needs a variety of minerals to stay healthy, some (1) _____ which we need to be careful about. One of these is salt, a substance (2) _____ many of us put on our food without thinking. Adults should eat no more than six grams of salt a day. That's approximately a teaspoon. Too much salt can increase the possibility of heart disease, (3) _____ which millions of people in the developed world die each year.

An easy way of reducing salt intake is to identify the types of food (4) _____ which we regularly add salt—fries, tomatoes, eggs, for example—and try to avoid these foods. More problematic is packaged food like soups or sauces (5) _____ a lot of salt is added to enhance the flavors because it is not always easy to read the salt content on the label. Busy people, for (6) _____ shopping is a chore to be completed as fast as possible, are unlikely to check the salt content of every item they choose. Fortunately, in many countries there are clearer food labels today, (7) _____ of which use color coding to indicate levels of particular substances in the food.

If you are one of the many people (8) _____ salt is an essential aid to flavor, try experimenting with other seasoning likes pepper, garlic, or lemon juice, none (9) _____ are as detrimental to our health as salt.

2 Rewrite the sentences with relative clauses so that they mean the same thing. The relative clauses all contain a preposition. Write a formal (F) or informal (I) sentence, as in the examples.

1 Do you know a good physical therapist? Can I go to them? (I)

Do you know a good physical therapist (that) I can go to?

2 We have just received a delivery of medical supplies. Payment is required for them. (F)

We have just received a delivery of medical supplies for which payment is required.

3 Professor Harris is unable to attend the lecture on nutrition. She was invited to it last week. (F)

4 There's a podcast on teenagers' health. You should really listen to it. (I)

5 What happened to that brochure on obesity? I saw it the other day. (I)

6 Patients should not become close to counselors. They might become dependent on them. (F)

7 Do you remember Samia, the medical student? I introduced you to her at the party. (I)

8 His new book is on a new treatment for asthma. There is currently no cure for it. (F)

3 Choose the correct option to complete the sentences. (–) means no article is needed.

1 If you aren't feeling right, go to – / *the* doctor and ask for *a* / *the* checkup.

2 *The* / – mental health is *a* / *the* huge concern for many societies today.

3 Some doctors believe that *an* / *the* aspirin a day is good for – / *the* heart.

4 Too much time using – / *a* computer without taking a break can result in injury to *the* / *a* wrist.

5 *My* / *The* ankle really hurts. I think I must have injured it when I was on – / *the* running track.

6 – / *The* elderly need a very specific type of *a* / – medical attention.

7 Some of *the* / – most common medical problems suffered by *the* / – teenagers are *the* / – asthma, allergies, and fatigue.

8 One of – / *the* major priorities for any government is *the* / – health of *the* / *a* nation.

4 Complete the text with the definite article, the indefinite article, and the zero article.

With (1) _____ advances in (2) _____ medicine and better nutrition, (3) _____ people are generally living longer these days, and more people are living to be older than 100. While (4) _____ official record for (5) _____ oldest person to have lived goes to Frenchwoman Jeanne Calment, who died at 122 in 1997, Carmelo Flores, (6) _____ Bolivian man who died in 2014, is said to have lived to (7) _____ ripe old age of 124. However, this claim has not been verified. (8) _____ problem is that (9) _____ birth certificates didn't become official in Bolivia until 1940, so there isn't (10) _____ official record of Flores's birth.

Even in his final years, Flores lived alone in (11) _____ hut high in (12) _____ Andes. He believed that (13) _____ diet was (14) _____ very important ingredient in his recipe for long life, in particular (15) _____ mushrooms and quinoa*.

quinoa *a seed grown in the Andes*

ADVANCED QUESTION TYPES

Tag questions are formed by changing a statement to a tag (i.e., from positive to negative, or negative to positive).

*You **haven't followed** the argument at all, **have** you?*

The positive can also be used in both the statement and the tag. This usually asks for confirmation.

*You **would** agree the smile is universal then, **would** you?*

Other less common forms of tag questions are:

***Someone** misled you about that gesture, didn't **they**?*

***Explain** that to me again, **would you**? / **will you**? / **could you**?*

Indirect questions can be asked to be polite or to soften a question. These start with an introductory phrase (e.g., *Can you tell me / I'd like to know…*) .

*What **would you use** here?* ⟶ ***Can you tell me** what **you'd use** here / **I'd like to know** what **you'd use** here.*

In the simple present and simple past, *do/does/did* is omitted in the indirect question.

***Does the journal use** a lot of jargon?* ⟶ *Do you know if **the journal uses** a lot of jargon?*

***Did the lawyer clarify** the wording?* ⟶ *Could you tell me if **the lawyer clarified** the wording?*

There is a second type of indirect question which asks for an opinion with *do you think*.

*Why **do you think** these gestures have an offensive meaning?*

Negative questions are formed by using the negative form of the auxiliary verb.

*Why **haven't** these ideas **become** more universally accepted?*

Yes/no questions in the negative are often used to ask for confirmation.

***Didn't** you **notice** the expression on her face?*

Echo questions are used to show surprise at a piece of information, or to ask someone to repeat something. The appropriate question word is used to ask about the piece of information.

A *We went to the Eden Project last month.*

B *You went **where**?*

SUBORDINATE AND PARTICIPIAL CLAUSES

Subordinate clauses add information to the main clause in a sentence and start with a subordinating conjunction (e.g., *since*).

←——— main clause ———→
Doctors have been washing their hands regularly

←——— subordinate clause ———→
***since** Semmelweis noticed the problem.*

Subordinate clauses are finite (i.e., the verb contains information about tense and person).

The subordinating conjunction provides a meaning connection between the main and subordinate clauses (i.e., in the example above, the meaning is one of time: *since*). Other meanings conveyed are reason (*because, as*), result (*so*), purpose (*so that*), and concession (*although*).

***Although** he proved his theory, he didn't publish it.*

The subordinate clause can come first, usually followed by a comma.

Participial clauses are similar to subordinate clauses, but the verbs in them are non-finite (i.e., they don't show tense or person). There are different types of participial clauses.

Present participial clauses use the present participle and have an active meaning. When they precede the main clause, they often express the idea of cause.

***Noticing** that fewer mothers died when giving birth at home, he decided to investigate…*

When they follow the main clause, they often express result.

*Pasteur and Koch proved the link between germs and disease, **leading** to the request… (which led to…)*

Note that present participial clauses can also be introduced by subordinating conjunctions.

*Noticing that fewer mothers died **when giving** birth at home…*

Past participial clauses use the past participle and have a passive meaning. They can be used alone or after subordinating conjunctions *when, once, until, although, if*, and *unless*.

***Discouraged** by the hostile reception, he decided to leave.*

***Although abandoned**, the building still showed potential.*

Perfect participial clauses use the present participle *having* + past participle. They have an active meaning and refer to the past.

***Having left** the hospital, he returned to Hungary.*

The negative of a participial verb is made by putting *not* in front of the participle.

***Not wanting** to accept responsibility for the deaths, the doctors rejected the argument.*

1 Rewrite the basic question or statement in the question form given in parentheses.

1 Do you know what this facial expression means? (negative question)

_____

2 What does this facial expression mean? (indirect question)

_____

3 Do you understand what this facial expression means? (positive tag question)

_____

4 What does this facial expression mean? (indirect opinion question)

_____

5 I don't understand what it means. (echo question)

_____

2 Put the words in the correct order to make questions.

1 You / tip and / understand / don't / tongue / you / ?
2 fascinating / differ / Isn't / how / it / languages / ?
3 the / Sorry, / what / on / ?
4 think / English / When / you / you / do / speak / I'll / like / ?
5 what / you / tell / expressions / mean / Can / kind of / you / me / ?

3 Complete the dialog with the questions from Activity 2.

A I know lots of expressions about the mind in English.
B (a) _____ I don't really know any.
A Yeah, well, something like "my mind goes blank," or the one I like is "on the tip of my tongue."
B (b) _____
A On the tip of my tongue.
B Oh, tongue. OK. But what does it mean?
A You don't know? (c) _____
B Yes, of course, but together I don't have a clue.
A I assumed you would because Spanish has a similar expression. It's like, when you can almost remember something, but not quite. So I could say "What's that actor's name? It's on the tip of my tongue."
B Ah, yes, we do have a similar expression, but it translates literally as "It's under my tongue."
A Oh, OK. (d) _____ Really interesting.
B (e) _____ I've been here for ages!

4 Rewrite the sentences using a subordinate clause instead of the participial clause.

1 Understanding the link between germs and infection now, doctors are much more careful.

Because they understand the link between germs and infections now, doctors are much more careful.

2 Not being healthy enough to go home, the patients had to remain in the hospital.
Because _____ .
3 Left to his own thoughts, the researcher realized where he was going wrong.
When _____ .
4 Having taken her final exams, she started working in the local hospital.
After _____ .
5 Antibiotics are being overused today, resulting in more resistant bacteria.
_____ , which _____ .

5 Complete the text with these words and phrases.

being used	breaking	depending on
having realized	Initially discovered	Not having
not using	Viewed	

I was recently in a remote area in East Africa when I fell, (1) _____ my leg badly. (2) _____ immediate access to an X-ray machine, I started to think about this vital tool that the developed world takes for granted. (3) _____ by Roentgen in 1895, the simple X-ray now contributes to speedy diagnosis in much of the modern world. Roentgen, (4) _____ the potential importance of his discovery, started testing it by X-raying his wife's hand. (5) _____ by many at first as an invasion of privacy, X-rays soon became used in medicine and by the military, (6) _____ on the battlefield as a way of locating bullets in soldiers who had been shot. However, (7) _____ harmful radiation for the clear imaging, it became obvious that X-rays needed to be used sparingly. It was only in the 1970s that a safe alternative to X-rays was found: (8) _____ dangerous radiation, magnetic resonance imaging allows clear images of the body without serious risk and is now the diagnostic tool of choice in many medical arenas.

6 Complete the second sentence so it means the same as the first.

1 I had a brilliant idea and wanted to tell the world!
Having _____ .
2 But since I'm not well-known in my field, I knew I'd have to find someone to advise me.
But not _____ .
3 After I'd identified the leading scientist in the field, I decided to write to her.
Having _____ .

IRREGULAR VERBS

INFINITIVE	SIMPLE PAST	PAST PARTICIPLE
arise	arose	arisen
beat	beat	beaten
become	became	become
bend	bent	bent
bet	bet	bet
bite	bit	bitten
blow	blew	blown
break	broke	broken
breed	bred	bred
bring	brought	brought
broadcast	broadcast	broadcast
build	built	built
burn	burned	burned
burst	burst	burst
cost	cost	cost
cut	cut	cut
deal	dealt	dealt
dig	dug	dug
dream	dreamed	dreamed
fall	fell	fallen
feed	fed	fed
fight	fought	fought
flee	fled	fled
forget	forgot	forgotten
forgive	forgave	forgiven
freeze	froze	frozen
grow	grew	grown
hang	hanged/hung	hanged/hung
hide	hid	hidden
hit	hit	hit
hold	held	held
hurt	hurt	hurt
keep	kept	kept
kneel	kneeled	kneeled
lay	laid	laid
lead	led	led
lend	lent	lent
let	let	let
lie	lay	lain
light	lit	lit
lose	lost	lost
mean	meant	meant

INFINITIVE	SIMPLE PAST	PAST PARTICIPLE
mislead	misled	misled
misunderstand	misunderstood	misunderstood
must	had to	had to
overcome	overcame	overcome
rethink	rethought	rethought
ring	rang	rung
rise	rose	risen
sell	sold	sold
set	set	set
shake	shook	shaken
shine	shone	shone
shoot	shot	shot
shrink	shrank	shrunk
shut	shut	shut
sink	sank	sunk
slide	slid	slid
smell	smelled	smelled
spell	spelled	spelled
spend	spent	spent
spill	spilled	spilled
split	split	split
spoil	spoiled	spoiled
spread	spread	spread
stand	stood	stood
steal	stole	stolen
stick	stuck	stuck
strike	struck	struck
swear	swore	sworn
tear	tore	torn
throw	threw	thrown
undergo	underwent	undergone
undertake	undertook	undertaken
upset	upset	upset
wake	woke	woken
win	won	won
withdraw	withdrew	withdrawn

WRITING

UNIT 1 An article

Choose an interesting title that summarizes the content of the article.

Engage the reader's interest with questions.

Sub-headings can make the article more interesting and easier to read.

Include personal information and examples to make your article more interesting.

Introduce separate points with words and phrases such as *First of all*, *Secondly*, and *Finally*.

Finish with an interesting or inspiring sentence.

How to excel at your sport

Reach for the stars

Have you always dreamed of being an Olympic swimmer? Of course, not everyone can win medals, but don't let that stop you. With practice and determination, you can make progress as a swimmer beyond your wildest dreams.

From small beginnings

I've been passionate about being a competitive swimmer ever since I was a small child. My dad used to take us to the local swimming pool every Saturday for swimming lessons. While the other kids were splashing around, I used every second of the time to practice my strokes. Soon, I started entering races, and even though I didn't win them all I kept improving my time. By the time I was 14, I was the fastest swimmer at my school, and now my burning ambition is to swim for my country.

Best tips for success

There are a few things you need to keep in mind if you really want to excel as a swimmer. First of all, no matter how talented you are, you need dedication in order to succeed. It isn't easy to get up every morning at 6:00 a.m. Nevertheless, with time you can overcome your dislike of getting up early and even start enjoying it! Secondly, you need a really good coach who can improve your technique and encourage you to do your best. And last but not least, you need to have a positive attitude.

Go for it!

Even if you don't take part in competitions, swimming is a great sport that people of all ages can enjoy. It is an exciting and rewarding activity, as well as a great way of staying in shape and making friends. So why not join your local swimming club now? Who knows, it could be the start of a life-long passion!

UNIT 2 A story

Set the scene for the story by describing the time, place, protagonist, and background actions.

Use a variety of narrative tenses and introduce the events and actions in a story with phrases like *At that moment* and *Just then*.

Notice how the repeated use of *would* emphasizes the main idea of the story.

A change of direction

One bright, sunny morning in mid-summer, Tarek was sitting on the deck behind his house, watching the birds flying in and out of the trees and chirping happily. He sipped his morning coffee and pondered his life. He had just taken his final exams at school and was anxiously awaiting the results. He had been hoping to study medicine in college, but he needed very good grades. He feared that the exams had not gone well.

At that moment, his mother stepped out onto the deck and handed him a large brown envelope. Tarek tore it open impatiently. He stared at the results and his heart sank. To his utter disappointment, he had scored three Fs—the worst possible result. He would never get into a good college now. He picked up the slip of paper with the results, crumpled it into a ball, and hurled it to the ground.

Just then, a bird swooped down and landed on the deck beside him. It seemed to study him carefully for a moment, and then it snatched the ball of paper in its beak and soared into the air and out of sight. A sudden thought came into Tarek's mind. He would travel. Yes, he would go to college—eventually. He would retake his exams—next year. But before that, he would travel and see the world. He drank his coffee and opened wide the door into his house.

Use adverbs (e.g., *happily, anxiously, impatiently*) to make your writing more colorful.

Describe emotional reactions.

Describing a change or turning point makes your story more interesting.

Your closing sentence can provide a conclusion or leave it open-ended for the reader to imagine.

UNIT 3 Informal emails

There are many fixed expressions in informal emails.

Remember to use contractions in informal emails.

Abbreviations, exclamation points, dashes, and ellipses are all common in emails. *BTW* means "by the way" and introduces an idea not directly related to the previous point.

To end an informal email, use an informal expression (e,g., *best wishes, lots of love,* etc.) or just write your name or initial. *xx* means "love" or "lots of love."

Use a range of phrasal verbs and informal expressions.

A Hello Sara,
How are things? Hope you're well. Sorry I haven't been in touch for so long. I've been up to my eyes with studying for my exams. Anyway, I'm emailing with a request. Some friends and I are organizing an event called "Songs for the Sea" for World Oceans Day on June 8th. It would be great if you could come and play a couple of songs. Let me know, and I'll email you with more details.
All the best,
Paul

B Hi Jo,
Thanks for your email. Sorry to hear you didn't pass your driving test—better luck next time… Anyway, this is just to let you know that I'm planning to go to an event called "Songs for the Sea" on Sat., the 8th. There's an excellent line-up—should be awesome. Do you want to come along? I could pick you up around 6 and then drop you off afterwards. BTW I have a new car—can't wait to show you!!
See ya!, Matt

C Hi Matt,
Good to hear from you. Glad to hear about the car!! Thanks for the invitation. I googled the event, and it sounds awesome. So, yeah, I'd love to come, and thanks for the offer of a ride! See you Saturday!
J xx

D Hi Sara,
Just a quick email to say thanks so much for playing at the event last Saturday. It was an amazing performance, and everyone loved the songs. I absolutely loved the last one—really moving. Thanks again, and let's get together soon. Will be great to catch up.
Write soon,
Paul

UNIT 4 A discussion essay

Start a discussion essay with a statement about the significance of the topic. It should be related to the title.

Remember to start your paragraphs with topic sentences that summarize the main idea.

Is Earth the only planet that has life?

The question of whether life exists outside our planet is one of the most fascinating questions in science. Are there primitive forms of life, such as bacteria, elsewhere in the universe? Are there more intelligent beings that may be trying to contact us? Robotic space probes and powerful telescopes, such as the Hubble Space Telescope, are helping scientists to answer these questions. Moreover, giant radio dishes are trying to detect signals from outer space.

Some important data has already been gathered. There is now strong evidence that water, which is probably necessary for life to exist, may have existed on Mars millions of years ago. Water has also been discovered on Europa, one of the moons of the planet Jupiter. Many planets exist outside our solar system, and research is being conducted to determine whether there could be water on them.

Many scientists argue that, statistically, Earth is unlikely to be the only planet in the universe with living beings on it. Yet despite all these investigations, no unambiguous evidence of extraterrestrial life has been found. Are we missing signals, are extraterrestrials unable or unwilling to talk to us, or is Earth really the only planet that has ever had life? In my view, there might be other forms of life in the universe, but it could be many more years before we find conclusive proof.

Introduce new points with words and phrases like *moreover, furthermore, in addition, additionally,* and *also.*

Use hedging expressions to say how sure you are about something and what evidence there is.

End the essay with a clear statement of your opinion, based on evidence.

UNIT 5 A formal letter to persuade someone to help

Begin a formal letter by stating your purpose.

Dear Ms. Vazquez:

I am writing to urge you to take action on behalf of the world's children at the upcoming UN World Summit.

The world produces enough food to feed the global population of seven billion people. Yet one person in nine goes to bed hungry every night, and about 45% of all child deaths are linked to malnutrition. Not only is this unjust, but it is also inexcusable in a world of plenty. These children need our help, and they need it now.

Include facts and statistics to inform the reader, and make your argument more persuasive.

Use strong language to emphasize the importance of the points you are making (e.g., *it is horrifying that…* , *it is incredibly important to…*).

It is horrifying that in many parts of the world, people are still suffering from malnutrition and hunger. In these situations, it is the children who suffer most. Only by getting enough food and a balanced diet can children grow up strong and healthy and develop resistance to disease.

Use emphatic structures to make your point clearly (e.g., *Only by -ing … can … , Not only is this unjust, but … *).

Right now, world leaders are preparing for the next UN World Summit. This is our chance to take action and help all the world's children. What we need to do is implement long-term policies, such as teaching people about nutrition, supporting small farmers, providing school meals, and ensuring that children under two get a balanced diet and enough to eat.

Be clear about the action you want the reader to take.

I call on you to put pressure on global leaders to tackle the challenge of child hunger at this summit. Together, we can change the fate of millions of children who need our help.

Make optimistic statements to emphasize solutions to the problems.

Yours sincerely,
Constanza Jara

UNIT 6 An opinion essay

In an opinion essay, state the arguments for and against different views, including one that is different from your own.

Schools have so many different functions that it is difficult to identify one single aim. On the one hand, it is probably true that, for many students the main purpose of their education is to find work. In my country, there is a great deal of unemployment among young people. As a result, there is increasing competition to obtain high scores on exams in order to go to a great college and have a successful career. On the other hand, most schools have other important goals as well.

In the second paragraph, explore the arguments against your own point of view.

There are strong arguments for the view that preparation for work is the key function of a school. Young people need skills to enter the workplace, so all students need to leave school with a good level of language and mathematical literacy and IT skills. Moreover, schools should equip young people to make a contribution to society. My school, for example, provides internships and vocational training that prepare students for the job opportunities that are available.

Support general statements with examples from your own experience.

However, I would question whether preparing students for work is the most important job of schools. I strongly believe that one of the key goals of education should be personal development, in other words helping students to reach their potential. In particular, schools should help students discover their strengths and passions, consider their aims in life, and set goals for the future. In my case, it was in an after-school club that I developed a strong interest in local wildlife. Now I am hoping to study ecology in college and work in nature conservation after I graduate.

In the third paragraph, outline your own views on the topic, using the language of personal opinions.

In the final paragraph, summarize both sides of the argument and state your own opinion.

In conclusion, it seems to me that although vocational training and academic success are important, the central focus of schools should be on personal development. Schools should enable students to develop their individual talents and interests; only in this way can they choose the right career path for the future and become valuable members of society.

UNIT 7 A report

Give your report a clear and informative title and use sub-headings for each section.

In the first paragraph, state the purpose of the report and summarize the questions asked.

Summarize the findings in the body of the report, using a variety of quantity expressions.

Use formal language (e.g., *expressed dissatisfaction with,* not *complained about*).

Use the final paragraph to summarize the findings and make a brief recommendation.

A report on the use of parks and green spaces

Purpose of the report
This report has been written to provide information on the results of an investigation into parks and recreation spaces in the town. Improvements have been introduced to these spaces over the last few years to make them more accessible and appealing to young people. The purpose of the survey was to determine how well the updates are meeting the needs of young people and to suggest further possible improvements. Students from schools and colleges across the town were asked about how they use the parks, their satisfaction with them, and their suggestions for improvements.

Use of the parks
It was found that the parks are used on a regular basis by just over half the students interviewed. The majority use the parks for exercise and sports, while approximately a third use the spaces as inexpensive and convenient meeting places. Virtually no one views the spaces as an escape from town life.

Opinions of interviewees
The vast majority greatly value the parks with sports facilities, in particular Breakspear Park with its swimming pool and soccer field. About half of the girls rated the cafe in Highfield Park very highly, and just over a third of all interviewees spoke approvingly about the parks that offered shelter against bad weather. Most interviewees expressed dissatisfaction with the less formal open spaces, which they felt were more appropriate for dog walkers. A sizeable minority of the interviewees were deeply disappointed that the running track in Taunton Park was overgrown. Virtually all of the interviewees heavily criticized the early closing times of the parks.

Recommendations
Overall, it appears that young people are relatively satisfied with the facilities at the parks, with the main exception of closing times. It is suggested that the parks should be closed two hours later, particularly in the summer, and that maintenance of the running track should be resumed as soon as possible.

UNIT 8 An essay comparing advantages and disadvantages

When comparing the advantages and disadvantages of two options, mention both options in the first paragraph.

In the second paragraph, list both the pros and cons of the first option.

In the third paragraph, list the pros and cons of the second option.

Finish by saying which of the two options you think is better, giving clear reasons for your choice.

There are many times in life when we struggle to find a solution to a problem. In these situations, it can be very helpful to talk the issue over with a good friend or to discuss it on an online forum. There are pros and cons to both alternatives.

There are many benefits to talking to a friend. First and foremost, a friend knows you very well and is concerned about your happiness and well-being. Another benefit is that they can easily understand what you are going through, because they are from the same generation. However, one possible disadvantage is that they may not question your attitude because they want to make you happy. Most importantly, a friend may not be experienced enough to give the right advice.

The main advantage of online forums is that they are anonymous, so it is easier to be open about your problem. Moreover, in an online forum you have the chance to read a variety of opinions from many different people. However, this has the possible disadvantage of creating confusion, so it is necessary to consider the advice critically. Another significant drawback is that people who post in online forums can sometimes write cruel and hurtful things.

Of course, no one can solve a problem for you; nonetheless, it is always helpful to get different perspectives on an issue. My own view is that the advantages of talking to a friend outweigh the disadvantages, as it is more personal, and by sharing a problem, you can feel less stressed out about it.

UNIT 9 A proposal

As in a report, give your proposal a title and use sub-headings.

In the introduction, briefly state what the proposal includes: the research, the findings, and recommendations.

In a proposal, the *Recommendations* section is longer than in a report.

Use bullet points to list your recommendations.

Use a variety of language to give recommendations. Use impersonal expressions and a formal style.

Give concrete examples (*for instance, such as, like* …).

Finish by stating the improvements that could be made if the proposal is implemented.

> ## Making links between the school and elderly people in the community
>
> ### Introduction
> This proposal is based on the results of a survey in which 35 people, all over the age of 65, were asked about their concerns and suggestions for greater involvement in our community. It outlines both difficulties experienced by the elderly and contributions they could make. It concludes by making recommendations on how the school could make positive links with older local residents.
>
> ### Challenges and opportunities
> The main difficulties that need to be addressed are loneliness and isolation. Many elderly people tend to feel out of touch with the local community and find it difficult to get out, either due to difficulties in getting around by walking or a lack of reliable public transportation. They would appreciate more support for their caregivers. In terms of opportunities, they are excited to share skills and support the school.
>
> ### Recommendations
> There are several steps that the school could take in order to involve local elderly residents in the community.
>
> - First of all, it would be useful to devote a certain number of school hours every month to visiting elderly people in their homes. This would build relationships and enable their visitors to learn more about their needs.
> - Secondly, it is recommended that elderly people be invited to the school to give talks, on local history for example, or to teach practical skills such as knitting or woodwork. In this way, the community would benefit from their skills and experience.
> - Third, students could provide support for families who have older family members living with them, for example, in the form of rides to the doctor.
> - Finally, the school might consider scheduling a small number of field trips to local attractions, where students could volunteer and accompany the elderly people.
>
> ### Conclusion
> By implementing these suggestions, the school could make positive links with elderly people. These are not just old people in need of help, they are people with amazing life experiences and talents to share. Involving students in this plan would benefit not only the older people, but also the students themselves.

UNIT 10 A review

A giant of Latin Music

Begin your review with a strong opening sentence to engage the reader's attention (e.g., describing the performer, the type of music or play, or the performance).

Last weekend's sell-out concert by Juan Luis Guerra proved beyond any doubt that he is a giant of Latin music. In the concert, given to launch his new album *Todo tiene su hora,* the singer from the Dominican Republic gave a thrilling performance, mixing nostalgia and novelty. The city stadium was packed with 9,000 fans of all ages who were loving every moment, singing along with old favorites and dancing to the infectious rhythms of salsa, merengue, and bachata.

Guerra opened the two-hour set by emerging theatrically from an old-fashioned telephone booth on stage and singing a new song, "Cookies & Cream," featuring catchy lyrics and a strong, energetic beat. This was followed by an exhilarating mixture of new tunes and classic hits such as "La bilirrubina" and "Ojalá que llueva café," accompanied by the artist's talented backing group, 440. These musicians also entertained the crowd during a break by Guerra with powerful instrumental solos and exciting choreography. Guerra ended the concert with a lengthy encore to satisfy his loyal fans, some of whom had crossed continents for a once-in-a-lifetime glimpse of the superstar.

For me, the most impressive aspect of Guerra's performance was his ability not only to energize the audience with the dance tunes, but also to move them with tender romantic ballads and social commentary. Such versatility is for me the hallmark of a great performer. Through his joyful music and lyrics, his modest stage presence, and his effortless rapport with the audience, Guerra conveys the message that life is good. I came away feeling uplifted and optimistic about the power of music to bring people together. It was an unforgettable and life-enhancing evening with a must-see performer. Don't hesitate to catch another concert on the tour if you can.

Begin your review with a strong opening sentence to engage the reader's attention (e.g., describing the performer, the type of music or play, or the performance).

In the first paragraph, give background information about the performer(s), the performance, and the audience.

In the second paragraph, focus on interesting details about the performance, using a variety of adjectives to convey your opinion.

In the final paragraph, evaluate the performance and give a personal opinion.

Describe the impact the performance had on you and how it has changed your ideas or feelings.

Make a recommendation about whether to see the performance or not.

UNIT 1

a dream come true (phr)	/ə ˌdrim kʌm ˈtru/
a glass ceiling (phr)	/ə ˌglæs ˈsilɪŋ/
affluent (adj)	/ˈæfluənt/
aspiration (n)	/ˌæspɪˈreɪʃən/
aspire to be (phr)	/əˈspaɪr tu bi/
audition (n)	/ɔˈdɪʃən/
be famous (phr)	/ˌbi ˈfeɪməs/
be successful (phr)	/ˌbi səkˈsɛsfəl/
broaden one's horizons (phr)	/ˌbrɔdən wʌnz həˈraɪzənz/
bureaucracy (n)	/bjʊˈrɑkrəsi/
burning ambitions (phr)	/ˌbɜrnɪŋ æmˈbɪʃənz/
catch sight of (phr)	/ˌkætʃ ˈsaɪt əv/
dedicated (adj)	/ˈdɛdɪˌkeɪtɪd/
dedication (n)	/ˌdɛdɪˈkeɪʃən/
devastated (adj)	/ˈdɛvəˌsteɪtɪd/
dive into (phr v)	/ˌdaɪv ˈɪntu/
do volunteer work (phr)	/ˌdu ˌvɑlənˈtir ˌwɜrk/
early retirement (n)	/ˌɜrli rɪˈtaɪərmənt/
envision (v)	/ɪnˈvɪʒən/
excel (v)	/ɪkˈsɛl/
favor (v)	/ˈfeɪvər/
fulfill (v)	/fʊlˈfɪl/
fulfill one's dream (phr)	/fʊlˌfɪl wʌnz ˈdrim/
genes (n)	/dʒinz/
go into (phr v)	/ˌgoʊ ˈɪntu/
go to college (phr)	/ˌgoʊ tə ˈkɑlɪdʒ/
grab an opportunity (phr)	/ˌgræb æn ˌɑpərˈtunəti/
inherent (adj)	/ɪnˈhɛrənt/
make a difference (phr)	/ˌmeɪk ə ˈdɪfərəns/
minimum wage (n)	/ˌmɪnɪməm ˈweɪdʒ/
never in one's wildest dreams (phr)	/ˌnɛvər ɪn wʌnz ˈwaɪldɪst ˌdrimz/
noticeable (adj)	/ˈnoʊtɪsəbəl/
overcome an obstacle (phr)	/ˈoʊvərˌkʌm æn ˈɑbstəkəl/
parental leave (n)	/pəˌrɛntəl ˈliv/
pass my driving test (phr)	/ˌpæs maɪ ˈdraɪvɪŋ tɛst/
premises (n)	/ˈprɛmɪsɪz/
prior to that (phr)	/ˈpraɪər tə ˌðæt/
pursue (v)	/pərˈsu/
pursue a goal (phr)	/pərˌsu ə ˈgoʊl/
raise a family (phr)	/ˌreɪz ə ˈfæmli/
realize one's potential (phr)	/ˌriəlaɪz wʌnz pəˈtɛnʃəl/
respectively (adv)	/rɪˈspɛktɪvli/
scholarship (n)	/ˈskɑlərʃɪp/
see the world (phr)	/ˌsi ðə ˈwɜrld/
set a target (phr)	/ˌsɛt ə ˈtɑrgɪt/
set up a business (phr)	/ˌsɛt ʌp ə ˈbɪznəs/
setback (n)	/ˈsɛtˌbæk/
state benefits (n)	/ˌsteɪt ˈbɛnɪfɪts/
status (n)	/ˈstætəs/
striking (adj)	/ˈstraɪkɪŋ/
subtle (adj)	/ˈsʌtəl/
survey (v)	/sərˈveɪ/
undertake a journey (phr)	/ˌʌndərˈteɪk ə ˈdʒɜrni/
unemployment rate (n)	/ˌʌnɪmˈplɔɪmənt ˌreɪt/
vision (n)	/ˈvɪʒən/
vocational	/voʊˈkeɪʃənəl/
(a) voluntary layoff (n)	/ˈvɑləntɛri ˈleɪˌɔf/
we made it (phr)	/ˌwi ˈmeɪd ɪt/

UNIT 2

accessible (adj)	/ækˈsɛsəbəl/
build up (phr v)	/ˌbɪld ˈʌp/
catch up with (phr v)	/ˌkætʃ ˈʌp wɪð/
come up with (phr v)	/ˌkʌm ˈʌp wɪð/
disastrous (adj)	/dɪˈzæstrəs/
dismay (n)	/dɪsˈmeɪ/
do away with (phr v)	/ˌdu əˈweɪ wɪð/
dull (adj)	/dʌl/
entertaining (adj)	/ˌɛntərˈteɪnɪŋ/
fascination (n)	/ˌfæsɪˈneɪʃən/
from scratch (phr)	/ˌfrəm ˈskrætʃ/
get hold of (phr)	/ˌgɛt ˈhoʊld əv/
get around to (phr v)	/ˌgɛt əˈraʊnd tʊ/
go out of one's way (phr)	/ˌgoʊ ˈaʊt əv wʌnz ˌweɪ/
gripping (adj)	/ˈgrɪpɪŋ/
grow out of (phr v)	/ˌgroʊ ˈaʊt əv/
hospitality (n)	/ˌhɑspɪˈtæləti/
intriguing (adj)	/ɪnˈtrigɪŋ/
lean on (phr v)	/ˈlin ˌɑn/
live up to (phr v)	/ˌlɪv ˈʌp tu/
long for (phr v)	/ˈlɑŋ ˌfər/
look forward to (phr v)	/lʊk ˈfɔrwərd tu/
moving (adj)	/ˈmuvɪŋ/
narrator (n)	/næˈreɪtər/
numerous (adj)	/ˈnumərəs/
overrated (adj)	/ˌoʊvərˈreɪtɪd/
patch (n)	/pætʃ/
sacred (adj)	/ˈseɪkrɪd/
sentimental (adj)	/ˌsɛntɪˈmɛntəl/
shatter (v)	/ˈʃætər/
sip (v)	/sɪp/
slow-moving (adj)	/ˌsloʊ ˈmuvɪŋ/
snatch (v)	/snætʃ/
soar (v)	/sɔr/
stick to (v)	/ˌstɪk tu/
thought-provoking (adj)	/ˈθɔt prəˌvoʊkɪŋ/
thrill (n)	/θrɪl/
touching (adj)	/ˈtʌtʃɪŋ/
trigger (v)	/ˈtrɪgər/
trilogy (n)	/ˈtrɪlədʒi/
witty (adj)	/ˈwɪti/
wrestle with (phr v)	/ˈrɛsəl ˌwɪð/

UNIT 3

a steep learning curve (phr)	/ə ˌstip ˈlɜrnɪŋ ˌkɜrv/
antibiotic (n)	/ˌæntibaɪˈɑtɪk/
antidepressant (n)	/ˌæntidɪˈprɛsənt/
antisocial (adj)	/ˌæntiˈsoʊʃəl/
biodiversity (n)	/ˌbaɪoʊdɪˈvɜrsəti/
biography (n)	/baɪˈɑgrəfi/
biology (n)	/baɪˈɑlədʒi/
blow one's mind (phr)	/ˌbloʊ wʌnz ˈmaɪnd/
buzz (n)	/bʌz/
climate change (n)	/ˈklaɪmət ˌtʃeɪndʒ/
coral (n)	/ˈkɑrəl/
coral reef (n)	/ˌkɑrəl ˈrif/
diversity (n)	/daɪˈvɜrsəti/
eco-friendly (adj)	/ˈikoʊˌfrɛndli/
ecology (n)	/iˈkɑlədʒi/
ecosystem (n)	/ˈikoʊˌsɪstəm/
ecotourism (n)	/ˈikoʊˌtʊrɪzəm/
endangered species (n)	/ɪnˌdeɪndʒərd ˈspiʃiz/
flood levels (n)	/ˈflʌd ˌlɛvəlz/
fossil fuels (n)	/ˈfɑsəl ˌfjuəlz/
geography (n)	/dʒiˈɑgrəfi/
geology (n)	/dʒiˈɑlədʒi/
geophysics (n)	/ˌdʒioʊˈfɪzɪks/
global warming (n)	/ˌgloʊbəl ˈwɔrmɪŋ/
greenhouse gases (n)	/ˌgrinhaʊs ˈgæsɪz/
habitat (n)	/ˈhæbɪtæt/
heritage (n)	/ˈhɛrɪtɪdʒ/
hyperactive (adj)	/ˌhaɪpərˈæktɪv/
hypersensitive (adj)	/ˌhaɪpərˈsɛnsətɪv/
macroclimate (n)	/ˈmækroʊˌklaɪmət/
macroeconomy (n)	/ˈmækroʊ ɪˌkɑnəmi/
macro lens (n)	/ˈmækroʊ ˌlɛnz/
mammal (n)	/ˈmæməl/
marine reserve (n)	/məˌrin rɪˈzɜrv/
microchip (n)	/ˈmaɪkroʊˌtʃɪp/
microscope (n)	/ˈmaɪkroʊˌskoʊp/
microsurgery (n)	/ˌmaɪkroʊ ˈsɜrdʒəri/
monolingual (adj)	/ˌmɑnoʊˈlɪŋgwəl/
monologue (n)	/ˈmɑnəlɑg/
monotonous (adj)	/məˈnɑtənəs/
oil refinery (n)	/ˈɔɪl ˌrɪfaɪnəri/
persistent (adj)	/pərˈsɪstənt/
polar ice-caps (n)	/ˌpoʊlər ˈaɪs kæps/
preservation (n)	/ˌprɛzərˈveɪʃən/
projection (n)	/prəˈdʒɛkʃən/
renewable energy (n)	/rɪˌnuəbəl ˈɛnərdʒi/
reproduce (v)	/ˌriprəˈdus/
sea defenses (n)	/ˈsi dɪˌfɛnsɪz/
stark (adj)	/stɑrk/
sustainable (adj)	/səˈsteɪnəbəl/
take for granted (phr)	/ˌteɪk fər ˈgræntɪd/
wilderness (n)	/ˈwɪldərnəs/
wreak havoc (phr)	/ˌrik ˈhævək/

UNIT 4

archeologist (n)	/ˌɑrkiˈɑlədʒɪst/
archeology (n)	/ˌɑrkiˈɑlədʒi/
authentic (adj)	/ɔˈθɛntɪk/
authenticity (n)	/ˌɔθɛnˈtɪsəti/
bacteria (n)	/bækˈtɪriə/
boundary (n)	/ˈbaʊndəri/
circumnavigate (v)	/ˌsɜrkəmˈnævəˌgeɪt/
clarity (n)	/ˈklɛrəti/
clear (adj)	/klɪər/
combat (v)	/ˈkɑmbæt/
conclusive (adj)	/kənˈklusɪv/
creativity (n)	/ˌkriˈtɪvəti/
curiosity (n)	/ˌkjʊriˈɑsəti/
curious (adj)	/ˈkjʊriəs/
detect (v)	/dɪˈtɛkt/
determine (v)	/dɪˈtɜrmɪn/
discovery (n)	/dɪˈskʌvəri/
endeavor (v)	/ɪnˈdɛvər/
endurance (n)	/ˈɛndərəns/
engage (v)	/ɛnˈgeɪdʒ/
ensure (v)	/ɛnˈʃʊr/
exhilarating (adj)	/ɪgˈzɪləˌreɪtɪŋ/
exploration (n)	/ˌɛkspləˈreɪʃən/
fleet (n)	/flit/
fragile (adj)	/ˈfrædʒəl/
fragility (n)	/frəˈdʒɪləti/
glory (n)	/ˈglɔri/
glow (v)	/gloʊ/
historian (n)	/hɪˈstɔriən/
humanity (n)	/hjuˈmænəti/
humid (adj)	/ˈhjumɪd/
humidity (n)	/hjuˈmɪdəti/
hypothesis (n)	/haɪˈpɑθəsəs/
intense (adj)	/ɪnˈtɛns/
intensity (n)	/ɪnˈtɛnsiti/
kid (v)	/kɪd/
landmark (n)	/ˈlændˌmɑrk/
launch (n)	/lɔntʃ/
listener (n)	/ˈlɪsənər/
map (v)	/mæp/
mission (n)	/ˈmɪʃən/
motivate (v)	/ˈmoʊtɪveɪt/
motivation (n)	/ˌmoʊtɪˈveɪʃən/
necessary (adj)	/ˈnɛsəˌsɛri/
necessity (n)	/nəˈsɛsəti/
network (n)	/ˈnɛtˌwɜrk/
pit (n)	/pɪt/
primitive (adj)	/ˈprɪmətɪv/
resolution (n)	/ˌrɛzəˈluʃən/
skepticism (n)	/ˈskɛptɪˌsɪzəm/
seek (v)	/sik/
sense (v)	/sɛns/
settlement (n)	/ˈsɛtəlmɪnt/
spin-off (n)	/ˈspɪnˌɔf/
stability (n)	/stəˈbɪləti/
stable (adj)	/ˈsteɪbəl/
trek (v)	/trɛk/

ultimately (adv)	/ˈʌltɪmətli/
unanimous (adj)	/juˈnænɪməs/
vegetation (n)	/ˌvɛdʒəˈteɪʃən/
vulnerability (n)	/ˌvʌlnərəˈbɪləti/
vulnerable (adj)	/ˈvʌlnərəbəl/

UNIT 5

address global issues (phr)	/əˌdrɛs ˌgloʊbəl ˈɪʃuz/
advocate (n)	/ˈædvəkət/
ambitious (adj)	/æmˈbɪʃəs/
anonymous (adj)	/əˈnɑnɪməs/
apathetic (adj)	/ˌæpəˈθɛtɪk/
bring about change (phr)	/ˌbrɪŋ əˌbaʊt ˈtʃeɪndʒ/
call on someone (phr v)	/ˈkɔl ˌɑn sʌmwʌn/
campaign (v)	/kæmˈpeɪn/
compliment (n)	/ˈkɑmplɪmənt/
condemn (v)	/kənˈdɛm/
confront (v)	/kənˈfrʌnt/
contented (adj)	/kənˈtɛntɪd/
contribute (v)	/kənˌtrɪbjut/
countless (adj)	/ˈkaʊntləs/
courageous (adj)	/kəˈreɪdʒəs/
coverage (n)	/ˈkʌvərɪdʒ/
criteria (n)	/kraɪˈtɪriə/
devastating (adj)	/ˈdɛvəˌsteɪtɪŋ/
discontented (adj)	/ˌdɪskənˈtɛntɪd/
disrespectful (adj)	/ˌdɪsrɪˈspɛktfəl/
face a challenge (phr)	/ˌfeɪs ə ˈtʃæləndʒ/
famine (n)	/ˈfæmɪn/
far from it (phr)	/ˌfɑr ˈfrʌm ɪt/
foundation (n)	/faʊnˈdeɪʃən/
globe (n)	/gloʊb/
hatred (n)	/ˈheɪtrɪd/
have an impact on (phr)	/ˌhæv æn ˈɪmpækt ɑn/
horrifying (adj)	/ˈhɔrɪˌfaɪɪŋ/
I didn't sleep a wink (phr)	/aɪ ˌdɪdənt ˌslip ə ˈwɪŋk/
idealistic (adj)	/aɪˌdɪəˈlɪstɪk/
immature (adj)	/ˌɪməˈtjʊr/
increase awareness (phr)	/ɪnˌkris əˈwɛrnəs/
index (n)	/ˈɪndɛks/
intolerant (adj)	/ɪnˈtɑlərənt/
irresponsible (adj)	/ˌɪrɪˈspɑnsəbəl/
it wasn't rocket science (phr)	/ɪt ˌwɑzənt ˈrɑkɪt ˌsaɪəns/
launch a campaign (phr)	/ˌlɔntʃ ə kæmˈpeɪn/
make an impact on (phr)	/ˌmeɪk æn ˈɪmpækt ɔn/
materialistic (adj)	/məˌtɪəriəˈlɪstɪk/
mature (adj)	/məˈtʃʊr/
modest (adj)	/ˈmɑdɪst/
nutrition (n)	/nuˈtrɪʃən/
outspoken (adj)	/ˌaʊtˈspoʊkən/
play one's part (phr)	/ˌpleɪ wʌnz ˈpart/

proportion (n)	/prəˈpɔrʃən/
raise awareness (phr)	/ˌreɪz əˈwɛrnəs/
random (adj)	/ˈrændəm/
realistic (adj)	/ˌrɪəˈlɪstɪk/
recreational (adj)	/ˌrɛkriˈeɪʃənəl/
resistance (n)	/rɪˈzɪstəns/
respectful (adj)	/rɪˈspɛktfəl/
responsible (adj)	/rɪˈspɑnsəbəl/
role model (n)	/ˈroʊl ˌmɑdəl/
run a campaign (phr)	/ˌrʌn ə kæmˈpeɪn/
shoulder to shoulder with (phr)	/ˈʃoʊldər tə ˈʃoʊldər wɪð/
single-minded (adj)	/ˌsɪŋgəlˈmaɪndɪd/
summit (n)	/ˈsʌmɪt/
supportive (adj)	/səˈpɔrtɪv/
tackle global issues (phr)	/ˌtækəl ˌgloʊbəl ˈɪʃuz/
take part (phr)	/ˌteɪk ˈpart/
the homeless (n)	/ˌðə ˈhoʊmləs/
tolerant (adj)	/ˈtɑlərənt/
top (v)	/tɑp/
trustworthy (adj)	/ˈtrʌstˌwɜrði/
twist (n)	/twɪst/
unambitious (adj)	/ˌʌnæmˈbɪʃəs/
unrealistic (adj)	/ˌʌnriˈlɪstɪk/
unsupportive (adj)	/ˌʌnsəˈpɔrtɪv/
upcoming (adj)	/ˈʌpˌkʌmɪŋ/
urge (v)	/ɜrdʒ/
volunteer (v, adj)	/ˌvɑlənˈtɪər/

UNIT 6

accessories (n)	/əkˈsɛsəriz/
advice on (phr)	/ədˈvaɪs ɔn/
approach to (phr)	/əˈproʊtʃ tu/
assumption (n)	/əˈsʌmpʃən/
attitude to (phr)	/ˈætɪˌtud tu/
ban on (phr)	/ˈbæn ɔn/
be given a warning (phr)	/bi ˌgɪvən ə ˈwɔrnɪŋ/
be punctual (phr)	/ˌbi ˈpʌŋktʃuəl/
bully (v)	/ˈbʊli/
bullying (n)	/ˈbʊliɪŋ/
challenge to (phr)	/ˈtʃæləndʒ tu/
change in (phr)	/ˈtʃeɪndʒ ɪn/
clash (n)	/klæʃ/
clash between (phr)	/ˈklæʃ bɪˌtwin/
clear up (v)	/ˌklɪr ˈʌp/
comparison between (phr)	/kəmˈpærɪsən bɪˌtwin/
comprehensive (adj)	/ˌkɑmprɪˈhɛnsɪv/
conclude (v)	/kənˈklud/
conflict between (phr)	/ˈkɑnflɪkt bɪˌtwin/
counterpart (n)	/ˈkaʊntərˌpart/
damage to (phr)	/ˈdæmɪdʒ tu/
decrease in (phr)	/ˈdikris ɪn/
detention (n)	/dɪˈtɛnʃən/

difference between (phr) /'dɪfrəns bɪˌtwin/
disruptive (adj) /dɪs'rʌptɪv/
distinct (adj) /dɪ'stɪŋkt/
drastic (adj) /'dræstɪk/
enforce (v) /ɪn'fɔrs/
fast forward (v) /ˌfæst 'fɔrwərd/
five consecutive years (phr) /ˌfaɪv kən'sɛkjətɪv ˌjɪrz/
focus on (phr) /'foʊkəs ɔn/
gap between (phr) /'gæp bɪˌtwin/
give a punishment (phr) /'gɪv ə 'pʌnɪʃmənt/
have a very long way to go (phr) /ˌhæv ə 'vɛri lɔŋ ˌweɪ tə ˌgoʊ/
impact on (phr) /'ɪmpækt ɔn/
improvement in (phr) /ɪm'pruvmənt ɪn/
inappropriate (adj) /ˌɪnə'proʊpriət/
increase in (phr) /'ɪnkris ɪn/
influence on (phr) /'ɪnfluəns ɔn/
innovative (adj) /'ɪnəˌveɪtɪv/
insight (n) /'ɪnsaɪt/
literacy (n) /'lɪtərəsi/
misbehave (v) /ˌmɪsbi'heɪv/
misbehavior (n) /ˌmɪsbi'heɪvjər/
need for (phr) /'nid fɔr/
norm (n) /nɔrm/
offensive (adj) /ə'fɛnsɪv/
peer (n) /pɪr/
principle (n) /'prɪnsəpəl/
punishment for (phr) /'pʌnɪʃmənt fɔr/
radically (adv) /'rædɪkli/
regime (n) /reɪ'ʒim/
respect for (phr) /rɪ'spɛkt fɔr/
responsibility for (phr) /rɪˌspʌnsə'bɪləti fɔr/
restorative approach (n) /rɪˌstɔrətɪv ə'proʊtʃ/
rise in (phr) /'raɪz ɪn/
set the tone (phr) /ˌsɛt ðə 'toʊn/
show disrespect (phr) /ˌʃoʊ ˌdɪsrɪ'spɛkt/
skip class (phr) /'skɪp 'klæs/
suspend (v) /sə'spɛnd/
take away privileges (phr) /ˌteɪk ə'weɪ 'prɪvəlɪdʒɪz/
talent for (phr) /'tælənt fɔr/
threat to (phr) /'θrɛt tu/
thrive (v) /θraɪv/
unthinkable (adj) /ʌn'θɪŋkəbəl/
vandalism (n) /'vændəˌlɪzəm/
vocational (adj) /voʊ'keɪʃənəl/
what is on their minds (phr) /ˌwɑt ɪz ˌɔn ðeər 'maɪndz/
workplace (n) /'wɜrkˌpleɪs/

UNIT 7

aha moment (phr) /ˌɑhɑ ˌmoʊmənt/
attributes (n) /'ætrɪˌbjuts/
breakdown (n) /'breɪkˌdaʊn/
car-centric (adj) /ˌkɑr 'sɛntrɪk/
carpool (v) /'kɑrˌpul/

collaborate (v) /kə'læbəreɪt/
communicate (v) /kə'mjunɪkeɪt/
commute (n/v) /kə'mjut/
commuter (n) /kə'mjutər/
commuting (n) /kə'mjutɪŋ/
component (n) /kəm'poʊnənt/
congested (adj) /kən'dʒɛstɪd/
congestion (n) /kən'dʒɛstʃən/
connection (n) /kə'nɛkʃən/
consumption (n) /kən'sʌmpʃən/
crossing (n) /'krɔsɪŋ/
drop someone off (phr v) /ˌdrɔp sʌmwʌn 'ɔf/
electrify (v) /ɪ'lɛktrɪfaɪ/
eye-opener (n) /'aɪ ˌoʊpənər/
formulate (v) /'fɔrmjəˌleɪt/
fumes (n) /fjumz/
gridlock (n) /'grɪdˌlɑk/
happen to (phr v) /'hæpən ˌtu/
imitate (v) /'ɪmɪteɪt/
imitation (n) /ˌɪmɪ'teɪʃən/
infrastructure (n) /ˌɪnfrə'strʌktʃər/
innovate (v) /'ɪnoʊveɪt/
innovation (n) /ˌɪnoʊ'veɪʃən/
journey (n) /'dʒɜrni/
justify (v) /'dʒʌstɪfaɪ/
lengthen (v) /'lɛŋθən/
maximize (v) /'mæksɪmaɪz/
memorize (v) /'mɛməraɪz/
obstacle (n) /'ɑbstəkəl/
originate (v) /ə'rɪdʒəneɪt/
overview (n) /'oʊvərˌvju/
paradox (n) /'pærədɑks/
prioritize (v) /praɪ'ɑrɪtaɪz/
purely (adv) /'pjʊrli/
purify (v) /'pjʊrɪfaɪ/
radical (adj) /'rædɪkəl/
rate (v) /reɪt/
regulate (v) /'rɛgjəˌleɪt/
replicate (v) /'rɛplɪkeɪt/
restless (adj) /'rɛstləs/
restrict (v) /rɪ'strɪkt/
resume (v) /rɪ'zum/
rush hour (n) /'rʌʃ ˌaʊər/
shaped (adj) /ʃeɪpt/
shuttle service (n) /'ʃʌtəl ˌsɜrvɪs/
simplify (v) /'sɪmplɪfaɪ/
smog (n) /smɑg/
stabilize (v) /'steɪbəlaɪz/
strengthen (v) /'strɛŋθən/
stuck (adj) /stʌk/
subsidize (v) /'sʌbsɪdaɪz/
subway (n) /'sʌbˌweɪ/
transportation (n) /ˌtrænspɔr'teɪʃən/
underlying (adj) /ˌʌndər'laɪɪŋ/
unify (v) /'junɪfaɪ/
urbanize (v) /'ɜrbənaɪz/
utilize (v) /'jutɪlaɪz/
vehicle (n) /'viɪkəl/
walker (n) /'wɔkər/

UNIT 8

adolescent (n) /ˌædə'lɛsənt/
assignment (n) /ə'saɪnmənt/
bed and breakfast (n) /ˌbɛd ænd 'brɛkfəst/
believe it or not (phr) /bɪ'liv ɪt ɔr ˌnɑt/
black and white (adj) /ˌblæk ænd 'waɪt/
brothers and sisters (n) /ˌbrʌðərz ænd 'sɪstərz/
brutal (adj) /'brutəl/
cheerful (adj) /'tʃɪrfəl/
come across (phr v) /ˌkʌm ə'krɑs/
conservative (adj) /kən'sɜrvətɪv/
consistently (adv) /kən'sɪstəntli/
couldn't care less (phr) /ˌkʊdənt kɛr 'lɛs/
distinctive (adj) /dɪ'stɪŋktɪv/
do my own thing (phr) /ˌdu maɪ ˌoʊn 'θɪŋ/
drawback (n) /'drɔˌbæk/
dual (adj) /'dul/
engage in (phr v) /ɪn'geɪdʒ ˌɪn/
even-tempered (adj) /ˌivən 'tɛmpərd/
facts and figures (phr) /ˌfækts ən 'fɪgərz/
first and foremost (phr) /ˌfɜrst ænd 'fɔrˌmoʊst/
fish and chips (n) /ˌfɪʃ ænd 'tʃɪps/
follow the crowd (phr) /'fɑloʊ ðə 'kraʊd/
foremost (adj) /'fɔrˌmoʊst/
generalization (n) /ˌdʒɛnərəlaɪ'zeɪʃən/
give me a thrill (phr) /ˌgɪv mi ə 'θrɪl/
here and there (phr) /ˌhɪr ænd 'ðɛr/
humility (n) /hju'mɪləti/
husbands and wives (n) /ˌhʌzbəndz ænd 'waɪvz/
impulsive (adj) /ɪm'pʌlsɪv/
influenced by peers (phr) /ˌɪnfluənst baɪ 'pɪrz/
insecurities (n) /ˌɪnsə'kjʊrɪtiz/
kick (n) /kɪk/
law and order (n) /ˌlɔ ænd 'ɔrdər/
loud and clear (phr) /ˌlaʊd ænd 'klɪr/
men and women (n) /ˌmɛn ænd 'wɪmɪn/
moody (adj) /'mudi/
name and address (n) /ˌneɪm ænd ə'drɛs/
nonetheless (adv) /ˌnʌnðə'lɛs/
odds and ends (n) /ˌɑdz ænd 'ɛndz/
outweigh (v) /'aʊˌtweɪ/
overwhelming (adj) /ˌoʊvər'wɛlmɪŋ/
peace and quiet (phr) /ˌpis ænd 'kwaɪət/
peer pressure (n) /'pɪr ˌprɛʃər/
perspective (n) /pər'spɛktɪv/
phenomenon (n) /fə'nɑməˌnɑn/
play it safe (phr) /ˌpleɪ ɪt 'seɪf/
prone to (adj) /'proʊn ˌtu/
rebellious (adj) /rɪ'bɛljəs/
reconcile (v) /'rɛkənˌsaɪl/
safe and sound (adj) /ˌseɪf ænd 'saʊnd/
self-conscious (adj) /ˌsɛlf 'kɑnʃəs/
self-controlled (adj) /ˌsɛlf kən'troʊld/
short and sweet (phr) /ˌʃɔrt ænd 'swit/
stereotype (n) /'stɛrioʊˌtaɪp/
thunder and lightning (n) /ˌθʌndər ænd 'laɪtnɪŋ/

torn between (phr)	/ˈtɔrn bɪˌtwin/
transition (n)	/trænˈzɪʃən/
trials and tribulations (phr)	/ˌtraɪəlz ænd ˌtrɪbjʊˈleɪʃənz/
undergo (v)	/ˌʌndərˈɡoʊ/
ups and downs (phr)	/ˌʌps ænd ˈdaʊnz/
wear and tear (n)	/ˌweər ænd ˈteər/
weigh the pros and cons (phr)	/weɪ ðə ˌproʊz ænd ˈkɑnz/
within a split second of (phr)	/wɪðˌɪn ə ˌsplɪt ˈsɛkənd əv/
worthy (adj)	/ˈwɜrði/

UNIT 9

account for (phr v)	/əˈkaʊnt ˌfɔr/
achievable (adj)	/əˈtʃivəbəl/
address (v)	/əˈdrɛs/
affordable (adj)	/əˈfɔrdəbəl/
alert (adj)	/əˈlɜrt/
assign (v)	/əˈsaɪn/
audible (adj)	/ˈɔdəbəl/
beneficial (adj)	/ˌbɛnɪˈfɪʃəl/
carbohydrate (n)	/ˌkɑrboʊˈhaɪˌdreɪt/
chronic (adj)	/ˈkrɑnɪk/
commonly (adv)	/ˈkɑmənli/
correlation (n)	/ˌkɔrəˈleɪʃən/
curable (adj)	/ˈkjʊrəbəl/
detrimental (adj)	/ˌdɛtrɪˈmɛntəl/
disposable (adj)	/dɪˈspoʊzəbəl/
drink plenty of water (phr)	/ˌdrɪŋk ˈplɛnti əv ˈwɔtər/
eat naturally (phr)	/ˌit ˈnætʃərəli/
edible (adj)	/ˈɛdɪbəl/
enhance (v)	/ɛnˈhæns/
enjoyable (adj)	/ɛnˈdʒɔɪəbəl/
experience firsthand (phr)	/ɪkˈspɪriəns ˌfɜrstˈhænd/
feasible (adj)	/ˈfizəbəl/
get enough sleep (phr)	/ɡɛt ɪˌnʌf ˈslip/
have a balanced diet (phr)	/hæv ə ˌbælənst ˈdaɪət/
horrible (adj)	/ˈhɑrəbəl/
in moderation (phr)	/ˌɪn ˌmɑdəˈreɪʃən/
inflatable (adj)	/ɪnˈfleɪtəbəl/
intake (n)	/ˈɪnteɪk/
isolation (n)	/ˌaɪsəˈleɪʃən/
keep an eye on (phr)	/ˌkip æn ˈaɪ ɑn/
label (v)	/ˈleɪbəl/
legible (adj)	/ˈlɛdʒəbəl/
lifelong (adj)	/ˈlaɪfˌlɔŋ/
loneliness (n)	/ˈloʊnlinəs/
longevity (n)	/lɔnˈdʒɛvəti/
machine-washable (adj)	/məˌʃin ˈwɑʃəbəl/
memorable (adj)	/ˈmɛmərəbəl/
moderate (adj)	/ˈmɑdərət/
moderation (n)	/ˌmɑdəˈreɪʃən/
nap (n)	/næp/
nutrient (n)	/ˈnutriənt/

nutritious (adj)	/nuˈtrɪʃəs/
obese (adj)	/oʊˈbis/
obesity (n)	/oʊˈbisəti/
occasional (adj)	/əˈkeɪʒənəl/
outlet (n)	/ˈaʊtˌlɛt/
plausible (adj)	/ˈplɔzəbəl/
practice the art of appreciation (phr)	/ˌpræktɪs ðə ˌɑrt əv əˌpriʃiˈeɪʃən/
preliminary (adj)	/prɪˈlɪmɪnɛri/
preventable (adj)	/prɪˈvɛntəbəl/
protein (n)	/ˈproʊtin/
rechargeable (adj)	/riˈtʃɑrdʒəbəl/
recyclable (adj)	/riˈsaɪkləbəl/
reduce (v)	/rɪˈdus/
refillable (adj)	/riˈfɪləbəl/
refined sugar (n)	/rɪˌfaɪnd ˈʃʊɡər/
refundable (adj)	/rɪˈfʌndəbəl/
relax (v)	/rɪˈlæks/
relieve stress (phr)	/rɪˌliv ˈstrɛs/
renewable (adj)	/rɪˈnuəbəl/
specifically (adv)	/spəˈsɪfɪkli/
stamina (n)	/ˈstæmɪnə/
stay active (phr)	/steɪ ˈæktɪv/
stem from (phr v)	/ˈstɛm ˌfrəm/
unaffected (adj)	/ˌʌnəˈfɛktɪd/
unprocessed foods (phr)	/ənˈprɑˌsɛst fudz/
visible (adj)	/ˈvɪzəbəl/
well-being (n)	/ˌwɛl ˈbiɪŋ/

UNIT 10

analogy (n)	/əˈnælədʒi/
analytical (adj)	/ˌænəˈlɪtɪkəl/
back up (phr v)	/ˌbæk ˈʌp/
backing (adj)	/ˈbækɪŋ/
bundle (n)	/ˈbʌndəl/
circuit (n)	/ˈsɜrkɪt/
concisely (adv)	/kənˈsaɪsli/
contrast (v)	/kənˈtræst/
convey (v)	/kənˈveɪ/
cookies (n)	/ˈkʊkiz/
doubtful (adj)	/ˈdaʊtfəl/
doubtless (adj)	/ˈdaʊtləs/
elaborate on (phr v)	/ɪˈlæbəˌreɪt ɑn/
empathy (n)	/ˈɛmpəθi/
engage (v)	/ɪnˈɡeɪdʒ/
eventful (adj)	/ɪˈvɛntfəl/
exclaim (v)	/ɪkˈskleɪm/
exquisite (adj)	/ɪkˈskwɪzɪt/
facial expression (n)	/ˌfeɪʃəl ɪkˈsprɛʃən/
fearful (adj)	/ˈfɪrfəl/
fearless (adj)	/ˈfɪrləs/
forget one's point (phr)	/fərˌɡɛt wʌnz ˈpɔɪnt/
forgetful (adj)	/fərˈɡɛtfəl/
fruitful (adj)	/ˈfrutfəl/
fruitless (adj)	/ˈfrutləs/
gesture (n)	/ˈdʒɛstʃər/

get across (phr v)	/ˌɡɛt əˈkrɑs/
giggle (v)	/ˈɡɪɡəl/
glimpse (n)	/ɡlɪmps/
heartless (adj)	/ˈhɑrtləs/
homeless (adj)	/ˈhoʊmləs/
hopeful (adj)	/ˈhoʊpfəl/
hopeless (adj)	/ˈhoʊpləs/
infectious (adj)	/ɪnˈfɛkʃəs/
jargon (n)	/ˈdʒɑrɡən/
jobless (adj)	/ˈdʒɑbləs/
lengthy (adj)	/ˈlɛŋθi/
lose my train of thought (phr)	/ˌluz maɪ ˌtreɪn əv ˈθɔt/
make eye contact (phr)	/ˌmeɪk ˈaɪ kɑntækt/
make up (phr v)	/ˌmeɪk ˈʌp/
meaningful (adj)	/ˈminɪŋfəl/
meaningless (adj)	/ˈminɪŋləs/
metaphor (n)	/ˈmɛtəfɔr/
mind goes blank (phr)	/ˌmaɪnd ɡoʊz ˈblæŋk/
misinterpret (v)	/ˌmɪsɪnˈtɜrprɪt/
neatly (adv)	/ˈnitli/
nostalgia (n)	/nɔˈstældʒə/
novelty (n)	/ˈnɑvəlti/
partially (adv)	/ˈpɑrʃəli/
pointless (adj)	/ˈpɔɪntləs/
powerful (adj)	/ˈpaʊərfəl/
powerless (adj)	/ˈpaʊərləs/
precise (adj)	/prɪˈsaɪs/
raging (adj)	/ˈreɪdʒɪŋ/
rational (adj)	/ˈræʃənəl/
regretful (adj)	/rɪˈɡrɛtfəl/
rephrase (v)	/ˌriˈfreɪz/
republic (n)	/rɪˈpʌblɪk/
run around (phr v)	/ˌrʌn əˈraʊnd/
scramble (n)	/ˈskræmbəl/
sheer (adj)	/ʃɪr/
see right through (phr verb)	/ˌsi ˌraɪt ˈθru/
skillful (adj)	/ˈskɪlfəl/
snap (v)	/snæp/
stable (n)	/ˈsteɪbəl/
startling (adj)	/ˈstɑrtəlɪŋ/
stick to the point (phr)	/ˌstɪk tu ðə ˈpɔɪnt/
summarize (v)	/ˈsʌməraɪz/
surge (v)	/sɜrdʒ/
sync with (phr verb)	/ˈsɪŋk ˌwɪð/
tactful (adj)	/ˈtæktfəl/
tactless (adj)	/ˈtæktləs/
tangle (n)	/ˈtæŋɡəl/
tasteful (adj)	/ˈteɪstfəl/
tasteless (adj)	/ˈteɪstləs/
tender (adj)	/ˈtɛndər/
thankful (adj)	/ˈθæŋkfəl/
thoughtful (adj)	/ˈθɔtfəl/
thoughtless (adj)	/ˈθɔtləs/
unrest (n)	/ʌnˈrɛst/
wasteful (adj)	/ˈweɪstfəl/
weave together (phr v)	/ˌwiv təˈɡeðər/
worthless (adj)	/ˈwɜrθləs/